"Robert McNally has added to John Muir's legacy in a way that will hook both conservationists and those with little interest in wilderness. At a time when the natural world has once again become the protagonist of our story, McNally breaks down the complicated and conflicted relationship with nature to show how our long-standing attitudes toward wild spaces grew from the limited perspective of an elite few. This is the story not of a single man but of a time, place, and culture that created a public figure who has hugely influenced how we interact today with the natural world—for good and ill."
—KATYA CENGEL, author of *From Chernobyl with Love*

"Robert Aquinas McNally throws back the curtain on John Muir and our deeply held beliefs about how the American wilderness came to be. A dogged researcher, McNally offers sometimes unsettling facts but steeps such accounts in a deep reverence for storytelling. As hard-hitting as it is lyrical, the profound truth at the heart of this book invites all of us to rethink what we've been told about Indigenous peoples."
—MELISSA FRATERRIGO, author of *Glory Days*

"The unique value of this groundbreaking study is its unflinching demonstration that John Muir's racial views were not peripheral—they were central to his whole conception of wilderness. Native Americans had 'no right place in the landscape,' Muir believed, if wilderness was to achieve its higher purpose as a space for white supplanters to contemplate its spiritual essence. *Cast Out of Eden* is a seminal work, written with remarkable sensitivity and compassion."
—JAMES J. RAWLS, author of *Indians of California: The Changing Image*

"*Cast Out of Eden* is a necessary read for everyone interested in John Muir. Like Muir himself in his quest to understand nature, McNally has gone deep to explore the man's writings within the turn-of-the-twentieth-century American zeitgeist. The result is the compelling story of a complicated figure and his place in shaping this country's vision of itself."
—MIKE WURTZ, head of the Holt-Atherton Special Collections and Archives, including the John Muir Papers, at the University of the Pacific

"A colorful portrait of the driven, politically savvy, and often ecstatic John Muir, and simultaneously a condemnation of his unwillingness or inability to transcend the racism of his era. . . . Robert Aquinas McNally shines a light on the attitudes that resulted in the failure not only of Muir but also of U.S. presidents, universities, the National Park Service, railroad tycoons, the Sierra Club, and others to acknowledge successful Native American stewardship of the landscape. The final chapter lays out contemporary efforts by government and Native peoples to overcome this history, part of the soul-searching, renaming, and re-envisioning today's world needs."
—MALCOLM MARGOLIN, cofounder of *News from Native California*, former director of Heyday Books, and author of *The Ohlone Way*

publication supported by a grant from

The Community Foundation for Greater New Haven

as part of the Urban Haven Project

ROBERT AQUINAS MCNALLY

CAST OUT
OF EDEN

The Untold Story of John Muir,
Indigenous Peoples, and the
American Wilderness

UNIVERSITY OF NEBRASKA PRESS

Lincoln

The University of Nebraska Press is part of a land-grant institution
with campuses and programs on the past, present, and future
homelands of the Pawnee, Ponca, Otoe-Missouria, Omaha, Dakota,
Lakota, Kaw, Cheyenne, and Arapaho Peoples, as well as those
of the relocated Ho-Chunk, Sac and Fox, and Iowa Peoples.

Library of Congress Cataloging-in-Publication Data
Names: McNally, Robert Aquinas, author.
Title: Cast out of Eden: the untold story of John Muir, indigenous
peoples, and the American wilderness / Robert Aquinas McNally.
Description: Lincoln: University of Nebraska Press, [2024] |
Includes bibliographical references and index. | Summary:
"Cast Out of Eden explores John Muir's role in the legacy
of racialized colonialism affecting U.S. wild lands and
points toward a way forward"— Provided by publisher.
Identifiers: LCCN 2023034950
ISBN 9781496227263 (hardback)
ISBN 9781496239198 (epub)
ISBN 9781496239204 (pdf)
Subjects: LCSH: Muir, John, 1838–1914. | Naturalists—United
States—Biography. | Nature conservation—Social aspects—
United States—History. | Public lands—United States—History. |
Indian land transfers—West (U.S.)—History. | Indians of North
America—Colonization. | Indians of North America—Government
relations—1869-1934. | United States—Race relations—History. |
United States—Environmental conditions. | BISAC: BIOGRAPHY
& AUTOBIOGRAPHY / Environmentalists & Naturalists | SOCIAL
SCIENCE / Ethnic Studies / American / Native American Studies
Classification: LCC QH31.M9 M295 2024 | DDC 333.72092
[B]—dc23/eng/20240116
LC record available at https://lccn.loc.gov/2023034950

Set and designed in New Baskerville ITC by N. Putens.

For my grandchildren,

Callahan, Maeve, and Devin,

in the hope that the America they inherit comes

to welcome all her peoples into

this land's wild wonders

And the Lord God planted a garden eastward in Eden; and there he put the man whom he had formed. And out of the ground made the Lord God to grow every tree that is pleasant to the sight, and good for food; the tree of life also in the midst of the garden, and the tree of the knowledge of good and evil. . . . And the Lord God said, Behold, the man is become as one of us, to know good and evil: and now, lest he put forth his hand, and take also of the tree of life, and eat, and live for ever: Therefore the Lord God sent him forth from the garden of Eden, to till the ground from whence he was taken. So he drove out the man; and he placed at the east of the garden of Eden Cherubims, and a flaming sword which turned every way to keep the way of the tree of life.

—Genesis 2:8–9, 3:22–24

CONTENTS

ILLUSTRATIONS

ACKNOWLEDGMENTS

Matthew Bokovoy, senior acquisitions editor at the University of Nebraska Press, helped right from the beginning as I struggled to shape a vague idea into this narrative. He went above and beyond in reading the draft from first page to last and offering both good ideas and validating enthusiasm.

The other beta readers, accomplished authors all, told me where the draft worked and where it didn't: Katya Cengel, a remarkable journalist and memoirist who is hard-nosed about facts and openhearted with the people she profiles; Melissa Fraterrigo, whose lyric prose finds beauty in hard truth and stuns me into admiration; Susan Harness, who turns heartfelt storytelling into justice-making; and Boyd Cothran, a historian and writer whose work demonstrates the power of molding a story to the truth of things. All are friends as well as coaches, and I owe them.

Jeffrey Ostler, professor emeritus at the University of Oregon, gave me a strategy for checking current values against historical realities. Clifford Trafzer, Costo Professor of American Indian Affairs at the University of California, Riverside, trusted me with a draft of his in-progress paper on John Muir's missed opportunity to learn Indigenous ways. Mark David Spence, who pioneered scholarship on the dispossession of tribal nations for the West's national parks, pointed me to the people I needed to talk to about the ongoing struggle of the Southern Sierra Miwuk Nation (SSMN) to win federal acknowledgment.

One of those people was Stephen Quesenberry of Hobbs, Strauss, Dean & Walker, who has led the legal side of the decades-long acknowledgment effort for SSMN. His work blends passion for the cause with indignation at injustice. Scott Gediman, the National Park Service ranger in charge of public affairs at Yosemite, laid out how the park works with the tribes who once called it home. Sandra Chapman, SSMN chair, made it clear that Yosemite's wonder began not with John Muir but with her ancestors, several millennia ago.

Shelly Davis-King shared her fieldwork on the historical and contemporary reality of the central Sierra Nevada's tribal peoples, as did Sandra Gaskell. Malcolm Margolin dug out the source for an important detail told in his revelatory *Deep Hanging Out.* Mike Wurtz, head of the Holt-Atherton Special Collections and Archives at the University of the Pacific, not only found photos I needed but also, both repeatedly and graciously, pointed me to unpublished Muir journals that had just the quotation I was trying to source. Tiana Williams-Claussen, head of the Yurok Tribe's condor restoration program, took precious time away from her work to help me understand the tribal roots and mythic meaning of that effort.

The University of Nebraska Press proved yet again that theirs is the best team in publishing. Heather Stauffer made sure that all the parts of the manuscript came together with accuracy and humor, then lent her sharp eye to the copyediting. Ann Baker kept everything straight and in order during the mind-numbing production process. Nathan Putens designed the eye-catching cover. Rosemary Sekora, a writer herself, again proved she is the on-the-ball publicity manager all authors long for and Tayler Lord brought her publicist's smarts to getting this book out there.

And how I owe my family. Over the years of writing this book all my grandchildren were born—Callahan, Maeve, Devin—bearing their special link between present and future. The grown-up members of my family reminded me over and over how we are all connected to far more than ourselves: Darren and Sara, Brian and Renee, Ali, Aimée and Arnaud.

Most important, I owe Gayle Eleanor, my partner. She has long been the world's best first reader, but that's just the beginning. Her very presence blesses me.

Prologue

THE VIEW FROM SHEEPY RIDGE, ONE

In the chill gloaming of early December 1874, a lean, lanky devotee of wild backcountry stood on the rim of Sheepy Ridge, a high point in California's remote northeast, and looked out. His name, then barely known beyond the circle of family and friends, was John Muir. Wearing his curly hair and beard long and vaguely combed, he was dressed practically: high lace-up boots, well-worn pants with suspenders, threadbare jacket and shirt, and battered broad-brimmed hat. Expecting something marvelous, Muir had stepped away from the campfire's warmth and light to behold a landscape new to him.

I, too, have stood in that spot, but nearly a century and a half later. I know the wide view Muir took in. To the north, Tule Lake would have stretched in a giant sheet into Oregon, its stillness slowly purpling as the light faded. To the right and south, uncut forests of old-growth yellow pine softened the contours of the volcanic enormity known as the Medicine Lake Highland. Straight ahead, on the eastern horizon, the first snows capped the far-off peaks of the South Warner Range. Muir likely felt none of the elation I experienced at this magnificent panorama. Rather, something dark welled up in him: unlike any other wild space he encountered before or after, this one creeped him out.

Try as he might, Muir could not take his eyes off the Lava Beds, which lay directly below him at the foot of the ridge in an ominous jumble of "yawning fissures," "clusters of somber pits," and "swelling ridges." Scattered bunch-grass and sagebrush barely softened the land's volcanic disquiet. "Deserts are charming to those who know how to see them—all kinds of bogs, barrens, and heathy moors," Muir wrote, "but the Modoc lava beds have for me an uncanny look." The retreating light only worsened his morbid feeling: "The sun-purple slowly deepened over all the landscape, then darkness fell like a death, and I crept back to the blaze of the camp-fire."

As the flames held back the dark, Muir had to be mulling over his strange reaction to this wild place. He had just devoted the better part of five years to living in Yosemite Valley, making long solo hikes into the Sierra Nevada's granite grandeur and extolling in his journals and newspaper accounts the infinite peace and myriad blessings of the high and the sublime. Were he able to look ahead to the next four decades, he would see his writings and advocacy on behalf of protected wilderness win such widespread public support that he would become known as the father of the nation's national parks. In time, better dressed and barbered than he was on Sheepy Ridge, he would camp out with President Theodore Roosevelt in Yosemite and show him the sights, welcome the friendship and backroom political support of railroad baron E. H. Harriman, and preside over the Sierra Club, the elite wilderness-preservation organization he helped found—all in the interest of preserving landscapes he considered untouched and sacred. Yet here he was, at the wild edge of just such a space, feeling his skin goosebump and his spine shiver. Muir must have been wondering why.

He got his answer the next morning, when the local rancher guiding him and his fellow adventurers led them down Sheepy Ridge and onto the Lava Beds. There the naturalist recognized that the roots of his dread lay not in the volcanic terrain's strangeness but in the human drama that had played out there. The rock walls of a military graveyard at the foot of the ridge enclosed the bodies of thirty U.S. Army soldiers who'd been "surprised by the Modocs while eating lunch, scattered in the lava beds, and [were] shot down like bewildered sheep."[1] Those buried battlefield casualties cast the deathly pall Muir had felt the evening before.

The firefight that necessitated the graveyard figured into a war that had broken out almost exactly two years earlier, when Modocs (Móatoknis) living off-reservation on Tule Lake's north shore were set upon by a U.S. cavalry patrol and driven into the Lava Beds, their traditional citadel against attack. "The true strongholds of Indians are chiefly fields of tall grass, brushy woods, and shadowy swamps, where they can crouch like panthers and make themselves invisible, but the Modoc castle is in the rock," Muir reported. For more than six months, the besieged Modocs held out against an American force that in the end outnumbered them twenty-to-one. They proved to be fierce and determined, fighting to save themselves and their homeland against invasion. The war claimed dozens of cavalry lives, including Brig. Gen. E. R. S. Canby, the only general officer to die in a western Indian war. His killing during peace negotiations, trumpeted in newspaper headlines across the country, raised the war into a cosmic struggle between the infernal evil of the Modoc insurgents and the celestial good of the United States.[2] In the end the spent Modocs surrendered, four leaders were hanged to avenge Canby's killing, and 153 survivors—women, children, and elders as well as fighters—were exiled to an Oklahoma reservation to punish their insurgency.

Aware from ubiquitous and lurid newspaper accounts of the horror on the Lava Beds, Muir easily imagined the terror soldiers felt in this battlefield, where uplifted black rock twisted into "the most complete natural Gibraltar I ever saw." Modoc riflemen in well-chosen sniping positions picked off advancing infantry so perfectly that return fire only wasted powder and lead. "They were familiar with by-ways both over and under ground, and could at any time sink out of sight like squirrels among bowlders," Muir claimed. When a soldier did catch a rare glimpse of his Modoc foes, they became less targets than objects of fear and loathing, a feeling Muir shared: "The few that have come under my own observation had something repellent in their aspects, even when their features were in sunshine and settled in the calm of peace; when, therefore, they were crawling stealthily in these gloomy caves, unkempt and begrimed and with the glare of war in their eyes, they must have looked very devilish."

The caves where the Modocs sheltered during the conflict harkened back to what Muir saw as humankind's primitive origins. The volcanic overhang that housed Kientpoos, the headman settlers dubbed Captain Jack, was littered with the bones of cattle slaughtered, butchered, and roasted during the war. His rocky abode provided "a good specimen of a human home of the Stone Age," Muir reported. Clearly he believed the Modocs had opted for savagery over the civilization offered by America's inexorable advance. And their "unkempt and begrimed" appearance argued for how "unnatural" they were, less wild than degraded and unredeemed. "The worst thing about them is their uncleanliness," Muir wrote about Native Americans in general. "Nothing wild is unclean."[3]

In the worldview Muir was spelling out in his writings, the wilderness offered a sanctuary where humans—largely of the white, Anglo-Saxon, Protestant persuasion—could fully experience their spiritual essence. Native Americans just got in the way. Their presence sullied the pure wilderness where civilized Euro-Americans could marvel at the ongoing miracle of Eden before serpent and apple. With the dangerous, dirty Modocs no longer cluttering up the view or posing a threat to visitors seeking wild enlightenment, this landscape in the shadow of Mount Shasta could now achieve its highest purpose. "The Shasta region is still a fresh unspoiled wilderness," Muir wrote, "accessible and available for travelers of every kind and degree. Would it not then be a fine thing to set it apart like the Yellowstone and Yosemite as a National Park for the welfare and benefit of all mankind, preserving its fountains and forests and all its glad life in primeval beauty?"[4]

Muir hardly invented this point of view. Rather, over the course of his long and active life, he reflected, channeled, and rarefied thinking that arose in Europe and flowered in a United States filling with immigrants, cloaking Anglo-Saxon Protestant supremacy in fake science. Manifest destiny necessitated the conquest and dispossession of Native Americans; Muir extended this ideology to the continent's wildest reaches.

Muir's story began not in the sublime spaces of the American West that he worshipped but in the Scottish Lowlands where he had been born thirty-six years before standing atop Sheepy Ridge. There a grim, religious fanatic believed that his path to salvation lay in a young, hungry country located across the Atlantic. The time had come for him to make his way there.

CAST OUT OF EDEN

PART **1**

A Voice Crying for Wilderness

For this is he that was spoken of by the prophet Esaias, saying,
The voice of one crying in the wilderness.

—MATTHEW 3:3

1

From Old World to New

The fulfillment of our manifest destiny to overspread the continent allotted by Providence for the free development of our yearly multiplying millions.

—JOHN L. O'SULLIVAN, 1845

It was an evening seemingly like any other in the deep Scottish winter of 1849. Eleven-year-old John Muir and younger brother David were nestled with their maternal grandfather beside the fire, catching a few warm minutes before heading off to study for school the next morning. Daniel Muir, the boys' father, entered the room where the fire's glow lit the far wall. "Bairns, you needna learn your lessons the nicht," he announced in a Scots dialect gone unusually ebullient, "for we're gan to America the morn!"[1]

When Muir told this story more than sixty years later, he remembered imagining a door opening to untold wonders. This eleven-year-old was trading flat grain fields along the windblown North Sea for a country green with promise. He envisioned a big-leafed canopy of sugar maples and imagined the sky above it filled with hawks, eagles, and passenger pigeons in sun-darkening numbers. Propelled westward by hope and social forces he little understood, the young John Muir was about to become an immigrant bent on becoming a settler.

His father, Daniel, was a man on a cosmic mission whose energy, if not its dogma, he would pass on to his eldest son. Years of seeking religious truth

3

had convinced Daniel that his personal path toward holiness led to North America. It was time to make the move God willed.

Born in 1804 in Manchester, England, where his soldier father was stationed, Daniel was orphaned as an infant. His sister, Mary, eleven years his elder, took him in after she married. Once he grew big enough, Daniel took on the endless toil of a farm laborer, a harsh existence that likely played into his soul-deep joylessness. It contributed, too, to his conversion as a teenager to evangelical religion, the emotional Calvinism that drew in Scotland's poor, landless, working-class masses. The newly hooked Daniel became God-guided. He set out to find the truest of the true while, like his father, he enlisted in the British Army and rose in the ranks. Stationed as a recruiter in the port town of Dunbar, east of Edinburgh, Sergeant Muir met and married Helen Kennedy, who had inherited a grain-and-feed store from her father. Daniel convinced Helen to buy out his enlistment contract, and he took on managing the store. Always a hard worker, he turned it into a small success, and the business became his alone when his wife died suddenly.

Daniel soon married another local young woman, Ann Gilrye, whose father was a prosperous meat merchant on Dunbar's High Street. Children followed quickly. First came Margaret and Sarah, then John, followed by David, Daniel Jr., and twins Mary and Annie, all born in Scotland. The last Muir child, Joanna, would arrive in the United States. Expanding the grain-and-feed business into the first floor of a larger building down the street, the energetic Daniel turned the floors above into domestic quarters. In his spare time he grew a garden and was "always trying to make it as much like Eden as possible," John recalled. Meanwhile, his family grew, his status rose, and he won election to the city council.[2]

Daniel's decision to leave success behind turned on religion. He had for some time been a member of the Dunbar congregation of the Secessionist Church, which split from the Church of Scotland over the issue of ministry. The Church of Scotland held that only landowners could participate in selecting ministers; the Secessionists argued that the landless, too, should have a say. Yet, as the years passed, Daniel came to believe that even this arrangement placed too much human mediation between the individual believer and God. The faithful should minister to themselves.

In this rebellious frame of mind, Daniel learned of Alexander Campbell, a Secessionist minister's son who was embracing radical religious democracy. A Scot born in Ireland's Presbyterian north, Campbell studied divinity at the University of Glasgow and then left to join his father, who had emigrated to Pennsylvania. The father-son preaching duo created a stir along the settlement frontier, offering their version of the American religious revival that led also to the Shakers, the Rappites, the Seventh-day Adventists, the Spiritualists, and the Church of Jesus Christ of Latter-day Saints. Calling themselves the Disciples of Christ, the Campbells and their followers flourished, soon becoming the fastest-growing denomination in the young republic.[3]

In 1847 Alexander Campbell returned to Scotland on a preaching tour and held forth in Edinburgh one hot August day. There, it is likely, Daniel Muir joined the sweaty, adoring audience. Finding in Campbell the charismatic leader he was seeking, Daniel soon converted to the radically egalitarian, evangelical Protestantism practiced by the Disciples of Christ. The Disciples looked beyond Europe and its entrenched hierarchies to democratic North America as the land promised to the young denomination's true believers.

Within five months, Daniel resolved to forsake the familiar and embrace this new world. On the morning of February 19, 1849, Muir headed off with three of his children, John among them, to make their way to America and prepare a home to receive the rest of the family. The first leg was a train trip to Glasgow, where Muir booked passage on the *Warren*, a three-masted, modest-sized packet ship built only two years earlier in Maine and registered in New York. The *Warren* sailed on a regular schedule between Glasgow and New York carrying both passengers and cargo. On February 24, five days after the Muirs left Dunbar, the ship sailed out of Edinburgh's Broomielaw Harbor toward the open Atlantic.[4]

The four Muirs and seventy-two other passengers on the *Warren* were adding to that year's thousands-strong wave of Scots emigrating to North America. All had given up on their homeland for reasons that ranged from financial to religious. Their future lay in becoming settler colonists.[5]

Say "colony," and contemporary Americans tend to think of the British Empire and India. India was, indeed, a colony. The British conquered the subcontinent with superior military force, took control of its resources and population, and put Indians to work producing wealth for Britain's benefit.

Some Britons lived in India to work in the armed forces and the colonial administration that kept the colony under the empire's thumb. Yet India's purpose was never to provide a new homeland for British immigrants. India was what academics call an "exploitation colony."

North America followed a different arc. In the first centuries after Columbus reminded Europe of the continent's existence, the French, the Spanish, the Dutch, and the English established various and competing exploitation colonies. As in India, the business model consisted of extracting resources—from beaver pelts and timber to sugar and tobacco—and exploiting Indigenous people to do the work. Sometimes Europeans traded with the locals, particularly for furs, and they relied on enslaved Indigenous labor far more than most contemporary Americans realize. When that supply fell short, enslaved Africans were imported beginning in the sixteenth century to close the labor gap, particularly in the plantation economy of the Caribbean and what became the southern United States.

The nature of the English-speaking colonies shifted slowly but inevitably through the seventeenth and eighteenth centuries. Fewer and fewer young men came to seek their fortunes and then return to Britain with a stash. Now families, even entire communities, crossed the Atlantic not only to take advantage of America's riches but also to claim new homes for themselves. They sought less what the land provided than the land itself. That shift gave birth to the "settler colony."

Once this exploitation colony became a settler colony, the locals only got in the way. For settler colonists to obtain full control of the land, its Indigenous inhabitants had to go. No longer were they a source of trade or labor; they had become a hurdle to be leapt, an impediment to be removed, a problem to be erased. "Settler colonialism," writes Australian anthropologist Patrick Wolfe, "destroys to replace."[6] This was the global shift the Muirs had signed up to advance: destroy to replace. First, though, Daniel Muir had to decide exactly where.

When he boarded the *Warren* with his three children, Daniel intended to head for the backwoods of what was then known as Upper Canada (now Ontario), a destination popular among Disciples of Christ. By the time the vessel docked in New York City, he had taken the advice of other Scots onboard and decided against Canada as too thickly wooded to be easily cleared and farmed. By the time he booked passage on another ship going up the Hudson to Albany, New York, and bought train tickets to Buffalo, he was wavering in choosing between Michigan and Wisconsin. A fellow Disciple from Dunbar convinced Muir that Wisconsin, which had been admitted to the union as a state only a year earlier, held the greater promise. Muir bought himself and his three children passage on a Great Lakes steamer to Milwaukee. From there the Muirs traveled in a farmer's hard-jolting wagon more than a hundred miles over bad, spring-muddy roads. They were headed toward the new state's frontier, the space where, according to the census, population density was less than two persons per square mile—a demographic that didn't count Native Americans.[7] Parking his children in a rented room in the village of Kingston, Muir soon located and purchased 160 acres of openly wooded land on the glacial Fountain Lake. The price was two hundred dollars, the minimum in those days and the equivalent of a mere five thousand dollars in contemporary currency. On the Wisconsin frontier, the promised land came cheap.

Muir bought his homestead from the Fox and Wisconsin River Improvement Company, a private company struggling to build a canal between the Fox and Wisconsin Rivers. The canal site lay near Portage, a village whose very name told of its history. A mushy mile of swamp separated the two rivers, and for centuries Indigenous canoeists had carried their light and nimble vessels from the one to the other, thus creating a watery trade route from the Mississippi Valley all the way to Lake Michigan at Green Bay. In the bustling days of the fur trade, French voyageurs recognized the strategic importance of the site and dubbed it Le Portage. When the United States took over, the name was anglicized to Portage. The beaver were gone by 1825, though, and the fur trade that had brought the French disappeared. By the time the Muirs arrived on what had become the American frontier, the only local furbearer of any commercial consequence was the lowly muskrat.[8]

Portage, Fountain Lake (known today as Ennis Lake), and the surrounding countryside had originally fallen within the extensive domain of the Ho-Chunks, a Siouan-speaking people also called the Winnebagos. They, along with their allies the Menominees, had seen their world collapse in the seventeenth and early eighteenth centuries with the arrival of the French and an influx of Algonquian and Haudenosaunee peoples from the east and north willing to fight to expand their territories. To survive, the Ho-Chunks accepted protection from the French and adjusted to the economics of the fur trade. At the same time, diseases spread by the French and compounded by war with the Indigenous newcomers sapped the Ho-Chunks' strength as a people.[9]

The situation continued to deteriorate following the War of 1812, when the United States took control of what would become first the territory, then the state, of Wisconsin. As more Euro-Americans poured in and seized land for themselves, Ho-Chunks took to killing settlers' livestock, sniping at travelers on the Fox River, and raiding unwelcome lead miners who raped Ho-Chunk women. The sexual assaults led to a limited and short-lived conflict dubbed with overdone grandeur as the Winnebago War of 1827. The much larger and more consequential Black Hawk War of 1832, which was fought across parts of what are now Iowa, Illinois, and Wisconsin, split the Ho-Chunk nation three ways. Some fought with Black Hawk's rebels, others joined forces with the Americans, and still others kept on fishing and hunting and tried to stay out of the line of fire. In the end they all lost.[10]

Government pressure to clear Wisconsin of its Native American inhabitants rose in the years following Black Hawk's defeat. The year 1837 proved to be the costliest for the Ho-Chunks. Tribal negotiators who traveled to Washington DC to bargain a treaty were held hostage all winter to pressure them into agreeing to the government's demands. In the spring they returned home with assurances that they could remain in Wisconsin another eight years before ceding their lands to the federal government, picking up stakes, and moving across the Mississippi River. Back at home, though, they learned that the eight years had been cut to only eight months—one more instance of the bad faith that drove the United States' dealings with Indigenous nations. When the deadline came and the Ho-Chunks were expected to move west, many rejected the agreement as invalid and stayed on in defiance. The next year, Gen. Henry Atkinson, who had commanded the American forces in the Black Hawk War, showed up with a military unit to drive the Ho-Chunks out in the Midwest's version of the Trail of Tears. But no sooner had the dispossessed Ho-Chunks been deposited on the far side of the Mississippi than some of them slipped back to the lands they and their ancestors had long called home. There they took up quiet, secretive lives.[11]

Not that there was much space for them to reoccupy. With every tribal cession of land and forced migration, more emigrants from eastern states and Europe appeared to stake their claims. In Wisconsin, the influx rose to a flood. Overall, the United States' population grew by a little over half between 1836 and 1850; Wisconsin grew by more than twenty-five times in those same years. The Muirs helped swell that great white wave of settler colonists aiming to seize a home of their own at Native Americans' expense.[12]

The Muir family's neighbors along the fast-filling frontier line were largely people of similar European origin. By 1850, one-third of Wisconsin's population was foreign-born, among them 3,527 Scots like the Muirs. Other nationalities came as well: Germans, Irish, English, Norwegians, French Canadians, Swiss, Dutch, Welsh, and Danes. They were drawn by the promise of fertile land made vacant and available by tribal treaties of cession and forced migration. Daniel Muir's Disciples of Christ flourished in the frontier culture of this expanding settler colony.[13]

The Disciples gave the nineteenth-century American dream a millennial cast in the West, a land promised to them as God's chosen people, much as the Hebrews envisioned Canaan. "To the Saxons in Europe, to the Anglo-Saxons in Britain, to the American Anglo-Saxons on this continent," Disciples of Christ cofounder Alexander Campbell proclaimed, "God has given the sceptre of Judah, the harp of David, the strength of Judah's Lion, and the wealth of the world." Tracing Anglo-Saxon origins through the Biblical generations to Noah's son Japheth, Campbell argued that Catholics were Christian in name only and that American political liberty depended on Protestantism. As for Native Americans, their pagan "war whoop and yell" stood in telling contrast with Anglo-Saxon Christian hymns; they were unbaptized heathens unworthy of occupying a rich and promising land like Wisconsin. To fulfill God's plan for spreading salvation and civilization worldwide, Native Americans, like the wild forest and the virgin soil, must give way. The Disciples of Christ were laying the foundation for the mashup of Protestant millennialism and militant American patriotism that was coming to be known as manifest destiny.[14]

Even as Daniel Muir, ever the faithful Disciple, labored to carve a farm from the Wisconsin woods, he took Campbell's dictates to heart. One of Muir's neighbors, a fellow Scot, lamented that it was pitiful to see landless Ho-Chunks scratching out a living that only became harder as more and more newcomers filled up what once had been their homeland. Daniel, son John wrote, "replied that surely it could never have been the intention of God to allow Indians to rove and hunt over so fertile a country and hold it forever in unproductive wildness, while Scotch and Irish and English farmers could put it to so much better use." These "industrious, God-fearing farmers" not only supported perhaps a hundred times more people on the same reach of land as the Ho-Chunks; they also were "at the same time helping to spread the gospel."

The critical neighbor lambasted as well the farming practices of Wisconsin settlers as unskilled and ignorant, abusing land on which educated agriculturalists could have raised five or ten times more per acre. To that accusation Muir's father had no answer, and John, who would later in life become an entrepreneurial agriculturalist himself, thought the critical neighbor had "the better side of the argument." Indeed, the conquest of Wisconsin served as an example of "the rule of might with but little thought for the right or welfare of the other fellow if he were the weaker; and that 'they should take who had the power, and they should keep who can,' as Wordsworth makes the marauding Scottish Highlanders say."[15]

Whatever sympathy John was feeling for the displaced Ho-Chunks faded in the day-to-day demands of making a living from the land. At the south end of the Muirs' homestead above Fountain Lake, John discovered a mound edged with grass-thatched Ho-Chunk burial sites along with more graves down the slope in the direction of the water. John, put behind the plow by age twelve, and his father accorded the graves and their inhabitants no special treatment. When the plow came to the graves, Muir remembered without any seeming regret that "we ploughed them down, turning the old bones they covered into corn and wheat."[16]

Not that living Ho-Chunks impressed the Muirs any more than the dead and buried. From time to time lone, nameless men appeared outside the kitchen door to beg for pork, flour, or matches, occasionally offering a fish in trade. One man stopped to sharpen a knife or tomahawk on the farmyard grindstone before asking for food and so frightened John's sister Sarah that she feared for her life until he walked off, the newly honed weapon tucked harmlessly in his belt.

Another Ho-Chunk shot a piglet along a trail that ran near the Muir home. Yet another made off with a workhorse named Nob and rode her to the town of Green Lake, some forty miles away, where he hoped to sell her. When a farmer thinking of buying the mare saw that she was shod, he accused the Ho-Chunk of horse theft and seized the animal. A month or two passed before the farmer located the Muirs and returned Nob. The thief, Muir recalled, must have treated her cruelly; whenever she passed near the spot where she had been rustled, her heart beat as hard as a thrumming partridge.

The family dog, Watch, qualified as a "a good judge of character," Muir wrote. One crisp winter morning John was walking with the dog north of Fountain Lake when Watch's nose questioned the air and his coat bristled. Racing upslope to get a view of the water, dog and boy spotted a Ho-Chunk hunter hefting a spear and moving in practiced silence from one muskrat den to another, listening closely and thrusting his weapon through the reedy walls at the least hint of rustling. If luck held, the hunter speared a muskrat destined to become meat on the table and a pelt worth a precious dime. It amazed John that Watch's keen smell detected the Ho-Chunk from a half-mile off. "Had the hunter been a white man, I suppose Watch would not have noticed him," Muir remembered.[17]

Scent also guided the mosquitoes that arose in hungry springtime hordes and displayed distinct preferences among the district's inhabitants. If they were hungry enough, "they would drink their fill from brown, smoky Indians, or from old white folk flavored with tobacco and whisky," Muir wrote. But what the pests preferred over all was white "boys full of lively red blood, and . . . girls in full bloom fresh from cool Scotland or England."

Still, the Ho-Chunks' skills in finding wild food amazed young John. Ho-Chunk hunters would walk directly up to a tree that looked like all the other trees in that patch of woods, chop into the trunk with their tomahawks, and pull out raccoons that John and his friends had no idea were denning there. The boys also spotted few deer even though their tracks were abundant. After the first winter snow, the boys often saw three or four

Ho-Chunks following a fresh trail of hoofprints like coursing hounds. The hunters were "noiseless, tireless," and their pursuit so dogged that rarely did they fail to run their quarry to ground and lay fresh venison on the fire.[18]

Muir's thoughts on the propriety of plowing up Indigenous graves, his dog's keen nose for tribal hunters, the preferences of mosquitoes for sweet-smelling Anglo-Saxon children, and the tireless tenacity of Ho-Chunk trackers appear in what some people consider his early writings. That's not quite right. In fact, Muir told the tales of his early days from the perspective of a seventy-one-year-old elder. He began what became *The Story of My Boyhood and Youth* in the summer of 1908, and the book itself was published in 1913, the year before he died.

Given his maturity, Muir could have repudiated the easy racism that plagued the Wisconsin frontier and became a bedrock of the expanding American republic. His own life contained testimony to the possibility of such a shift. The middle-aged Muir displayed a compassion and insight toward the Indigenous peoples of southeast Alaska and the Arctic that was remarkable for his time. Yet, as he was writing about his early years long after these head-turning northern experiences, he returned to that earlier time and its fast belief that Indigenous peoples had to be supplanted and would soon fade away. Although Muir had long ceased to follow the Disciples of Christ, the spirit of Alexander Campbell's teaching guided him still. The world belonged to the Anglo-Saxons of North America and Europe, who were chosen by God to cleanse the world and bring its many pagans and primitive peoples to civilization. While Muir was composing the story of his early years, the trope of the "vanishing" American Indian was all the cultural rage. Muir played into that story as he reconstructed the narrative of how he had started out in a Wisconsin where the last Ho-Chunks were inevitably fading into oblivion.

What most held Muir's fascination as a Wisconsin youngster was the wild sans its human inhabitants, whether Euro-American or Indigenous. "Oh, that glorious Wisconsin wilderness!" he wrote of his earliest days on the Fountain Lake homestead. "Everything new and pure in the very prime of spring when Nature's pulses were beating highest and mysteriously keeping time with our own!" Muir was discovering a world unlike any he had known in Scotland: "Everything about us was so novel and wonderful that we could hardly believe our senses except when hungry or while father was thrashing us."[19]

Hacking the farm out of the Fountain Lake woods made for endless body-breaking labor, and as the eldest son John took up much of the burden. Workdays stretched to sixteen or seventeen hard, sweaty hours. And Muir worked those long days under the domination of a father who intimidated his children with descriptions of the hellfire that would burn young sinners for eternity. When such sermons failed to instill what Daniel considered good behavior, he beat his children. In the language of the time, he was a strict disciplinarian; these days, Daniel Muir would be labeled physically abusive. For young John the Wisconsin woods became an escape and refuge from endless work and arbitrary punishment: "but those terrible fire lessons quickly faded away in the blithe wilderness air; for no fire can be hotter than the heavenly fire of faith and hope that burns in every healthy boy's heart."[20] Wilderness would retain its aura of sanctuary and refuge throughout Muir's life.

When eight years of farming exhausted the soil and reduced the grain crop at the Fountain Lake farm, Daniel moved his family to another site, a few miles to the east, and began again the hard labor of turning forest into farm. The family dubbed this new place Hickory Hill for its many trees. The high, dry site with no springs, creeks, or lakes needed a well to be habitable, and Daniel put John to the task of digging through the sandstone to the water table with hammer and mason's chisel. The bore had reached some eighty feet deep when Daniel lowered his son in a wooden bucket one morning to resume work. Nearly oxygen-free gas had gathered overnight in the bore's bottom and quickly overwhelmed John. He passed out, then startled awake. Hearing his father calling from up top, a confused John fumbled his way back into the bucket. Daniel raised him to the surface, where he finally gasped the clear, clean air he needed.

A stone mason neighbor taught Daniel how to dissipate the gas by dumping water down the shaft and dropping a bundle of brush or hay on a light rope again and again to mix the gas with air. Confident that these measures would work, Daniel sent John back down the hole to finish the job. "Father never spent an hour in that well," John wrote later in a line fairly dripping with resentment at the danger his clueless and authoritarian parent had put him in.[21] Now nineteen years old, tall and lean and drawn toward a wider and less laborious world, the son was building toward a break.

As the old song goes, "How ya gonna keep 'em down on the farm, After they've seen Paree?" Muir's first lesson in the possibility of escape came from a source a tad less elegant than the city on the Seine: the Wisconsin state fair.

2

A Widening World Darkens

And Saul arose from the earth; and when his eyes were opened, he
saw no man: but they led him by the hand, and brought him into
Damascus. And he was three days without sight, and neither did
eat nor drink. . . . And Ananias went his way, and entered into the
house; and putting his hands on him said, Brother Saul, the Lord,
even Jesus, that appeared unto thee in the way as thou camest, hath
sent me, that thou mightest receive thy sight, and be filled with the
Holy Ghost. And immediately there fell from his eyes as it had been
scales: and he received sight forthwith, and arose and was baptized.

—ACTS OF THE APOSTLES 9:8, 17–18

On the Fountain Lake farm it fell to young John Muir to hoe the crops to
keep weeds down, hard work that made for a long, back-breaking day. The
laborious task became much simpler when Daniel Muir put up the money
for mechanical cultivators. His son took that lesson to heart: by devising a
contraption that makes the job easier, the future brightens.[1] Muir was a fan
of technology as well as nature, and he demonstrated a self-taught talent
for inventing it.

Determined to pursue a newfound love of Shakespeare and Milton and
to invent the next big thing, Muir cut his sleep to only five hours per winter
night and rose early to both read and tinker. First came a self-setting sawmill,
then a series of "waterwheels, curious door locks and latches, thermometers,
hygrometers, pyrometers, clocks, a barometer, an automatic contrivance for

feeding the horses at any required hour, a lamplighter and a fire-lighter, an early-or-late rising machine, and so forth." Displaying an inborn knack for engineering, Muir moved on to a timekeeper that told the day of the week and date as well as hour and minute. The contraption could be adapted to wake him at the time of his choosing, then start a fire for warmth or light a lamp for reading.

Muir's inventions impressed neighbors, who pronounced the boy a genius sure to rise in the world. One nearby settler encouraged Muir to exhibit his work at the upcoming state fair, noting that surely his clever machines would earn him a good-paying job in a machine shop. Bucked up and determined, Muir headed to Madison, Wisconsin's capital, carrying under his inventive arm two clocks and a small thermometer fashioned from hickory wood. With his machines on exhibit in the fair's Temple of Arts building, this farm-boy-turned-inventor won raves in the press and a cash prize.[2]

Norman Wiard, another inventor at the fair, sensed a kindred tinkering spirit in Muir and offered him a job in his Prairie du Chien machine shop. Muir soon found he was learning little he didn't already know in Wiard's small operation, and he moved on to a new position where he traded work for meals and devoted his free time to studying science. When he made little headway in self-education, Muir returned to Madison hoping to enter the University of Wisconsin: "I was desperately hungry and thirsty for knowledge and willing to endure anything to get it."[3]

Muir's palpable desire proved persuasive. Although he had had no formal schooling since Scotland, he talked the acting president of the university into admitting him into the preparatory department where he could polish his academic skills. Muir advanced to the university as a freshman in February 1861, just as the United States was tumbling toward the chaos of the Civil War.

In the sheltered, immigrant enclave around Portage where Muir grew up, the issues at stake in the looming war looked distant and abstract. To begin with, Muir felt more allegiance to Scotland than to the United States, as did many of the neighbors. The Disciples of Christ held themselves at a theological arm's length from the terrible struggle about to break upon the country. Disciples disapproved of war and championed nonviolence and pacifism, a position Muir echoed. "This war seems farther from a close than ever," he wrote in a letter after hostilities had erupted. "How strange that a country with so many schools and churches should be desolated by so unsightly a monster." In the cycle of life, leaves yield their green to wither and die, "but may the same be said of the slaughtered on the battle field?" he asked rhetorically.[4]

Nor did slavery constitute an evil so great that taking up arms against it was justified. Many Disciples of Christ leaders opposed the peculiar institution, though they generally did not favor immediate emancipation. Others were equivocal or even supportive of slavery. Founder Alexander Campbell argued that nothing in the New Testament forbade enslavement and that slaveholders as well as abolitionists could be Disciples. He saw slavery as a political question and not a moral issue demanding Christian attention.[5]

The outbreak of war in April 1861 suddenly and dramatically changed Madison and the university. The state fairgrounds turned into an army training center named Fort Randall after the state's Republican—and enthusiastically prowar—governor. Some seventy thousand recruits passed through the camp on their way to the battlefield over the course of the conflict and endured endless drills and discipline. Sex workers and liquor sellers took every possible advantage of the displaced, bored, and horny young men. Muir, disturbed by Camp Randall's licentious atmosphere, visited recruits he knew as friends from Portage and Prairie du Chien, and he urged them to hold to the straight, narrow, and evangelical Christian path. Camp Randall showed him, too, direct evidence of war's horrors. Approximately twelve hundred Confederate prisoners of war were held at the camp under such bad conditions that 140 of them died. Muir witnessed their suffering in the camp hospital and considered heading off to medical school at the University of Michigan to learn how to alleviate such misery.[6]

The war had another consequence. With so many of Wisconsin's young men volunteering for the army, falling student enrollment slashed the university's revenue. "Our University has reached a crisis in its history," Muir wrote to his sister Sarah and brother-in-law David, "and if not passed successfully, the doors will be closed, when of course I should have to leave Madison for some institution that has not yet been wounded by our war-demon."[7] Rescue for Muir and the University of Wisconsin did come—from expropriated Native American land.

The Morrill Act, also known as the Agricultural College Act, was signed into law by Pres. Abraham Lincoln in 1862, Muir's second academic year in

Madison. The new law promised each state between 90,000 and 990,000 acres, based on the size of its congressional delegation, as long as the state agreed to conserve and invest the principal raised from the land grant and to establish a university-level agriculture department. What the law did not say was that the land to be distributed—nearly eleven million acres in total, an area larger than all of Maryland or two-thirds of West Virginia—had been taken from tribal nations under coercion, force, and dubious treaty. The government of Wisconsin accepted its Morrill grant of 235,530 acres of formerly Ojibwe and Menominee land in 1863, and in 1866 the state designated the University of Wisconsin as the beneficiary of what became a $303,349 endowment. Like the "frontier" created by forcing Indigenous people from their territories, the "free" land the university received was taken to benefit Euro-Americans at the expense of Native Americans. That was how settler colonialism worked, and it kept John Muir in school.[8]

In his two and a half years at the university, Muir took no regular curriculum. Instead he studied where his interests led, primarily botany and geology with some chemistry and mathematics. All were taught by Ezra Carr, a physician who served as the university's sole science instructor. Muir leavened this rich diet with a side of classical Latin and Greek. In the process, he discovered field botany and built a mystical relationship with the discipline and its practice. Muir learned to look beyond the colorful wonder of flowers in order to perceive "their inner beauty, all alike revealing glorious traces of the thoughts of God, and leading on and on into the infinite cosmos. I wandered away at every opportunity, making long excursions round the lakes, gathering specimens and keeping them fresh in a bucket in my room to study at night after my regular class tasks were learned; for my eyes never closed on the plant glory I had seen."[9]

Muir's botanical passion was fueled in part by his budding relationship with Jeanne Carr, Ezra Carr's wife, who was an adept amateur botanist as well as an enthusiast for the writings of Ralph Waldo Emerson. Growing up in New England, she had known the great Transcendentalist personally. Emerson offered a world of light in place of Calvin's darkness and held forth a profoundly religious view of the natural world. Muir received even more Emersonian influence from James Davie Butler, Muir's classics professor,

who counseled his students to take up Emerson's discipline of keeping commonplace books. Muir set to journaling his many wanderings, a practice he
followed for the rest of his life.[10]

Soon Muir's satisfaction from books and classes was falling short. Something bigger, something cosmic, called to him from beyond Madison and
its wartime chaos and into the wider world's wonders. Muir dreamed of
wandering free and loose in the remote regions of the continent during
a three-week camping and botanizing trip across Wisconsin and into Iowa
with two college friends in summer 1863. Embarking on such an odyssey to
regions unknown meant saying goodbye to Madison. He reflected, "I was
only leaving one University for another, the Wisconsin University for the
University of the Wilderness."[11]

First, though, Muir went back to Portage and the Fountain Lake farm,
where he stayed with his sister Sarah and brother-in-law David Galloway, who
had purchased 120 acres of the property from Daniel Muir.[12] A few months
before John Muir's return, the United States Congress passed the Civil War
Military Draft Act to swell the ranks of a Union Army steadily depleted by
disease and battle. Concerned that his name could appear on a draft list, Muir
lingered to learn his fate. After several months of waiting, he still had not
been called. As the spring of 1864 promised warmth and thaw, Muir decided
to head for Canada. Across the border, the chaos of war would be less disturbing to his pacifist soul, and he could explore a new land and its botany.

Muir began his trek close to the point where Lakes Huron, Michigan, and
Superior merge, then headed south, botanizing as he went, into what is now
Ontario. He traveled light, sleeping rough without blankets and relying on
bread bought from settlers' kitchens. Thus fortified, he was "able to wander
many a long, wild mile, free as the winds in the glorious forests and bogs,
gathering plants and feeding on God's abounding, inexhaustible spiritual
beauty bread." He confessed obliquely to just one instance of fear. "Only
once in my long wanderings was the deep peace of the wilderness savagely
broken," Muir wrote. It happened about midnight when the campfire in the
maple woods burned low. "I was awakened by the awfully dismal howling of
the wolves, and got up in haste to replenish the fire."[13]

When several months of tramping used up almost all his money, Muir
settled for the winter in Trout Hollow, near Meaford on the southeast shore

of Lake Huron, and took a job in a rake factory. Muir's inner inventor reemerged, and he struck a deal with the owners to improve the factory's machinery in return for half the increased revenues. Ever the clever industrial engineer, Muir built a self-feeding lathe that nearly doubled output. Then, in a humbling twist of fate, the fortune he was in line to make went up in smoke when the factory burned to the ground in late February 1866. Wiped out financially, Muir trudged back into the United States, which had become a different place after the Union's Civil War victory and Lincoln's assassination almost a year earlier.[14] In the months to come, Muir would receive an on-the-ground lesson in the racial realities of a reunited America.

It began in Indianapolis, then an industrial boomtown on the tamed flatlands of central Indiana. Soon after he stepped off the train, Muir found work in a factory that produced wooden hubs and spokes for wagon wheels and handles for plows. Although the job made him one more automaton in a faceless urban proletariat, Muir was "determined not to leave until I have made my *invention mark*." He saw his labor as part of an advancing racial hierarchy; Scots like him were "the salt of the earth—the salt of *machines*." And, as he admonished his brother Daniel in a letter, "the streets must be trodden not by 'black Gentoos [Hindus] & pagan Turks' but by the white and fixin loving peoples of the sons of Japheth [Noah's third son]." Summoning the biblical genealogy that Disciples of Christ founder Alexander Campbell invented to underscore Anglo-Saxon dominance, Muir placed himself at the tip of the spear in civilization's conquest of dark-skinned heathendom.[15]

That connection to his faith led Muir to devote Sunday mornings to the Disciples congregation in the city. In the afternoons, his hunger for the wild led him out of Indianapolis's industrial wasteland to tramp about surviving pockets of oak and hickory forest. Muir needed green as much as God.[16]

In a frightening way, he discovered too how much he needed light. In the factory, as he was using a file to shorten the stretched band of a newly installed circular saw, a slip of the hand drove the tool's point deep into his right eye. The eye shut in shock from the blow. When Muir opened it, aqueous humor—the jellylike substance that fills the eyeball's interior—slipped into his palm in a warm, wet glop. "My right eye is gone," Muir murmured to himself, "closed forever on all God's beauty." Still seeing well enough to walk to his boardinghouse, he took to his bed. Soon his left eye, too, dimmed and went out.[17]

Muir suffered from classic sympathetic ophthalmia. First described by Hippocrates more than twenty centuries earlier, the condition is now thought to be an autoimmune response to proteins from the injured eye circulating through the body. The immune system reads them as foreign and attacks with inflammation that swells, damages, and blinds the uninjured eye. Sometimes the blindness resolves over time, but sometimes it persists.[18]

Confined to an unlit room, unable to read the poets he admired or to saunter in the woodlands he loved, Muir prepared to face the worst: "I was in total darkness and feared that I would become permanently blind." His Disciples of Christ faith held that all things and events evidenced God's hidden hand, but "during these dark weeks I could not feel this, and, as for courage and fortitude, scarce the shadows of these virtues were left me. The shock upon my nervous system made me weak in mind as a child," he confided to Jeanne Carr.[19] For months he was enveloped in this dark night of the soul.

Rescue came, slowly. He recalled how "the lonely dark days of waiting were cheered by friends, many of them little children. After sufficient light could be admitted, they patiently read for me, and brought me great handfuls of the flowers I liked best." As the world and his own soul lit up with sight's slow return in both eyes, Muir underwent conversion, like Saul in Damascus. "Now had I arisen from the grave," he wrote to Jeanne Carr. Seeing the world anew, he realized that the sterile, synthetic world of factory and industry left him spiritually hungry. He needed "to store my mind with the Lord's beauty and thus be ready for any fate, light or dark."[20]

A new pilgrim had been set on a mystical path that would in time lead to the grandeur of Yosemite Valley. First, though, he determined to head south. Another continent invited exploration.

"How intensely I desire to be a Humboldt!" Muir exclaimed to Jeanne Carr while he focused on making better rake handles. Alexander von Humboldt, said by his contemporaries to be the most famous man on earth after Napoleon, was not only a brilliant scientist and philosopher of nature but also a long-distance walker with a penchant for the wild side. Born a Prussian nobleman, he spent five years at the turn of the nineteenth century traveling in the Americas, tramping in Venezuela's rainforests to record their blazing botanical diversity, and climbing Ecuador's Chimborazo volcano—20,548 feet in altitude and thought then to be the highest mountain on Earth—to grasp the cosmic mural of nature's interwoven unity.[21]

Muir longed to complete his own version of such a vision quest among South America's wild marvels. "For many a year I have been impelled toward the Lord's tropic gardens of the South. Many influences have tended to blunt or bury this constant longing, but it has outlived and overpowered them all," he wrote. As light returned to Muir's world, he saw his chance. "I bade adieu to mechanical inventions, determined to devote the rest of my life to the study of the inventions of God." He sketched out a vague itinerary, proposing "to go South and see something of the vegetation of the warm end of the country, and if possible wander far enough into South America to see tropical vegetation in all its palm glory."[22] On September 1, 1867, Muir said goodbye to Indianapolis and boarded a train that took him to the Ohio River across from Louisville, Kentucky. There he commenced to walk south, ever south.

Muir planned to cross Kentucky, Tennessee, North Carolina, and Georgia to Florida and reach the Gulf of Mexico. From there he figured on finding a boat to Cuba and then sailing on to South America. "My plan," he made clear, "was simply to push on in a general southward direction by the wildest, leafiest, and least trodden way I could find." He traveled both focused and light. A change of underwear, a bar of soap, a comb. And he carried four books: the verse of Robert Burns to nourish his Scottish soul; John Milton's *Paradise Lost* to sing to him of the central biblical drama of Eden's loss; the New Testament to connect him to his faith as a Disciple; and Alphonso Wood's fat and utilitarian *A Class-Book of Botany* to identify the plants he saw. Finally, he added a press to preserve the botanical specimens he collected and a journal to record his impressions and thoughts.[23]

Muir sought out "the inventions of God." On this long hike that set the pattern for his later explorations of the Sierra Nevada, he encountered many a natural revelation: "the Cumberland Mountains, the first real mountains that my foot ever touched or eyes beheld"; insight into the complicated life stories of plants ("How little we know as yet of the life of plants—their hopes and fears, pains and enjoyments!") and the divinity of botany ("Oh, these forest gardens of our Father! What perfection, what divinity, in their architecture!"); and, in the style of Humboldt, the cosmic unity of the wild world ("There is not a fragment in nature, for every relative fragment of one thing is a full harmonious unit in itself"). If Muir had had his druthers, he would have avoided civilization altogether except for the necessity of fetching bread every few days.[24] Despite Muir's desire to travel like a holy hermit rejecting the human-made world and embracing only the divine, the South's social, political, and racial reality would prove unavoidable.

The region was yet reeling from the Civil War. Somewhere around three hundred thousand people had died in the beaten Confederacy, the Southern economy was burned and broken, and millions of African Americans had been emancipated. The wild wanderer was encountering an America unlike anything in his experience as immigrant and student.

Back in Wisconsin, Muir had precious little contact with African Americans. As of 1860, there were but twelve hundred Black residents among the state's population of almost 776,000, or a tiny 0.15 percent. Even those few were hardly welcome. In 1861 a white mob dragged a Black man accused of murder from a Milwaukee jail cell and lynched him. In 1863, while Muir was attending the university and the Civil War raged on, legislators in Madison introduced several bills seeking to block further Black immigration into the state. The bills failed, but the racist sentiment behind them lived on.[25]

Muir's lack of familiarity with African Americans changed on his second day in Kentucky, when he prepared to cross the Rolling Fork River. He started to ford on foot when a Black woman on the opposite bank called to him to stop, warning that that the current was too deep and fast. If he kept on, he would "'sartain [*sic*] be drowned,'" so "the cautious old soul" set off to fetch a horse. A stilt-legged white horse appeared, ridden by a "little sable n—— boy." Muir swung up behind him. "I mounted behind little N——. He was a queer specimen, puffy and jet as an India rubber doll and his hair was matted in sections like the wool of a merino sheep." The horse made it across despite its double load and deposited Muir on the far bank. Too bad, he thought, that the horse failed to throw them into the stream, since a bath would have benefitted both of them. He mused, "I could swim and little Afric looked as if he might float like a bladder."[26]

Racist as Muir's stereotypes and language were, he did talk to African Americans at length. On his way to Mammoth Cave he overtook an old Black man driving an ox team and hitched a ride for a few miles. They chatted all the while. The Black teamster told Muir how war had come to the very road they were on. "'Right heah,' said he, 'is where the Rebs was a-tearin' up the track, and they all a sudden thought they seed the Yankees a-comin', obah dem big hills dar, and Lo'd, how dey run,'" Muir recorded in his journal. When Muir asked whether the man would like to see a return of "these sad war times," the old man made it clear he was against any more fighting. Something in his manner impressed Muir, and he observed that "many of these Kentucky n———s are shrewd and intelligent, and when warmed upon a subject that interests them, are eloquent in no mean degree."

Muir decided that shrewd and intelligent though they were, Blacks lacked the least work ethic. "The n———s are easy-going and merry, making a great deal of noise and doing little work," he wrote. "One energetic white man, working with a will, would easily pick as much cotton as half dozen Sambos and Sallies." It never occurred to Muir that he was witnessing resistance to hor-rific working conditions, even after he learned from a plantation owner that labor following emancipation actually cost less than it had under slavery. Black people were legally free, but they still got the short end of the economic stick.[27]

As he neared Athens, Georgia, Muir discovered that Black field hands lived in old slave quarters, worked the same antebellum fields, and made only seven to ten dollars a month. Muir knew how miserable that wage was; he had earned four times that much at the Indianapolis wagon wheel fac-tory. Athens, though, impressed Muir as "the most beautiful town I have seen on the journey." Part of its charm arose from its Black residents, who were "well trained and are extremely polite. When they come in sight of a white man on the road, off goes their hats, even at a distance of forty or fifty yards, and they walk bare-headed until he is out of sight."[28]

Ever the garrulous wanderer, Muir took a break from his hike to settle in for a long, informative chat with a young Black man. He heard an "eloquent narrative of coon hunting, alligators, and many superstitions." A train had run off the track nearby, and the young man assured Muir that the "ghosts of the killed may be seen every dark night." As for whites in the vicinity, they were typified by the household of Dr. Perkins, who took Muir in for a night and whom Muir described as "a thoroughly characteristic Southern family, refined in manners and kind, but immovably prejudiced on everything connected with slavery."[29]

Muir's fears mounted on nights he failed to find a hospitable house like the Perkins' and had to camp in the woods by himself. He sought out "a dry spot on which to sleep safely hidden from wild, runaway n——s." Often he decided against the welcome warmth and dancing light of a fire, rationalizing that he "did not dare to make a fire for fear of discovery by robber n——s, who, I was warned, would kill a man for a dollar or two."[30]

Muir's fear soon became real, or at least so he thought. In a lonely stretch of north Florida, Muir ran into a "large, muscular, brawny young n——, who eyed me with glaring wistful curiosity." Certain that the man wanted to rob him, Muir made a point of saying he had nothing worth stealing. Still, the young man insisted Muir had to be carrying money and blocked his way, eyeing his pockets in a search for weapons. "Do you carry shooting-irons?" the man asked, his quavering voice betraying his criminality as amateur. The unarmed Muir put his hand into a back pocket, strode up close enough to the young man to glare into his eyes, and threatened, "I allow people to find out if I am armed or not." The chastened tyro stood aside, and Muir passed on, convinced that "this was evidently a narrow escape."[31]

Crossing swamp country, Muir kept a wary eye out for alligators but took solace from a gator hunter who advised him that the big reptiles were "extremely fond of n——s and dogs, and naturally the dogs and n——s are afraid of them." Feeling less of a reptilian target, Muir wished the alligators well: "Honorable representatives of the great saurians of an older creation, may you long enjoy your lilies and rushes, and be blessed now and then with a mouthful of terror-stricken man by way of dainty!"[32]

As Muir walked south, he passed judgment on the backward people he met, most especially the irretrievably dirty, no matter the color of their skin. Long-haired mountain men who had fought as Confederate guerrillas were to him uncouth and uncivilized. When a party of loggers felling longleaf pines for ships' spars hospitably fed Muir on pork and hominy, he noted that "for downright barbarism these Florida loggers excel." And there was a backwoods couple sick with malaria and dirty in a way Muir had never seen. He wrote, "The dirt which encircled the countenances of these people did not, like the common dirt of the North, stick on the skin in bold union like plaster or paint, but appeared to stand out a little . . . , the most diseased and incurable dirt that I ever saw, evidently desperately chronic and hereditary."[33]

The dirt got even worse. On his way to Gainesville, Florida, with night fallen around him, a thirsty Muir stumbled toward a light burning in the piney woods, hoping for water and fearing that he could be headed into a "camp of robber n——s." Rather, he found a Black couple sitting in a clearing lit up by a log fire. "I could see their ivory gleaming from the great lips, and their smooth cheeks flashing off light as if made of glass," Muir wrote. "Seen anywhere but in the South, the glossy pair would have been taken for twin devils, but here it was only a n——and his wife at their supper."

The two offered Muir the water he hoped for. While asking them about the road to Gainesville, he noticed a "black lump of something lying in the ashes of the fire." The woman bent over the lump, seemingly made of rubber, and said, "'Come, honey, eat yo' hominy.'" With that invitation, "the rubber gave strong manifestations of vitality and proved to be a burly little n—— boy, rising from the earth naked as to the earth he came." Muir hardly believed his eyes. "Birds make nests and nearly all beasts make some kind of bed for their young; but these n——s allow their younglings to lie restless and naked in the dirt." That marked them as less than natural to Muir, who proclaimed: "Man and other civilized animals are the only creatures that ever become dirty."[34]

As to Indigenous people along his route, Muir had little to say for the simple reason that most of them had either been killed or force-marched west. Only once did evidence of this past draw his attention. As Muir hiked through Murphy, North Carolina, the local sheriff, a man named Beale, stopped the shabbily dressed, feral-bearded, road-dusty Muir just to make sure he was no carpetbagger looking to pick over the carcass of the South. Satisfied that Muir was harmless and even radiated a certain hobo charm, Beale invited the pilgrim to his home for the night. The next day, Beale showed Muir "the site of Camp Butler where General Scott had his headquarters when he removed the Cherokee Indians to a new home in the West."[35]

That had happened in 1838 when Pres. Martin Van Buren, determined to finish the work of the Indian Removal Act of 1830, dispatched Winfield

Scott to hurry the Cherokees (DhBΘGƏT, Anigiduwagi) on their way to present-day Oklahoma. The Cherokees resisted removal, arguing fiercely that the push to get them off their lands was illegal. Scott didn't care. He drove the Cherokees into transit camps like Butler, imprisoned them with little food and no clean water through an unusually hot and dry summer, then drove them westward over what became known as the Trail of Tears. Before removal, the Cherokees numbered twenty-two thousand to twenty-three thousand. By the time they reached Oklahoma after a thousand-mile walk through a bad winter, an estimated four thousand people had died from dysentery and other diseases, malnutrition, exposure, and the occasional gunshot or bayonet thrust. One soldier who took part in the campaign and later served in the Civil War, where he saw "men shot to pieces and slaughtered by the thousands," made it clear that "the Cherokee removal was the cruelest work I ever knew."[36] The Cherokees agreed.

Muir clearly grasped at least the cruel outlines of this history. He may also have known that Ralph Waldo Emerson, his philosophical guiding light and an abolitionist, had protested Cherokee removal in a public letter to President Van Buren. Yet Muir, in using the words "new home" to describe Scott's mission, cast Cherokee removal in an undeservedly warm, domestic light. Indeed, what little evidence remained of now-removed Cherokees left the ever-fastidious Muir unimpressed. He found Sheriff Beale's well-tended, flower-bedecked house to be a perfect example of North Carolina's transition "from the wigwams of savages to the clumsy but clean log castle of the thrifty pioneer."[37] In Muir's eyes the Cherokees had to go.

After leaving southwest North Carolina, Muir angled across Georgia and along the Savannah River to the city of the same name, where he planned to pick up money his brother was sending from Wisconsin. The funds had yet to arrive when Muir reached Savannah. Hungry and broke, he looked for a place to camp and wait for the money. He wanted somewhere free from insects and snakes. There was another concern as well: "idle n——s were prowling about everywhere, and I was afraid." For his safe haven he chose the Bonaventure graveyard outside town since "'there,' thought I, 'is an ideal place for a penniless wanderer. There no superstitious prowling mischief maker dares venture for fear of haunting ghosts, while for me there will be

God's rest and peace.'" Several days passed before the money arrived. By then Muir was down to his last quarter and faint with hunger. He celebrated his sudden riches by buying and eating a whole tray of gingerbread from "a very large n—— woman," then topped off the tangy sweet with a regular restaurant meal. "Thus my 'marching through Georgia' terminated handsomely in a jubilee of bread," he wrote, harkening back to Sherman's March to the Sea during the Civil War.[38]

With his blood sugar rising, Muir noticed many signs of that war around Savanah, not only "on the broken fields, burnt fences, mills, and woods ruthlessly slaughtered but also on the countenances of the people." Older people who had lived through the conflict continued to "bear in sad measure the ineffaceable marks of the farthest-reaching and most infernal of all civilized calamities"—war.[39]

Muir used some of his replenished bankroll to buy passage on a steamship to the port of Fernandina, Florida. The vessel ferried Muir past a thick, entangled, coastal forest certain to stop any hiker and put him ashore in the tropically flowery land that he had long dreamt of. Soon he found that, too, impassable. "Florida is so watery and vine-tied that pathless wanderings are not easily possible in any direction," this walker of walkers decided. He followed the rail line to cross the state, emerging at the town of Cedar Key on the Gulf of Mexico.[40]

Cuba came next on the itinerary, yet there was a two-week wait for a ship that would be taking on a load of lumber for Galveston, Texas, where Muir could likely find a ship sailing to Havana. He took a short-term job at a sawmill to pass the time and replenish his wallet. Lodging with his boss's family, a Mr. and Mrs. Hodgson, Muir began feeling weaker and more lethargic by the day before finally collapsing at work. Feverish and bed-bound by an apparent attack of malaria, he spent three months recuperating under the Hodgsons' generous care.

Once he was strong enough, Muir read through and updated his journal. He had stopped making entries after Savannah, and he wanted to bring his notes up-to-date, particularly around his stay in the Bonaventure cemetery. He turned that time of hunger and loneliness into a transformative experience of wild nature interwoven with life and death. Instead of an ordeal of hunger, his time there became a mystical experience where "everything seemed divine."[41]

One thing he did not alter was the way he referred to the people he had encountered along the way. Some of the whites he met he named: Dr. Perkins, the resolute supporter of slavery; Beale, the North Carolina sheriff; Mr. and Mrs. Hodgson, the couple who kindly took in this sick traveler. Yet none of the African Americans he met bore a name in his journals or his later manuscripts. Not the woman and the child who ferried him across the Rolling Fork River; not the teamster on the oxcart; not the young man who opined on alligators and ghosts; not the wannabe strong-arm robber; not the campfire couple with a child emerging from the ashes. Cherokees received the same anonymity: General Winfield Scott had a name; Chief John Ross did not.

Not until January did Muir feel strong enough to buy passage on the *Island Belle*, a schooner bound for Cuba. He disembarked in Havana and hoped to hike his way out of the city and into the tropical paradise just beyond, but he discovered that he was still too weak to travel far under his own power. Muir remained in Havana for a month, admiring the city's exuberantly tropical vegetation and taking careful notes of his new surroundings.

Euro-Cubans, on the whole, impressed him although he described them as "superfinely polished, polite, and agreeable in society, but in their treatment of animals they are cruel." Black Cubans, many of whom would remain enslaved until the 1880s, made a different impression on this former Wisconsin farm boy. "In Havana I saw the strongest and the ugliest n——s that I have met in my whole walk. The stevedores of the Havana wharf are muscled in truly giant style, enabling them to tumble and toss ponderous casks and boxes of sugar weighing hundreds of pounds as if they were empty," Muir wrote. "The countenances of some of the n—— orange-selling dames express a devout good-natured ugliness that I never could have conceived any arrangement of flesh and blood to be capable of."[42]

Weak as he was, Muir still resolved to push on. He planned to find passage to the northern coast of South America, hike toward the headwaters of the Orinoco River in the mountains of Venezuela, then continue to an Amazon tributary. There he intended to build a raft or skiff and float the world's largest river to the sea. "It seems strange that such a trip should ever have entered the dreams of any person, however enthusiastic and full of youthful daring," Muir wrote from the vantage point of advanced years, "particularly under the disadvantages of poor health, of funds less than a hundred dollars, and of the insalubrity of the Amazon Valley."[43] Then again, Muir never thought small or safe.

Unable to find passage south, Muir flipped directions and plans. California became his new destination. Since no ships sailed to the West Coast from Havana, he first headed to New York City on a schooner carrying oranges. There he located passage to San Francisco via the Isthmus of Panama and bought a ticket in steerage. That cheap choice proved appalling. He lamented, "Never before had I seen such a barbarous mob, especially at meals."[44]

There was but one bright spot in the long journey from East Coast to West. As the passengers traveled by railcar across Panama, Muir fell in love with the tangled, flowering jungle that overshadowed the pale remnants he had seen in Florida and Cuba. And Black Panamanians stood in marked contrast to the people of color Muir had met in the South. "N——s of Panama [are] much superior to those of North America in form and cleanliness," he wrote in his journal. "Simple and natural in habits and [they] enjoy more than [the] artificially refined. Their open cane sheds are among bananas and palms, and whatever be their sufferings, they are exempt from [the] pain and degradation of want. [Females have] musical voices and nearly handsome children, naked." If Muir knew that Afro-Panamanians had been free since 1851, in marked contrast to still-enslaved Afro-Cubans and just-emancipated African Americans, he did not say so.[45]

Back aboard ship on Panama's Pacific side, Muir and the other passengers made their way up the coast to San Francisco and landed in late March 1868. Muir spent but one night in the city. Come morning, he set off walking, stopping to ask a man carrying carpenter's tools for the nearest way out of town. Unsure what this odd stranger was looking for, the man replied, "But where do you want to go?" Muir said, "Anywhere that is wild."[46]

So began his trek across California to Yosemite. John Muir was heading home.

3

The Ungodliness of Dirt

Most Indians I have seen are not a whit more natural in their lives than we civilized whites. Perhaps if I knew them better I should like them better. The worst thing about them is their uncleanliness. Nothing truly wild is unclean.

—JOHN MUIR, 1911

John Muir was always on the lookout for the Garden of Eden. Such a fan of John Milton's *Paradise Lost* that he packed the epic along on his thousand-mile walk, Muir hoped to find Eden in the wild lands of the South. Here and there on that trek he encountered intimations of that primordial landscape. First came Kentucky's forests, which he extolled as "the Eden, the paradise of oaks." Then the Hiwassee River, along the border of Tennessee and North Carolina, offered "its forest walls vine-draped and flowery as Eden. And how fine the song it sings!" And in Cuba, when frightened by a "snake" that turned into a long, looping vine, Muir called down upon it "the curse of Eden, 'Upon thy belly shalt thou go and dust shalt thou eat.'"

Now, as he walked south from San Francisco into California's wilds, Muir again felt he was discovering a place barely removed from the first days of creation. The air tasted so celestial that he understood how the original human couple experienced their surroundings. "The sky was perfectly delicious, sweet enough for the breath of angels; every draught of it gave a separate and distinct piece of pleasure. I do not believe that Adam and Eve ever tasted better in their balmiest nook," he opined. Spring runoff and

31

singing birds laid down paradise's soundtrack as "hundreds of crystal rills joined song with the larks, filling all the valley with music like a sea, making it Eden from end to end."[1]

Muir's embrace of Eden was more than a literary trope. As a good Disciple of Christ, he understood the primal garden as the opening scene of humankind's long biblical morality play. When Adam and Eve shared the apple, they cut themselves off from God and were cast out of Eden. Now humankind, as descendants of Creation's first couple, was working to find a way back. Muir's long walks contributed to this pilgrimage of return.[2]

Muir was hardly unique in centering his thinking about the wild and natural on the return to Eden. As environmental historian Carolyn Merchant points out, "The Garden of Eden story has shaped Western culture since earliest times and the American world since the 1600s. We have tried to reclaim the lost Eden by reinventing the entire earth as a garden." Henry David Thoreau fit himself into this tradition when he depicted Walden Pond as Eden. "Perhaps on the spring morning when Adam and Eve were driven out of Eden," he wrote, "Walden Pond was already in existence . . . and covered with myriads of ducks and geese, which had not heard of the fall." Drawing on ancient traditions that depicted the soul of the wild world as female, Thoreau cast nature as both spotless virgin and nurturing mother. Muir borrowed this thinking and expanded it. Thoreau's Eden was a green New England farmscape of cultivated fields, tended orchards, and selectively harvested woodlots, while Muir saw untamed nature—raw and exuberant—as Eden's recreation.[3] To that primal place he was now heading.

Muir's escape from San Francisco took him through the Santa Clara Valley toward what is now the city of Gilroy. There he turned east to cross the Diablo Range over Pacheco Pass and descend into the San Joaquin Valley just as its spring wildflower bloom burst forth. An ecstatic Muir proclaimed the valley "the floweriest piece of world I ever walked, one vast, level, even flower-bed, a sheet of flowers." The San Joaquin Valley in bloom outdid even Florida, that land named for its flowers.[4]

Muir thought he was beholding an Eden-like landscape, natural and pristine, but he was seeing nothing of the kind. In reality, he was feasting his eyes on the gathering grounds of the Miwok and Yokut peoples. These

Indigenous nations actively burned and pruned their homelands to favor desired seeds, bulbs, and greens. Muir was indeed looking at a garden, but not the untouched Eden, fresh from the creating hand of God, that he imagined. Never did he come to understand how Indigenous stewardship had shaped the purportedly wild landscapes he most admired.[5]

Muir made his way through the San Joaquin flower fields to the Merced River, knowing that if he followed the flow upstream he would come to Yosemite. While convalescing from his eye injury in Indianapolis, Muir had read a brochure on this gem of the Sierra Nevada.[6] Now he planned to see it for himself.

Muir's introduction to Yosemite was far more pedestrian than the heavenly glory he ascribed to it in his later writings. Traveling with a Cockney immigrant named Chilwell he had met on the passage from New York, Muir reached Yosemite Valley in early May 1868, about a month after leaving San Francisco. In those days, grizzlies still prowled California's backcountry, and even the milder-mannered black and cinnamon bears sometimes proved perfect jerks. Fearful, Muir and Chilwell armed themselves with a used shotgun and decided to try it out. Muir loaded a charge of birdshot while Chilwell took cover in a flimsy shanty. Muir, who had never used a firearm before, unwisely chose the shanty as his target. The blast pierced the wall and drove a piece of birdshot into Chilwell's shoulder. Fortunately, this caused no more than a minor wound. Now chastened but still armed, the two tenderfeet slept on the valley floor, poked around here and there, and made their way to Mariposa Grove for a gander at its giant sequoias. When their funds began running out, Muir and Chilwell headed back downhill. Muir never said what became of the shotgun, but thereafter he always tramped and traveled unarmed.

Given his years of farming experience in Wisconsin, Muir quickly found work as a seasonal hand. When fall arrived, John Connell, an Irish immigrant colorfully nicknamed Smoky Jack, offered Muir a job caring for his flock through the winter in Twenty-Hill Hollow. The oval, well-watered depression lies in the plain between the Merced and Tuolumne Rivers. Ringed by grassy knobs and spanning less than a mile, it offered good grazing for Connell's eighteen hundred sheep. In the mornings, the animals streamed out of their corral into the hills; in the evenings, they returned, largely on their own.

Muir wasted no love on sheep, but tending the wintering flock was an easy task that left him time to botanize through California's green winter and take note of nature's many details, including three distinct meadowlark songs.[7]

In this seemingly unspectacular locale miles from Yosemite's grandeur, Muir underwent a soul change. "Never," he wrote later, "shall I forget my baptism in this font." Perched atop one of the hills, Muir watched as "the Hollow overflowed with light, as a fountain, and only small, sunless nooks were kept for mosseries and ferneries. . . . Light, of unspeakable richness, was brooding the flowers. Truly, said I, is California the Golden State—in metallic gold, in sun gold, in plant gold." In that instant, Muir folded his being into a larger, cosmic reality. "Presently," he continued, "you lose consciousness of your own separate existence; you blend with the landscape, and become part and parcel of nature."[8]

The landscape Muir most hoped to become part and parcel of was the Yosemite high country, a realm that, as befits a man who had once endured total blindness, he would name the Range of Light. And sheep, those miserable creatures Muir loved to hate, would get him there.

Pat Delaney, a rancher whose sharp face Muir compared to Don Quixote's epic visage, stopped by Twenty-Hill Hollow and offered to hire the Scotsman. Muir's job would be to accompany Delaney's flock to the Merced and Tuolumne headwaters and ensure that the summer-long operation was well managed. Muir signed on. The out-and-back trip would take him into the very stretch of mountains he wanted to see firsthand. Importantly, it would give him a botanist's close-up look at successive vegetation zones as he, and the sheep, gained altitude.

Muir would not go it alone. A hunter he knew lent him Carlo, a St. Bernard savvy in mountain living, herding sheep, and guarding campsites. Billy, a man Muir called "proud," served as shepherd. And, to help drive the flock through the brushy foothills for the first few days, the crew was rounded out with "a Ch——and a D——Indian." The guard dog and shepherd bore names in Muir's account, yet these two men, the one Chinese and the other Native American, did not.[9]

Fleeing famine and war, Chinese men had immigrated into California by the thousands for the late 1840s gold rush. In the early 1850s the newly formed State of California passed laws to favor native-born miners by imposing hefty monthly fees on foreigners. An 1862 law added to this discrimination by requiring Chinese laborers who worked in anything other than a few prescribed occupations to pay yet another monthly levy that ate into their poor earnings. As a result, many Chinese workers left gold mining and took jobs as cooks, laundrymen, or field hands. The nameless Chinese man accompanying Delaney's summering flock was one such repurposed miner.[10]

As for the anonymous Native American, Muir gave him a tribal identity that existed only in the Euro-American mind. The term "Digger" arose in California and the Great Basin as a loose, pejorative moniker for largely unrelated Indigenous peoples who used digging sticks to harvest roots, tubers, and fiber. Once the "D——" gloss entered the vocabulary of settler colonialism, it served as a convenient racist shorthand that characterized Native Americans as dirty, lice-ridden, and lazy. The rhyme with the N-word slur for Blacks added to the term's nastiness. When the crew camped their first night out and gathered to eat, Muir noticed that "the Indian kept in the background, saying never a word, as if he belonged to another species." In a manner of speaking, he did.[11]

As the flock climbed above the foothills and into the first mountain forests, Muir entered ecstasy. "How glorious a conversion, so complete and wholesome. . . . In this newness of life we seem to have been so always," he penciled in his notebook. "I must drift about these love-monument mountains, glad to be a servant of servants in so holy a wilderness."[12]

Traveling through Brown's Flat on the divide between the Merced's North Fork and Bull Creek, Muir met "the adventurous pioneer David Brown," a part-time gold miner, part-time bear hunter, and the shallow valley's namesake. A band of tribal people had taken up residence at the edge of the valley. They had learned to respect the white hunter and seek Brown's guidance, according to Muir, and they looked to him for protection against robber bands who came over the Sierra crest on raids "to plunder the stores of the comparatively feeble D——s and steal their wives."[13]

Again, Muir fell into commonplace stereotypes about Native Americans. He chose to see Brown as a white savior on the order of Dances With Wolves or Tarzan bestowing wisdom, leadership, and tactical skill on dark-skinned "savages." In fact, Brown's tribal neighbors were less feeble than unarmed.

California law at the time prohibited Indigenous people from owning fire-arms, so settling close to a white man equipped to take on grizzlies made good tactical sense.[14]

One of the Native Americans staying at Brown's Flat appeared suddenly in the middle of the flock's campsite before anyone noticed he was there. The apparition took Muir aback. "I was seated on a stone, looking over my notes and sketches, and happening to look up, was startled to see him standing there, grim and silent within a few steps of me," he recalled. The man was "as motionless and weather-stained as an old tree-stump that had stood there for centuries." After the initial shock, Muir expressed admiration that "all Indians seem to have learned this wonderful way of walking unseen." He attributed the "wild Indian power of escaping observation" to Native Americans' long experience with hunting and fighting.

And, Muir realized, this mode of moving lightly across the land meant that tribal peoples left little trace and did less harm. They had inhabited this country for a long while, yet "heavier marks have not been made. Indians walk softly and hurt the landscape hardly more than the birds and squirrels, and their brush and bark huts last hardly longer than those of woodrats." Euro-Americans struck a powerful contrast. They stormed through California's gold-mining regions like wrecking balls—blasting bedrock, re-channeling streams and rivers, slashing timber, washing whole hillsides to the sea—and all in "a few feverish years." Muir lamented, "Long will it be ere these marks are effaced," even with nature lending a hand and "patiently trying to heal every raw scar."

Yet another tribal resident showed up in the campsite's center so stealthily that even the dogs failed to notice her arrival. This woman caught Muir's eye less for her light tread than her sorry appearance. "Her dress was calico rags, far from clean," he noted. "In every way she seemed sadly unlike Nature's well-dressed animals, though living like them on the bounty of the wilderness. Strange that mankind alone is dirty." It would have been far better if, instead of arraying herself in civilization's castoffs, she dressed in fur, grass, or bark so "she might then have seemed a rightful part of the wilderness; like a good wolf at least, or bear." Costumed as she was, she became something degraded and unsaved in Muir's perspective. "From no point of view that

I have found are such debased fellow beings a whit more natural than the glaring tailored tourists," he wrote.[15]

The separation of fallen humankind in the form of dirty Indigenous people from the unfallen, Edenic wild was absolute. There was nature, and there were Indigenous people. In Muir's view the latter had nothing to do with the former.

Delaney's flock and its various attendants and guardians were following a route to and over the Sierra crest known as the Mono Trail. It started in Big Oak Flat, east of the contemporary town of Groveland, and made for Tamarack Flat on the north of Yosemite Valley before climbing to the rock-bowled lake now called Tenaya. The next major destination was Tuolumne Meadows, then Mono Pass at a breathless altitude of 10,600 feet, followed by a sharp descent toward Mono Lake and its rain-shadow desert. Since the late 1850s, gold seekers had been using this route to reach mines on the eastern Sierra Nevada slope. It was hardly the miners' discovery, however. The Mono Trail had been charted over millennia by Indigenous peoples who used it to cross the Sierra between Yosemite and Mono Lake and trade goods back and forth.[16]

As Muir climbed with Delaney's flock, he grew more and more ecstatic with this ever rockier and more rarified world. Trusting nature's beneficence, he crept to the slippery edge of Yosemite Falls to peer down into the valley and its great granite monoliths. It was three thousand feet to the bottom, a fall fatal many times over, yet Muir neither quailed nor held back. Under the spell of such a scene, "one's body seems to go where it likes with a will over which we seem to have scarce any control," he remembered. Midday cloudbursts with their flashing lightning and pealing thunder felt so sublime that Muir longed to experience the Sierra's fierce winter storms. He sensed the presence of the Divine all around. "Nature as poet, an enthusiastic workingman, becomes more and more visible the farther and higher we go; for the mountains are fountains—beginning places, however related to sources beyond mortal ken."[17]

Various distractions disturbed his mystic reverie: the sheep with their stupid, meadow-munching ways; Billy the shepherd, "a queer character and hard to place in this wilderness," whose long-unwashed pants added new layers of grease and grime daily; and the deer-hunting Indigenous man from the Mono Lake side of the mountains, who traded venison for flour, sugar, tobacco, whiskey, and needles. "A strangely dirty and irregular life these dark-eyed, dark-haired, half-happy savages lead in this clean wilderness," Muir reported. He envied only their steady intake of "pure air and pure water." All the rest was a mess.[18]

Recognizing Muir's longing for the wild, Delaney suggested that he explore nearby Bloody Canyon. Muir accepted the chance to hike through the steep defile that loses some four thousand feet in only four miles. The canyon earned its name either for the many sharp stones that cut the legs of descending horses or for the red slates coloring the rock walls. Muir tied a notebook and bread to his belt and set off for the pass, which lay close to where the flock was camped east of Tuolumne Meadows. Botanizing as he went, dawdling to contemplate every plant he identified, and taking no heed of time, a light-hearted Muir was "sauntering" as he called it, a usage he borrowed from Henry David Thoreau. Muir signed on to Thoreau's idea that "saunter" came from the Middle Ages when French-speaking pilgrims bound for the Holy Land said they were on the way to "*la Sainte Terre.*" That etymology is unlikely, but the word captured well the sense of the sacred that Muir cultivated on his long walks.[19] Wrapped in reverie, he summited Mono Pass and started down the canyon where "the huge rocks began to close in around me in all their mysterious impressiveness."

No sooner had he entered the pass's narrow defile then "suddenly a drove of beings, hairy and gray, came in sight, progressing with a kind of boneless wallowing motion, like bears." Muir might have stepped aside to let them pass, but he wrote that "I never turn back" and refused to give way, particularly when he was in no mood to welcome "so grim a vision." Slowly it dawned on him that these strange creatures were nothing more than Indigenous people from the Mono Lake area dressed in rabbit skins and headed toward Yosemite Valley to barter for acorns, a staple food on the western slope of the Sierra. They were "mostly ugly, and some altogether hideous," as well as altogether filthy. They could not pass by too quickly for Muir's taste as he watched until, "viewed at a little distance, they formed mere dirt-specks in the landscape, and I was glad to see them fade out of sight." When night came and Muir bedded down nearby, his anxiety rose. "I experienced a feeling of uncomfortable nearness to the furred Monos," and he passed "a whole night . . . full of strange voices, and I gladly welcomed the purple morning" to make his escape.[20]

After completing the saunter to Mono Lake and returning to the sheep camp, Muir explored his alpine surroundings further and grew ever more jubilant over the High Sierra's craggy wonderland. "All the wilderness seems to be full of tricks and plans to drive and draw us up into God's Light," he wrote and dubbed the Sierra Nevada as the Range of Light.

Still, man cannot live on light alone—there were the sheep to consider. As the weather cooled into September, Delaney, Muir, Billy, and their many animals descended to the lowlands and winter pasturage. Muir returned as a man changed by the pilgrimage. "I have crossed the Range of Light," he reflected, "surely the brightest and best of all the Lord has built; and rejoicing in its glory, I gladly, gratefully, hopefully pray that I may see it again."[21]

He would, of course. Muir stayed in Yosemite Valley that very winter and for most of the following four years, and he sauntered through the Range of Light's many canyons, peaks, glaciers, watersheds, and forests. Yet, in his account of that first trip to the high country, Muir laid down key notions of wilderness and the human place in it that continue to shape the way Americans behold wild landscapes.

First comes sacred space, the place where the Divine manifests itself. In the European tradition, sacred space led to sanctuary—an area marked off and separated from the landscape, dividing the small sacred from the larger secular. Another way considers the entire earth, not just designated parts of it, sacred. As Chief Seattle (Sealth) told the governor of Washington State, "Every part of this soil is sacred in the estimation of my people." No matter where you stood in Chief Seattle's world, your feet rested on holy ground, an idea woven into many Indigenous cultures. Although certain places focus divine power, like South Dakota's Black Hills for the Lakotas (Lakhótas) and Arizona's San Francisco Peaks for the Hopis and Navajos (Dinés), the whole planet was and is sacred.[22]

Disciple of Christ that he was, Muir followed the Western tradition of segregated sanctuary. He borrowed the language of ecclesiastical architecture to describe, among other mountains, Cathedral Peak as "a majestic temple of one stone, hewn from the living rock, and adorned with spires and pinnacles in regular cathedral style. . . . I hope some time to climb it to say my prayers and hear the stone sermons." In defining sanctuary by its boundaries, Muir made it clear that only some space was sacred and the rest was not. As author and critic of the wild Rebecca Solnit writes, "To say that Yosemite is Eden is to say that everywhere else is not." For Muir, the wild temple became a stand-in for Creation's garden, and the land outside it comprised the secular realm where humankind was consigned after the serpent, the apple, and the Fall.[23]

Muir made it clear that sacred wilderness had to be defended against the invading secular. When God sent Adam and Eve packing, he stationed cherubims and a flaming sword at Eden's entrance to keep them from slipping back in. Seeing the damage done by grazing sheep in a Sierra meadow, Muir advocated this biblical strategy for the high country. "One might reasonably look for a wall of fire to fence such gardens," he wished, for "as far as I have seen, man alone, and the animals he tames, destroy these gardens."[24]

Thus, to preserve the Range of Light's sacred sanctuary, Indigenous people had to be cast out. Their bodies and lives were physically woven into the wilderness. They hunted woods and plains and fished streams, harvested wild rye and pine nuts and acorns, built huts and houses, burned meadows seasonally to favor rabbits and deer and thin the thickets of shade-loving trees. As Muir saw it, tribal peoples desecrated nature's sacred spaces. Yosemite's Eden was a temple for contemplation, not a homeland. The Indigenous residents had to go.[25]

As John Muir began elaborating his vision of an Indigenous-free wilderness in the summer of 1869, he had little idea what the Native Californians he found so dirty and distasteful had been through before he first laid eyes on them. Their story entails violence so catastrophic that grasping its historic horror requires a concept rooted in contemporary international law: genocide.

PART **2**

East of Eden

And Cain talked with Abel his brother: and it came to pass, when
they were in the field, that Cain rose up against Abel his brother,
and slew him. . . . And Cain went out from the presence of the
Lord, and dwelt in the land of Nod, on the east of Eden.

—GENESIS 4:8, 16

4

Yosemite's Genocidal Backstory

In the wild gold years of 1849 and '50, the Indian tribes along the western Sierra foothills became alarmed at the sudden invasion of their acorn orchard and game fields by miners, and soon began to make war upon them, in their usual murdering, plundering style. . . . The Yosemite or Grizzly Bear tribe, fancying themselves secure in their deep mountain stronghold, were the most troublesome and defiant of all.

—JOHN MUIR, 1912

Exactly one century before Muir's sheepherding summer in the Sierra, Spaniards pushing north from Mexico arrived in the bay they called San Diego to colonize Alta California in the name of the crown. From that imperial moment on, violence centered European conduct toward Native Californians.

Spanish soldiers at Mission San Diego used their off-duty time to chase, corner, and rape Kumeyaay women while killing men who dared stand in their way. Small wonder that outraged Kameyaays attacked the colonial outpost, burned it to the ground, and killed a Franciscan padre. The determined Spanish rebuilt and kept expanding northward along the coast to just beyond San Francisco Bay. They drove local tribes into the missions and baptized them as Catholic neophytes who were forced to work the fields and faced pursuing soldiers if they tried to escape. Along El Camino Real and its system of twenty-one missions, death by malnutrition, severe physical punishment, and military raids spread hand in hand with the Gospel. In addition, European diseases like smallpox, measles, and syphilis traveled out from the missions along long-used Indigenous trade routes and took a toll both inland and along the coast. The pattern continued even after Mexico won its independence from Spain and secularized the missions. Overall, California's Indigenous population fell from an estimated 310,000 in 1769 to 150,000 by 1846, the final year of Mexican control.[1]

Some colonizers welcomed the trend by arguing that the colony would be better off without the colonized. In a petition to Gov. Pío de Jesús Pico, a group of Los Angeles's prominent Mexican citizens complained about the danger posed by the increasing spread of sexually transmitted diseases among their Indigenous subjects. The Mexicans saw the public-health issue as good news, claiming that disease would "exterminate their race" and that the demise would be "beneficial to the city." Some colonizers did not wait for contagion to take its toll. Along the frontier of control, paramilitaries sometimes executed Native Californians en masse and even massacred whole villages, as Alférez Moraga did to the Suisun rancheria of Sespesuya. Still, such horrors were more unusual than commonplace. The Spaniards and Mexicans wanted to dominate and exploit a terrorized and intimidated Indigenous population as an effectively enslaved labor pool. They killed to keep their subjects in line rather than to wipe them out.[2]

This atrocious dispensation took a turn for the worse on July 7, 1846, soon after the outbreak of the Mexican-American War when Commodore John D. Sloat sailed the warship *Savannah* into Monterey Bay and declared California a U.S. possession. Sloat likely didn't realize that his nation had just absorbed the largest and densest Indigenous population of any American state or territory. Indeed, despite the catastrophic decline in population, Native Californians at the time outnumbered non-Natives ten to one—150,000 to 15,000. Native Californians were also culturally diverse, comprising some one hundred distinct linguistic groups and about five hundred village-based states, typically small and typically local. The tribes tipped more toward peace than war and lacked warrior societies that could mount and sustain ongoing conflict. As a result, non-Natives—American and European immigrants, Spanish-speaking Californios and Mexicans—called the shots. They had the guns, the remains of the secularized mission system, and extensive farming and ranching lands. This was exploitation colonialism carried over from the Spanish and Mexican days: a small minority from a home country extracting wealth from the colony through forced Indigenous labor. Cruelty and repression reigned as methods of control, but the colonizers needed the colonized and their strong backs.[3]

California ceased to be an exploitation colony soon after the 1848 discovery of gold in the Sierra Nevada foothills. In no time, the world rushed in—Americans from every state and territory in the union, Mexicans, South Americans, Europeans, Chinese—and flipped the state's demographic balance. In only eleven years, the non-Native population increased twenty-five times over and became the majority. Every new arrival lessened the demand for Indigenous labor as settlers needing a grub stake were happy to take the farming, ranching, and mining jobs Native Californians had been doing. And as the gold deposits were depleted, land became the principal source of California's wealth. Driving tribal people off and occupying the dispossessed real estate made it easier for newcomers to monetize timber, minerals, and agricultural potential. California was launching the fastest, most radical settler-colonial enterprise yet in the United States.[4]

From the beginning, mass violence played a leading role. In April 1846 Capt. John C. Frémont ordered his seventy-six heavily armed soldiers and scouts—the legendary Kit Carson among them—to attack a large gathering of Wintus on the Sacramento River near modern-day Redding. Local American settlers claimed the Wintus were staging a war dance; in fact they were fishing the spring salmon run. Hawken rifles accompanied by handguns and sabers easily bested spears, bows, and arrows. No one counted the dead Wintu women, children, and men, who likely numbered in the hundreds. Frémont lost not a man in what was less a fight than a "perfect butchery" as scout Kit Carson called it.[5]

Three years later, events around Clear Lake and along the Russian River showed again how well-organized violence could clear the land of its burdensome Native Californians. Andrew Kelsey and Charles Stone, who ran a cattle ranch near the lake, treated the local Eastern Pomo and Clear Lake Wappo peoples as personal serfs and slaves. They kept them on starvation rations, whipped any who stepped out of line, raped women and girls at will, and killed for the most trivial of reasons. When one of the ranchers' horses went missing in December 1849, the Natives knew the punishment would be terrible. Five men banded together to bushwhack Kelsey and Stone before they even knew the horse was gone.

The retribution for those killings, exacted by vigilante posses and U.S. Army units, took as many as a thousand Indigenous lives over the following months. Few of those slain—who again included women and children—had anything to do with the deaths of Kelsey and Stone.[6]

The Sacramento River and Clear Lake massacres set a precedent: massive, anti-Indigenous violence on the least pretext, a pattern that would repeat again and again up, down, and across California. At the same time, the state was stripping Native Californians of legal protection. New statutes—one titled with cruel irony as "An Act for the Government and Protection of Indians"—denied the right to vote by limiting citizenship to white males; legalized *de jure* custodianship of Indigenous minors and convict leasing, thereby creating slavery by another name; permitted corporal punishment like whipping; and disallowed trial testimony by tribal people against Euro-Americans. As long as no white person was willing to testify against them, settlers could get away with murder, mayhem, and rape. And they did.[7]

Meanwhile, special commissioners appointed and funded by the federal government were in the process of negotiating eighteen treaties with 119 tribal signatories that set aside 7.488 million acres as reservations. At first California's political leaders accepted this effort as good policy, but by the time the last treaty was signed and the whole package went to the U.S. Senate for ratification, the political winds had shifted entirely. California's congressional delegation lobbied against the agreements as indulgently generous to the undeserving tribes. Meeting in a closed-door executive session, the Senate unanimously rejected the treaties and filed them under a secrecy order in an obscure archive far from public view. There they would remain until early in the next century.[8]

The Senate's action meant the federal government was stepping aside and allowing California's political class to do what it wanted. And what it wanted was extermination.

On January 7, 1851, Peter Burnett, California's first civilian governor, addressed the legislature on the state of the state. He brought a racist backstory to the governor's office. As an immigrant from the Little Dixie region of northwestern Missouri, where his family owned slaves, Burnett first dove into politics in Oregon. There he championed excluding free Blacks from the state and whipping those who refused to leave, an idea he embraced in California as well after he moved south. Burnett also signed into law the onerous 1850 tax on foreign miners that targeted Latin American and Chinese gold seekers. Later in life, he would lobby enthusiastically for the 1882 Chinese Exclusion Act.[9]

Burnett focused the bulk of his 1851 address on the tribes, naming them as the greatest impediment to California's progress and enrichment. Experience, he said, had demonstrated that Euro-Americans and Native Americans, owing to the laziness and avarice of the latter, "cannot live in the same vicinity in peace." That reality left settlers with but one option: "The two races . . . must ever remain at enmity. That a war of extermination will continue to be waged between the races until the Indian race becomes extinct must be expected. While we cannot anticipate this result but with painful regret, the inevitable destiny of the [Indigenous] race is beyond the wisdom or power of [the white] man to avert."[10]

The governor's speech drew considerable criticism, not for its endorsement of Indigenous extermination, but for its tedious length and verbosity. Truth be told, Burnett tended to drag on and on and on. The criticism must have stung, for two days after committing to a war of extermination, Burnett resigned the governorship.[11] His departure made no difference to the state's rush toward genocide, although no one at the time would have called it that. The legal category defining the atrocity Burnett invoked in 1851 would not be created for nearly another century.

Although the crime of one group of people seeking to exterminate another likely reaches far back into prehistory, it lacked its own name until the mid-1940s. Raphaël Lemkin, an international lawyer and a refugee from the Nazi invasion of his Polish homeland, wanted to define the systematic extermination of Jews, Slavs, Roma, Sinti, and other minority groups as a unique and especially heinous crime against humanity. Lemkin combined the Greek word *genos*, meaning "race" or "tribe," with the Latin root-*cide*, meaning "killing," to create *genocide*.

"Generally speaking, genocide does not necessarily mean the immediate destruction of a nation," he wrote. "It is intended rather to signify a coordinated plan of different actions aiming at the destruction of essential foundations of life of national groups, with the aim of annihilating the groups themselves."[12] After the war ended, Lemkin tirelessly lobbied the United Nations General Assembly to include his concept of the "crime of crimes" in international law. The UN did just that in 1948 by defining genocide as a legal matter and empowering its prosecution.

Given how genocide entered the legal lexicon, the Holocaust shapes the way the word is used, referring to actions that are centrally planned and organized, swift, efficient, and massive. This is hardly the only model for how one group of people can exterminate another, a reality that Lemkin himself pointed out. Nazi genocide was but "an old practice in modern development," he wrote, citing Rome's destruction of Carthage in 146 BCE and the obliteration of Magdeburg in Europe's Thirty Years' War as two examples. When death overtook him, Lemkin was working on a book about historical genocides, including those aimed at destroying the Americas' Indigenous peoples.[13]

Under international law, a prosecutor seeking to convict an alleged perpetrator of genocide must make two proofs. The first turns on demonstrating the intention to destroy a national, ethnic, racial, or religious group. The second requires evidence of acts designed to carry out that intention, which can range from outright murder to removing children from the targeted group.[14]

Peter Burnett's 1851 public declaration of "a war of extermination" laid out California's goal. In short order state legislators put California's money where Burnett's mouth was. Over the next several years, the state floated $1.5 million in bonds—the equivalent of $58 million today—at an attractive interest rate to fund Indigenous extermination. These bonds became the largest line item in the state's budget.[15] Clearly California meant to wipe out its Indigenous peoples; the intention was obvious. As for the second proof, that evidence would mount, atrocity by atrocity, over the remainder of the nineteenth century.

Twenty-four militias funded by those state bonds hunted down Native Californians, usually on the pretext of punishing livestock rustling or avenging the rare killing of Euro-Americans, then transported survivors to reservations where food was nonexistent and health conditions proved lethal. Militiamen received generous compensation for time and materials, including horses, food, and ammunition. The U.S. Army added to the effort by mounting one killing campaign after another. All the while, local posses and vigilante groups slaughtered Native Californians at will and with impunity.[16]

By the time John Muir landed in San Francisco in 1868, Native California's population had been cut from 150,000 twenty years earlier to about 30,000.[17] When Muir crossed the San Joaquin Valley to Yosemite, he was entering a landscape that was anything but the pristine Eden he assumed it to be. The California genocide had ravaged this spectacular region and its ancient human presence. And the killing was not yet over.

One reason Peter Burnett endorsed genocide as the path to California's salvation came from a series of unfortunate events in Mariposa County, which includes Yosemite Valley. As a county so large that it took up one-fifth of the state and was later broken into all or part of eleven other counties, Mariposa encompassed the Sierra Nevada foothills' southern mining district. Lured by the sparkle of the goldfields, miners, ranchers, farmers, traders, and market hunters overran the area in the late 1840s and early 1850s and ravaged it. Mining waste trashed rivers and their tributaries, deer and elk disappeared from forests and meadows, and loosed hogs rooted up oak groves. Retreating into the high country to avoid deadly encounters with armed settlers and struggling to keep themselves fed, various tribal bands turned to stealing horses, mules, and cattle for food. Now and again, confrontations with Euro-Americans over livestock turned deadly. The rumor mill blew these stories into tales of horror worthy of the most lurid dime novels. In one case, purportedly "shown by unmistakable evidence," one of the dead "had been skinned by the merciless fiends while yet alive."[18]

As anti-Indigenous panic rose with each new spine-tingling exaggeration, the Mariposa County sheriff raised a large posse in early 1851 and led an attack on a village occupied by several tribes, likely gathered for a religious ritual and said to number around four hundred people. The posse employed a tactic standard for village raids. Before dawn, riflemen surrounded the encampment. As the sun rose, they fired into the village, and then, when the guns' barrels were fouled with black powder residue, they charged with pistols, knives, and hatchets for up-close killing. The Mariposa posse claimed that it took out between forty and fifty warriors, and then burned huts and food stores, losing only two dead and four wounded, more likely by friendly fire than bows, arrows, and spears.[19]

When the smoke cleared, the sheriff sent off a letter asking for state assistance to Gov. John McDougal, who had risen from lieutenant governor with Burnett's surprise resignation. McDougal was eager to boost his political prominence by fast, decisive action, and Mariposa County offered an ideal opportunity. The governor authorized the sheriff to raise a force of two hundred militiamen funded by the state.

Among the men recruited into the Mariposa Battalion was Lafayette Bunnell, a twenty-seven-year-old man eager for action. Born in New York and raised in Michigan and Wisconsin, Bunnell apprenticed to his physician father for a time, served in the Mexican-American War, then made the long trek to California for the gold. In time he went back to Wisconsin, purchased an honorary MD from a shady and short-lived medical school, and practiced medicine for a living, including serving as a surgeon with a volunteer cavalry unit during the Civil War. But before that, in 1851, he was a young man unrestrained by the Hippocratic oath and aggrieved at what the tribes were doing to his neighbors, "hardy, resolute pioneers" all. Bunnell's motivation was less than entirely altruistic; he stood to make good money running the tribes to ground. The pay scale, from private to major, ranged from five to fifteen dollars a day, equaling or bettering what a man could make at mining.[20]

Chosen to lead Bunnell and the Mariposa Battalion was James Savage, a shadowy character who, had Joseph Conrad set *The Heart of Darkness* in California, would have made a perfect Kurtz. Savage ran a string of trading posts in the San Joaquin Valley and Sierra foothills between what is now Yosemite and Sequoia, worked mines with crews of minimally compensated Native Americans and kept the gold for himself, took wives from several tribes so that family ties to the people he exploited sheltered him from retribution, and happily used violence against anyone, particularly uppity tribal people, who got in his way. As greedy as he was brutal, Savage grew so wealthy and self-inflated that he crowned himself *el rey tulareño*, king of the Tulares.[21]

With the settlers' tide rising, Savage's ties to the people he used for his own profit began to fray. His wives told him that nearby tribes were banding together to drive out the invading miners. Indeed, each tribal nation was connected to all the others by shared ceremony, intermarriage, and a robust trade network that stretched from the Pacific to the Great Basin and carried news as well as acorns and obsidian. Nothing frightened settlers as much as the prospect of a general Indigenous uprising. Savage himself became a target when an attack on his Fresno River trading post killed three of his clerks and cost him all his trade goods. Seeking revenge, Savage wanted to crush the rebellion and restore his top-dog prerogative.[22]

Savage impressed Bunnell, not as the devotee of greed and violence that he was but as a frontier superhero who had emerged from a James Fenimore Cooper novel into real life. "No dog can follow a trail like he can. No horse endure half so much," Bunnell recorded in his memoir of the Mariposa Battalion. "He sleeps but little, can go days without food, and can run a hundred miles in a day and night over the mountains and laugh for hours over a camp-fire as fresh and lively as if he had just been taking a little walk for exercise."[23]

One rumor making the rounds in Mariposa County had it that a band of particularly egregious horse thieves occupied a mountain hidey-hole far up the Merced River. Savage dispatched an envoy to this secretive tribe to summon its people out of the mountains and send them to a reservation on the Fresno River in the hot, dry San Joaquin Valley flatlands. The band's headman, Tenaya, arrived at the militia's camp to tell Savage that he and his people had all they needed and wanted for nothing. They preferred to remain in the mountains where they were born and where "the ashes of our fathers have been given to the winds." Savage was unswayed; this tribe, like the others, had to get down to Fresno River. Tenaya reluctantly agreed that he and his people would surrender and move. But when no one else from the tribe came in, Savage resolved to take a portion of his force and, with Tenaya as unwilling guide, climb to the deep valley where the tribe lived, round up the entire band, and drive them down to the reservation. The battalion did meet a few dozen of Tenaya's people descending through the late-March snow, and the headman claimed this small group represented his entire tribe. No one else remained in the villages upstream on the Merced, Tenaya said, so slogging uphill through the deepening snow was a hard, cold waste of time. Savage dismissed Tenaya's claim, and he and his men pushed ahead. And so the Mariposa Battalion, with Savage at its head and Bunnell in its ranks, became the first Euro-Americans to enter what is now known as Yosemite Valley.[24]

The sight of the valley from a high point sent Bunnell into seraphic transport. He exclaimed, "I have here seen the power and glory of a Supreme being; the majesty of His handy-work is in that 'Testimony of the Rocks.'"[25] He wanted to memorialize the "discovery" of this place with a name suitable to its godly grandeur.

In fact, it was already known as Ahwahnee and had been occupied for nearly six millennia. In the last decade of the eighteenth century, some terrible plague, likely brought to California by Spaniards and Mexicans and carried onward by tribal traders, swept through Ahwahnee and killed about one-third of the people then known as Ahwahneechees after their homeland. Fearing that the pestilence arose from the valley itself, the survivors fled over the Sierra crest to the Mono Lake domain of the Kutzadika'as, with whom they had long been trading partners. The refugees settled in. Tenaya was born there, the son of an Ahwahneechee chief and a Kutzadika'a mother. When he grew to early manhood, Tenaya and a number of Ahwahneechees returned to the valley sometime between 1805 and 1820 to reclaim their birthright territory. They welcomed refugees from other Miwok groups, Kutzadika'as, Monaches from the upper elevations of the western foothills, Yokuts from the Central Valley, and mission neophytes of various tribes on the run. These people called themselves Yosemites, a name Bunnell thought meant "grizzly bears." His etymology was mistaken—the word meant "those who kill" in the Miwok tongue and referred not to the place but the people's reputation for toughness. Despite the mistranslation, Bunnell's name for the valley stuck.[26]

It might seem that Bunnell was honoring the original inhabitants with the name Yosemite, but in fact he was erasing them. By replacing the name Ahwahnee with a moniker of his own selection, Bunnell made a seeming bow to the place's Indigenous reality while turning its long-term occupants into something nostalgic, something sure to vanish into history's fading mists.

As soon as the Yosemites knew the Mariposa Battalion had entered the valley, they fled. Only one old woman remained behind, Bunnell claimed, too aged to climb the rocky, precipitous trail and escape. He likened her to a "vivified Egyptian mummy. This creature exhibited no expression of alarm, and was apparently indifferent to hope or fear, love or hate." Bunnell saw her as subhuman, a primitive throwback, "a peculiar living ethnological curiosity." Savage tried to get her to tell him where the rest of the tribe had gone, but the old woman gave him nothing more than a knowing, catch-them-if-you-can smile.[27] Bunnell did not record what became of her.

Almost certainly it went badly. The invasion in 1851 "was a massacre," Della Hern, a tribal elder and basket weaver, told a *Mariposa Gazette & Miner* reporter 136 years later. She had not been there, of course, but her great-grandfather, whom Euro-Americans nicknamed Captain Sam, and his family had been. They passed their firsthand story down to their descendants. As they told it, news of the approaching militia had panicked the Yosemites. Knowing full well the Euro-American penchant for violence and their superior weaponry, the Yosemites packed up food and other necessities and made an eastward dash into the High Sierra. Sam's two little daughters were too young to travel so far so fast, and his parents too old, so he hid the four-some in the rocks and warned them not to move a muscle. True to type, the militiamen rampaged through the empty village and hunted down anyone who stayed. The two little girls escaped detection, but the raiders rooted out the elderly pair. The miners-turned-militiamen looped ropes around their necks and hoisted their frail bodies into a tree. They were hanging there still when Sam and the rest of the family returned.[28]

Since the militiamen had neither the time nor the supplies to pursue the escaping Yosemites into the high country, Savage ordered his men to burn huts and food caches, destroying shelter and sustenance even as a snowstorm approached. Then the battalion headed back toward Mariposa, planning to convey Tenaya and the surrendered members of his band to the Fresno River reservation. The headman had the last laugh, however. In the middle of the night he and his people slipped away and hightailed it for home.[29]

In May the Mariposa Battalion, this time under the command of Capt. John Boling, returned to Ahwahnee with the goal of rounding up Tenaya and his band and ensuring that this time they made it to the reservation. Again the village sites were empty but for a few flitting shadows, until the militiamen moved up the valley, weapons at the ready. Assured that they would be safe, five Yosemites came out of hiding and surrendered, among them two of Tenaya's three sons and his son-in-law. Seizing another chance to bestow a name, Bunnell dubbed a nearby triple-peaked prominence the Three Brothers.

The safety promised to the prisoners turned out to be a ruse. Boling sent out Tenaya's elder son and son-in-law with his scouts to locate the headman and convince him to give himself up. When one of the three remaining Yosemite hostages ran into the safety of the woods, Boling had the remaining two roped back-to-back and tethered to an oak in the middle of camp. Soon they untied each other and sprinted for the trees. The guards, hot to kill, were hoping for this chance. One hostage made it to safety through the gunfire, but Tenaya's youngest son was cut down.

The body was still lying in its pooled blood when the captured Tenaya came in with several militiamen. At the sight of his dead child the headman's lips quivered, and he gave Boling a look meant to kill. Tenaya maintained a "moody silence and extreme taciturnity for several days afterward," according to Bunnell, who appeared surprised at the depth of feeling this father expressed over his son's violent death. His amazement increased when Tenaya broke his silence to lament the murder of his son, scold Captain Boling, and call down vengeance on Boling and all Euro-Americans: "You may kill me, sir, Captain, but you shall not live in peace. I will follow in your foot-steps, I will not leave my home, but be with the spirit among the rocks, the waterfalls, in the rivers and the winds; wheresoever you go I will be with you. You will not see me, but you will fear the spirit of the old chief, and grow cold."

Boling found the display amusing. Bunnell, though, reported that he "began to have almost a genuine respect" for the headman. That benevolent feeling evaporated when, just a half hour later, Bunnell saw Tenaya tuck eagerly into a bowl of pork and beans "with the appetite of a hungry animal. . . . I now saw only a dirty old Indian."[30]

Bunnell was convinced that he was beholding not a fellow human being from a different culture but a specimen of a separate species. His evidence for this belief: lice. Euro-Americans had little to fear from the bloodsuckers that infested Native Americans, according to Bunnell, since they disliked white blood and soon abandoned their new hosts. "To me this is quite suggestive," he wrote, "when considered as evidence of a diversity of origin of the races." He was convinced that "each separate race has parasites indigenous to that race, although the genus may be common to each."[31]

Given the stark differences he perceived between the races, Bunnell saw no reason to "cater to the taste of those credulous admirers of the NOBLE R—— MAN, the ideal of romance, the reality of whom is graded low down in the scale of humanity." Native Americans had only themselves to blame for their conquest, expulsion, and even extermination. "The savage is naturally vain, cruel and arrogant," Bunnell declared. "His treachery is to him but cunning, his revenge a holy obligation, and his religion but a superstitious fear." Tenaya "appeared unconscious of his own wrong-doing, and of the inevitable fate that he was bringing upon himself and his people."[32]

Since most Euro-Americans considered Native Americans an inferior species fated to vanish before the advance of a "superior" people, naming objects and landmarks after the displaced consigned the expiring race to nostalgic memory. Much as Bunnell had erased Ahwahnee to create Yosemite, he elicited the names of landmarks from Tenaya and created his own—often mistaken—English versions of what he thought they meant: Mirror Lake, Vernal Falls, El Capitan, Nevada Falls, North Dome, Royal Arches, Half Dome, and Bridalveil Falls, among others.[33] And he made quite the show of bestowing a special honor on Tenaya.

The headman told Boling that those of his people who escaped had made it over the Sierra crest to seek sanctuary among the Kutzadika'as. Boling didn't believe him and ordered the battalion to follow the Yosemites' trail into the high country, once again forcing Tenaya to act as guide. Sure enough, the militia came upon a village "resting in fancied security, upon the border of a most beautiful little lake." The battalion surrounded and rushed the encampment, captured the refugee Yosemites without a fight, and led them under guard back to the Fresno River reservation. On the journey down, Bunnell proposed to Boling that the lake be named after Tenaya. "Here, probably, his people had built their last wigwams in their mountain home," Bunnell wrote. "From his lake we were leading the last remnant of his once dreaded tribe, to a territory from which it was designed they should never return as a people." Boling agreed. Bunnell, pleased with himself and expecting praise and gratitude, told Tenaya what he had done. The old chief was unimpressed. "It already has a name," he said, "we call it Py-we-ack."[34] Tenaya understood full well Bunnell's power game, and he was having none of it.

Deposited on the Fresno River reservation, the Yosemites found the hot, dry flatland unappealing and the rations unappetizing and scant. A few weeks there were enough for Tenaya. He asked for and received permission to take his people back to their long-time home in Ahwahnee in return for a guarantee of no further trouble. All went well and peaceably until May 1852 when a small group of miners from the foothills decided to take a prospecting tour of Ahwahnee. Perhaps they did not know that an earlier band of prospectors had murdered an unarmed Yosemite boy. To avenge that killing, the Yosemites ambushed the second group of miners, killing two and wounding another. A U.S. Army contingent responded by slipping into Ahwahnee at night and capturing five Yosemite men. Convinced that they had the killers—no matter whom they caught, such patrols always asserted they had snared the bad guys—the lieutenant in charge ordered the men to be shot on the spot. By that time Tenaya and the Yosemites had packed up and were heading over the mountains yet again to take refuge among the Kutzadika'as. The army gave chase, but the Yosemites outran the soldiers, who soon tired in the spring snow and called off their wet, cold pursuit.[35]

The Yosemites' sojourn with the Kutzadika'as was said to have ended badly. In Bunnell's telling, Tenaya and some of his men stole horses from the Kutzadika'as, who did not take kindly to the theft. They attacked, and the headman fell along with several of his men. Another, and more likely, account attributes Tenaya's death to a gambling dispute.[36]

As accurate as he may have been in recounting the Mariposa Battalion's maneuvers, marches, and murders, Lafayette Bunnell got almost everything about the Yosemites themselves wrong. His memoir makes the tribe sound like a homogenous band headed by a single leader who exercised autocratic control over his subjects. The reality was vastly more complicated. Research into Yosemite Valley's archaeology reveals at least nine ceremonial sites and almost forty seasonal camps and year-round villages. Social organization was every bit as complicated as the physical layout. Oral histories passed down through the Southern Sierra Miwuk Nation, the descendants of the Yosemites, identify eighteen lineages from eleven cultural groups, each cycling annually through villages and hunting-and-gathering grounds. Leadership comprised forty to forty-five captains, chiefs, appointed chiefs, and dance captains.[37] In other words, Tenaya was hardly a solitary dictator. Behind and around him stood a complicated phalanx of leaders with varying responsibilities and areas of influence among a people embedded in a tightly woven net of social and cultural connections. There was nothing "primitive" about the Yosemites.

Not that Bunnell and the Mariposa Battalion had an interest in grasping the political and cultural reality of the people they were invading, killing, and dispossessing. Reducing the Yosemites to a "savage" tribe made it that much easier to rain down violence and take their lives and land.

Murder, whether by gun, knife, or hatchet, was hardly the only mode of genocide that affected the Yosemites and the other California tribes. Pushed off their hunting, fishing, and gathering grounds, tribal peoples who had once sustained themselves abundantly now faced malnutrition and starvation. The loss of homelands, with all the spiritual and cultural connections they embodied, triggered such diseases of despair as depression, alcoholism, and suicide. Infectious illnesses flourished as well, not because Native Americans were constitutionally vulnerable to imported microbes but because—as the COVID-19 pandemic made clear—contagious disease cuts deepest along a society's fault lines to sicken the poor and the marginal.[38] Everything that could kill them did and at such a scale that, in less than two decades, four out of five Native Californians disappeared.

For all that, the Yosemites survived as a people and have proved themselves resilient through the more than century and a half since the Mariposa Battalion's invasion. Their story of creation—in which Coyote fashions humans after consulting with the other animals about the best body plan—is rooted in the dramatic landforms of Ahwahnee. Unlike Euro-Americans who imported the Genesis creation story from Middle Eastern mythology, the Yosemites and the Ahwahneechees before them traced humankind's origin to the very place they lived—until, of course, the Mariposa Battalion removed them from the landscape that served as their scripture.[39]

The Yosemites were not the only Ahwahnee-area tribe battered by the California genocide. The Central Sierra Miwok peoples lived to the north, over the divide between the Merced and Tuolomne Rivers, particularly around the valley that came to be known as Hetch Hetchy, and assumed an outsized place in John Muir's last years. And at least four ethnic groups

57

from the eastern side of the Sierra lived either permanently or seasonally in parts of what would become Yosemite National Park. The California genocide cost them their long-held lands and resources, both physical and spiritual, and established a pattern for what, over time, evolved into the national park system.[40]

John Muir played a key role in developing the park system's ethos. Yet in the fall of 1869, with Pat Delaney's sheep parked on their winter range and the prospect of idle time before him, he wasn't thinking so far ahead. Muir longed to plunge into pure, pristine nature fresh from the Creator's hand, and he hoped to find this wild paradise in Yosemite Valley. With winter chasing away even the few hardy tourists who made the strenuous trek up the Merced River, he looked forward to savoring Yosemite's wonderland of granite, snow, and splendid isolation. Lean and fit, his beard long and dark, thirty-one-year-old John Muir was prepared for this moment. Eden was calling him home.

5

Return to the Garden

I have spent every Sabbath for the last two months in the spirit world, screaming among the peaks and outside meadows like a n—— methodist in revival time.

—JOHN MUIR TO JEANNE CARR, JULY 29, 1870

Buddying up with a young orphan he had met at Delaney's ranch, Muir walked back to Yosemite, the place that would become his questing soul's new center as he sought to recover the virginal innocence of unfallen nature. His saunters around Yosemite soon lifted him to the spiritual ecstasy he sought. "I used to envy the father of our race, dwelling as he did in contact with the new-made fields and plants of Eden," Muir made clear, "but I do so no more, because I have discovered that I also live in 'creation's dawn.'"[1]

And as it turned out, Yosemite offered more than nature alone. Muir encountered three individuals there who proved significant to the arc of his life. The first gave him a way to make a living, then turned on him, nudging Muir into the next, public phase of his career. Then came a revered personage Muir eagerly wished to befriend yet found better read than met. The third became a soul friend who figured into Muir's private and public life on science, nature, and race for more than three decades.

And beyond these three were other people, far more numerous and Indigenous all, whom Muir failed to see. Their absence, too, figures into this part of the story.

At the time of Muir's return Yosemite Valley was but five years into its new legal status as a preserve "for public use, resort, and recreation"—a purpose granted by the Yosemite Act of 1864. That federal law mandated that the state of California administer the property through a nine-member commission headed by the governor. Yosemite was not yet a national park, and it was far smaller than today's preserve, encompassing only the valley proper, a mile back from its rim, and the nearby Mariposa Grove of giant sequoias.[2] Still, it was on the way to becoming a prestige destination for Victorian eco-tourists.

The first arrived in 1855 as a party of three men led by English immigrant James Hutchings, who had come for the gold rush and stayed for the tourist trade. He founded *Hutchings' California Magazine* to publicize the valley as a spectacular destination and later wrote and self-published a detailed guidebook to the region. To complete his business plan and profit from the influx he was promoting, he acquired a hotel close to Yosemite Falls. Accommodations at the Hutchings Hotel were rough. Mere curtains separated one "room" from the next, and the dining hall earned well under four stars. Yet people came, more every year, even though getting there was a piece of work.[3]

To reach Yosemite Valley from San Francisco in the early 1860s, tourists first caught a steamboat across San Francisco and San Pablo Bays and up the San Joaquin River to Stockton. Next came a joint-jarring jostle by stagecoach for seventy-five miles to Coulterville, a mining town in the Sierra Nevada foothills. Guards brandishing double-barreled weapons came along to fend off highwaymen, lending a Wild West air to the journey. Next, travelers saddled up and rode almost thirty dusty, sun-beaten miles to Mariposa, then pushed on the next day to a ranch where the small town of Wawona now sits. Visitors often explored the Mariposa Grove for a day before riding twenty more miles for their first view of Yosemite Valley at Old Inspiration Point. A long downgrade on a rough trail took them into the valley and its welcome if rude hospitality.[4] Many hoped, no doubt, that the beer was cold.

The tourist boom prompted Hutchings to hire Muir. Hutchings had invested in a sawmill to provide dressed logs and finished lumber for the ramshackle hotel's many repairs, and he wanted to add cottages to expand capacity. As an experienced millwright, Muir had the skills to erect the building, install and tune the machinery, dam the creek below Yosemite Falls for a millrace, and get the saw humming. He even turned the sawmill into his rent-free home. "I sleep in the mill for the sake of hearing the murmuring hush of the water beneath me, and I have a small box-like home fastened beneath the gable of the mill, looking westward down the Valley," Muir wrote to his sister Sarah. He fitted his retreat with windows: one in the roof for a view of South Dome and another on the roof's other side to keep upper Yosemite Falls in view, plus a wall window opening onto the valley's forest.[5]

For two years Muir would work for Hutchings. He devoted his days off and the snow season to exploring the high country and building the fund of experience that filled the many writings of his later life and earned him a local reputation as a wilderness guide.[6]

Short, bald, and more crotchety by the year, Hutchings was married to a much younger woman, Elvira, who gave birth to three children and would in time abandon her family to seek her own way in the world. As she warmed to that rending decision, she found a sympathetic listener in Muir. Always a man who valued friendship, the backcountry wanderer offered the lonely wife a sympathetic ear. However drawn he was to Elvira, Muir was far too prudish to countenance an affair. Still, when she did escape her marriage, Hutchings blamed Muir for alienating his runaway wife's affections. The two men sparred for months until Muir abruptly quit the sawmill job in the summer of 1871 and headed into the mountains. He could afford to. Ever the frugal Scot, Muir had put hundreds of dollars aside. Now he had other peaks to climb.[7]

Muir was still sawing downed logs into lumber when Ralph Waldo Emerson arrived in Yosemite trailing an entourage fit for the best-known American public intellectual of the time. Muir very much wanted to make the acquaintance of the writer and philosopher he saw as prophet and spiritual brother. "I had read his essays, and felt sure that of all men he would best interpret the sayings of these noble mountains and trees. Nor was my faith weakened when I met him in Yosemite," Muir remembered. "He seemed as serene as a sequoia, his head in the empyrean; and forgetting his age, plans, duties, ties of every sort, I proposed an immeasurable camping trip back in the heart of the mountains." That trek never came to be. Emerson was a lover of nature at many arms' length—one who preferred a roof over his head to a starlit night in a sequoia grove—and his companions nixed sleeping outdoors as too hazardous for the great man's sixty-eight years. Indeed, Emerson "was past his prime, and was now as a child in the hands of his affectionate but sadly civilized friends, who seemed as full of old-fashioned conformity as of bold intellectual independence," Muir complained. Yet when Emerson's party rode out of Mariposa Grove on their way back to San Francisco Bay, the great man turned his horse, doffed his hat, and waved goodbye. A bereft Muir returned to the big trees, built a fire of the blazing sort he loved, and bedded down, "lonesome for the first time in these forests."[8]

Emerson did not forget Muir and sent along the two volumes of his essays as a gift. Muir carried those books with him when he was sauntering in the mountains, marking passages and adding notes, even sketching a pine tree in a page margin. Muir often disagreed with Emerson; he penciled "no!" again and again next to the text.[9] Yet the two men shared a vision of nature as a font of spiritual experience and wisdom. Emerson modeled something else for Muir: a philosophically respectable white supremacy.

Emerson served, in the words of historian Nell Irvin Painter, as the "philosopher-king of American white-race theory." Drawn heavily from Scottish writer Thomas Carlyle, who carried the racial and nationalist thinking of German Romanticism into English literature, Emerson's writings amounted to the most complete statement to date of the ideology later termed Anglo-Saxonist or Nordic. As Emerson saw it, real and true Americans descended from the Saxon-Norse who had conquered England and carried their blend of forward energy, manly violence, and physical beauty to the New World. Emerson counted himself and his true followers among the heirs of this racial lineage. The rest of the people who called America home, those who were other than Anglo-Saxon, counted for nothing.[10]

"The American is only the continuation of the English genius into new conditions, more or less propitious," he wrote. "England has inoculated all nations with her civilization, intelligence, and tastes." The reason for England's world dominance was the immutable reality of race, a word that in the mid-nineteenth century meant much the same as "species" now.

"We anticipate in the doctrine of race something like that law of physiology that whatever bone, muscle, or essential organ is found in one healthy individual, the same parts or organ may be found in or near the same place in its congener," he declared, "and we look to find in the son every mental and moral property that existed in the ancestor." The evidence was obvious, Emerson continued: "Race is a controlling influence in the Jew, who, for two millenniums, under every climate has preserved the same character and employments. Race in the n—— is of appalling importance."

As Emerson saw it, Europeans comprised no single white stock but a variety of separate races. The Irish, Catholic and poor, were of an inferior sort; Hungarians and Poles fell into the same low zone. As for the English, their dominance rose from the favorable mixing of Celtic, Saxon, and Norse blood, a pedigree that blessed them with an inheritable mix of physical, intellectual, and moral traits bound to propel them to the pinnacle of the world's racial hierarchy. Real Americans shared this pure English ancestry—a position that an upper-crust, Harvard-educated New Englander like Emerson found comforting. To his privileged club no Irish, no Eastern Europeans, no Africans, no Asians, and no Native Americans need apply. "I think it cannot be maintained by any candid person that the African race have ever occupied or do promise ever to occupy any very high place in the human family. Their present is the strongest proof that they cannot," Emerson argued. "The Irish cannot; the American Indian cannot; the Chinese cannot. Before the energy of the Caucasian race all the other races have quailed and done obeisance."

Emerson's animus against the perceived lower varieties of humankind embraced the poor in general. He explained, "The worst of charity is, that the lives you are asked to preserve are not worth preserving. The calamity is the masses. I do not wish any mass at all, but honest men only, facultied men only, lovely & sweet & accomplished women only; and no shovel-handed Irish." Without a doubt, humanity's physical and spiritual progress required aristocracy: "Men of aim must lead the aimless; men of invention, the uninventive."[11]

Emerson built his view of nature on this racist elitism. He set humankind apart from nature, much as the God of Genesis had done when he cast Adam and Eve out of Eden. Emerson saw the wild as the lost spiritual source that hungry souls were seeking. "Nature is made to conspire with spirit to emancipate us," he wrote. "Know then that the world exists for you." Nature nurtured the human capacity for enlightened goodness. "Nature is loved by what is best in us. It is loved as the city of God," Emerson asserted. "Man is fallen; nature is erect and serves as a differential thermometer, detecting the presence or absence of the divine sentiment in man." Only a minority of humans, however, enjoyed this advanced capacity to grasp nature's divinity. He explained, "To the intelligent [person] nature converts itself into a vast promise, and will not be rashly explained. Her secret is untold." Only those blessed with abundant intellect could grasp what nature offers. "Nature is the incarnation of a thought," Emerson claimed, "and turns to a thought again, as ice becomes water and gas."[12]

As John Muir sat by evening campfires on his tramps through the High Sierra and read Emerson's essays again and again, he turned these ideas over and over. He disagreed with Emerson that nature existed to serve human purposes; soon he would argue that nature served only itself.[13] But the racist elitism and white supremacy in Emerson's books seeped into his own thinking. It would emerge, newly dressed for a changing world, in Muir's later decades.

The baptism in wild mysteries that Muir hoped to share with Emerson came to pass in the unexpected person of a scientist and, like Muir, a new Californian: Joseph LeConte. Two elements brought LeConte and Muir together: light and ice.

The light came at Tenaya Lake soon after the two met and took off into the Yosemite high country. Following supper and a chat around the campfire, they sauntered through a pine grove toward the lake and perched on a rock reaching out into the water. Bathed in a full moon and the high-altitude vault of sparkling summer stars, the surrounding mountains glowed, and their illuminated forms danced in the water's "unstable mirror." At first, the two chatted, then they fell silent as, in Muir's words, "earth and sky were inseparably blended and spiritualized, and we could only gaze on the celestial vision in devout, silent, wondering admiration." LeConte, too, was moved. The "grand harmony made answering music in our hearts," he recalled. The two new friends contemplated for a silent hour. That experience of awe shared beyond words captured Muir's lifelong reverence for LeConte. "The lake with its mountains and stars, pure, serene, transparent, its boundaries lost in fullness of light, is to me an emblem of the soul of our friend," he told a memorial gathering after LeConte's death almost thirty years later.[14]

The ice that joined LeConte and Muir had to do with glaciers. Long saunters through the High Sierra convinced Muir that glacial forces had played a huge hand in shaping the range's peaks and valleys, that living glaciers still plowed the range's alpine reaches, and that Yosemite Valley itself resulted from massive glacial sculpting. As he rode along with LeConte, Muir laid out his evidence so impressively that his friend was persuaded. LeConte had studied at Harvard with Louis Agassiz, the geologist who first promoted the idea of enormous glaciers sheeting the earth in past ages, so he already understood that glaciation did much to shape the earth's surface.[15] As Muir pointed out moraines, grooves, and polishing from glaciers long gone, LeConte nodded in agreement.

Not everyone was of the same mind. Josiah Whitney, California's most prominent scientist at the time, dismissed Muir's ideas, published soon after his meeting with LeConte, as campfire science. He knew full well that the Sierra Nevada showed evidence of glaciation, but the idea that ice had removed enough rock to carve out Yosemite Valley struck him as ludicrously over the top. The valley had formed, he was sure, from massive subsidence, a catastrophic downward slip of rock.[16]

Time was to prove Muir and LeConte right and Whitney wrong. Yet that success was not what bound the two friends together. Their connection formed at a level well below the thin air of academic theory. Theirs was a bond revealed by their quiet hour at Tenaya Lake and what led up to it.

Jeanne Carr, Muir's Wisconsin mentor, was now living in Oakland after her professor husband joined the faculty of the newly formed University of California. LeConte had just begun teaching there as well, and Jeanne found him marvelous. She described him as "gold seven times refined, i.e., in geological science, in botanical (general), in music, in landscape love, in poetry, in self forgetfulness, in adoration—*a Christian soul.*" When she learned that LeConte was planning to lead a student group on a trip across the Sierra Nevada to study science in the field, she told LeConte to be sure to look Muir up, then she sent Muir a letter alerting him to the professor's coming. The two met at Hutchings's sawmill. Soon recognizing Muir as "a gentleman of rare intelligence, of much knowledge of science, particularly botany," LeConte proposed that he come along on the trek. Muir accepted. LeConte's backcountry manner soon convinced Muir that he had found a worthy companion. "Sinewy, slender, erect, he studied the grand show, forgetting all else, riding with loose, dangling reins, allowing his horse to go as it liked," Muir remembered. "He had a fine poetic appreciation of nature, and never tired of gazing at the noble forests and gardens, lakes and meadows, mountains and streams."[17]

LeConte came to the Yosemite trek with a telling backstory. Born in 1823, he grew up on a large plantation in Georgia's coastal lowlands. This was a happy world, LeConte remembered, owing to his father's "just, wise, and kindly management of his two hundred slaves." Just to be sure that the slaves stayed in line, however, his father joined other planters to form a mounted police force that chased down African Americans abroad at night without passes—something of a Ku Klux Klan on training wheels. The pairing of wisdom and whip was salutary, LeConte argued: "There never was a more orderly, nor apparently a happier, working class than the n——s of Liberty County as I knew them in my boyhood."[18]

LeConte was drawn to study natural history and science after spending much of his boyhood hunting and fishing in the lowlands' forests and swamps. Following college, he entered New York City's College of Physicians and Surgeons, now the medical school of Columbia University. Although little interested in practicing medicine, he saw a medical degree as "the best preparation for science." LeConte did practice for two and a half years in Macon, then, upon learning that famed Swiss geologist Louis Agassiz had been appointed to a professorship at Harvard, he headed to Cambridge to earn the credentials needed to teach geology and zoology at the university level. LeConte worked at Agassiz's side, absorbed science under his fierce mentorship, and took in his long, philosophical talks. "To explain how much I owe to him, it is only necessary to say that for fifteen months I was associated with him in the most intimate personal way, from eight to ten hours a day, and every day, usually including Sundays," LeConte recalled.[19]

The first major lesson LeConte took from Agassiz was his theory of historic ice ages that sculpted mountains and shaped continents. The second was evolution "not by *organic forces within,* but according to *an intelligent plan without*—an evolution not by *transmutation* of species, but by *substitution* of one species for another." In other words, God lurked in the machine and shaped it to his ends by creating one species then replacing it later with a new, more advanced model. There was no transition from one species to another, no intermediate trial-and-error steps, but successive, separate, specific creations. The third lesson, built on Agassiz's evolutionary theory, was what LeConte called scientific sociology. It depicted society as "an organized body, and therefore subject to the laws of organisms. Society, too, passes by evolution from lower to higher, from simpler to more complex, from general to special, by a process of successive differentiation." Humankind begins in barbarism and evolves into civilization.[20]

Agassiz expanded this thinking into a theory of race while LeConte was his student. Before coming to America in 1846, the Swiss scientist considered that all humans originated from one creation, just as the book of Genesis recounts. Whatever the differences among different groups of humans, all were one species under the skin. But Agassiz's first experiences with African Americans shocked him into rethinking this belief. "Nonetheless, it is impossible for me to repress the feeling that they are not of the same blood as us," he wrote home to his mother in Switzerland. "In seeing their black faces with their thick lips and grimacing teeth, the wool on their heads, their bent knees, their elongated hands, their large curved nails, and especially the livid color of their palms, I could not take my eyes off their face in order to tell them to stay far away."[21]

Driven by repulsion and holding to his view of species as immutable thoughts in the Creator's mind, Agassiz argued more and more forcefully that each human race—Caucasian, Arctic, Mongol, American Indian, Negro, Hottentot, Malay, and Australian by his accounting—resulted from a separate creation and that each was a distinct, immutable species. Holding to any other position, Genesis notwithstanding, was "contrary to all the modern results of science," he declared.[22]

Agassiz was hardly alone in depicting human races as separately created species. The foundation for this line of thinking in the United States was laid by Samuel George Morton's *Crania Americana*. A physician by training, Morton based his book on a study of some six hundred Indigenous skulls from the Americas. Indians, as he called them, understood abstract reasoning but little, learned poorly, and were "restless, revengeful, and fond of war, and wholly destitute of maritime adventure." Given its impaired intellectual capacity, "[the Indian's] mind appears to be different from that of the white man," he wrote, "nor can the two harmonise in their social relations, except on the most limited scale."[23]

Types of Mankind by Morton's one-time student J. C. Nott and diplomat George Gliddon picked up where *Crania Americana* left off. Each race formed a separate species. "Let us assume, with Agassiz and Morton, that all mankind do not spring from one pair, nor even each race from distinct pairs; but . . . men were created in *nations*, in the different zoological provinces where history first finds them," they reasoned. Racial conflict advanced evolution. "Human progress has arisen mainly from the war of races," which put the dominant on top and kept the inferior down. "Nations and races, like individuals, have each an especial destiny: some are born to rule, and others to be ruled. And such has ever been the history of mankind. No two distinctly marked races can dwell together on equal terms," Nott and Gliddon maintained. "Observe how the aborigines of America are fading away before the exotic races of Europe."[24]

Agassiz found this thinking so congenial that he contributed a global map of wildlife zones—and human races—to *Types of Mankind.* His prestigious presence added to the book's commercial success. Given his leading position across Europe and North America and his willingness to go public with his ideas, Agassiz reinforced the "scientific" racism of the pre-Civil War era that justified the enslavement of Africans and the extermination and dispossession of Native Americans.[25]

LeConte drew deeply from Agassiz's mentorship throughout his own long scientific career. Agassiz's thinking about ice ages helped prepare his mind to welcome Muir's hypothesis on the glacial origin of Yosemite Valley. And the Swiss scientist's position on evolution and society, shaped by unmitigated racism, gave a "scientific" slant to how LeConte, the son of slaveholders, addressed the same deeply American issues.

After he finished his studies at Harvard in 1851, LeConte returned to Georgia and began teaching, landing finally at South Carolina College (now the University of South Carolina) in Columbia. At first wary of secession, LeConte signed on to aid the Confederate cause soon after the shelling of Fort Sumter marked the beginning of the Civil War. He had decided that the conflict was "an honest difference of opinion as to the nature of our government." Slavery, he was saying, was beside the point. LeConte served the Confederacy as the chemist for a medicine-manufacturing operation and later filled the same role in an explosives factory. As the war turned against the South and Sherman's Union army bore down, LeConte rescued his relations from their plantation on the Georgia coast and, in a harrowing journey through an embattled land, delivered them to the temporary safety of Columbia. When Sherman's soldiers sacked and burned much of the city, LeConte and his family hid. They sought a new refuge every day, "for it was our policy never to use the same place twice, as we might be observed and betrayed by some prowling n——."[26]

As bad as the war was, Union occupation after Appomattox proved worse. In LeConte's eyes, Reconstruction came down to "the intolerable insolence of the n——s suddenly set free with all their passions not only uncontrolled but often even encouraged" by Union agents. LeConte himself was relieved to be free of the burden of managing slaves on the two thousand acres of land he still owned, but in his view the utter unreliability and total laziness of free Blacks made profitable farming impossible. "They have no ambition to improve, and live almost like animals," he wrote. "I bore the iniquities of the government as long as I could, but when the n—— legislature began to talk about what they were going to do to the University, I thought it time to quit."[27]

Joseph and his brother John headed for the brand new University of California, then but a single campus, located first in Oakland and later in Berkeley. In 1868 the university came off the drawing board with a Morrill Act grant of more than one hundred fifty thousand acres of what had been Native Californian land that the university turned into an endowment of more than $740,000.[28] Eager to tie their futures to this flush academic enterprise, the LeConte brothers moved to the eastern shore of San Francisco Bay and took up professorships. The LeContes were in only their second academic year when Joseph enlisted nine of his students for an expedition to explore the Sierra Nevada's geology and biology firsthand. On that trip he and Muir shared Tenaya Lake in the moonlight and began their lifelong friendship.

At first glance, they appeared an unlikely pair. LeConte had been born to an upper crust of land, money, and slave-supported gentility, while Muir came from people who accumulated little from their own hard labor. LeConte was highly educated and an accomplished academic, while college-dropout

Muir was largely self-taught. Yet, as that hour of moonlit awe along Tenaya Lake showed, they shared intellectual and spiritual ground.

Both had experienced mystical conversions that convinced them of the divinity at the cosmos's core. Both saw Darwin's evolution as cogent scientific theory, but they insisted that God's intelligent design, not the clawed and toothed fight for fitness, drove the creation of species including humankind. This agreement on the basics gave them a great deal to discuss when they got together to talk, as they often did. Muir spent many evenings with the LeConte brothers and their families in the "queer old house in Oakland" they shared. The three kicked around everything from Muir's explorations of the Yosemite backcountry to the arcana of physics—John LeConte's specialty. Almost certainly those many hours of conversation turned now and again to race. The issue was top of mind for Joseph LeConte.[29]

Besides his many technical papers, LeConte wrote about racial issues for the general public. Always framing his work in ostensibly scientific rhetoric, he unfurled an argument for why Euro-Americans occupied the top and Blacks and Native Americans existed on the bottom. No burning crosses and white hoods for LeConte; it all turned on science and data. Or so he assured his readers.

Charles Darwin, LeConte implied, had it wrong. Ever since the publication of *On the Origin of Species*, conservative Christians saw evolution by natural selection as little more than competitive chaos and an argument against the existence of God. LeConte took the opposite tack. In fact, he argued, evolution proved there was a God, and the creation of species demonstrated the deity's ongoing urge toward perfection. He reasoned that "the law of gravitation is naught else than the mode of operation of the divine energy in sustaining the cosmos—the divine method of sustentation; the law of evolution naught else than the mode of operation of the same divine energy in originating and developing the cosmos—the divine method of creation." Race pointed to inherited differences among groups of humans that played a role in God's long-range plan. "On account of the extreme slowness of the process, the divine patience of nature, varieties pass into races, races into species, species into genera," Le Conte wrote. "*Primary races* correspond to *races* or permanent varieties, and race-aversion is an evidence that the tendency to mix is much weakened though not destroyed.

They are commencing species, though not true species—they interbreed, but not freely."[30]

Interbreeding countered evolution's upward movement, as he concluded, "It seems certain that the mulatto has not the physical health and endurance of either the white or the n—— race." This diminished vigor explained why mixed-race people suffered far more from hereditary diseases than either parent race, he asserted. "I regard the light-haired blue-eyed Teutonic and the n—— as the extreme types, and their mixture as producing the worst effects."[31]

Evolutionary creation, LeConte made clear, achieved its climax in humankind then changed focus. No longer was evolution merely physical; now it entered an advanced, social phase. "But more and more, as civilization advances, this higher and distinctively human factor becomes more and more dominant, until now, in civilized communities, it takes control of evolution," LeConte declared. "Reason, instead of Nature, now assumes control, though still using the methods and factors of Nature. This *free*, self-determined evolution of the race, in order to distinguish from the *necessary* evolution of the organic kingdom, we call progress."[32] What society looked like became a matter of divine concern, and leaders who wished to align with the will of God had to shape their societies to the form God intended.

Since the races differed in moral status, and since God guided evolution, the Divine dictated that the morally superior race rules the inferior. Whenever races came into contact, the outcome depended on their evolutionary status. If the lower race "be in the early stages of race-evolution, and therefore plastic, docile, imitative, some form of subordination will be the result; if, on the other hand, it be highly specialized and rigid, extermination is unavoidable. The N—— is probably the best type of the former and the American Indian of the latter." In fact, Euro-Americans owed it to Blacks and Indigenous people to rule them. LeConte claimed, "The sacredness of all rights, because the right most apt to be violated, is the right of the weak and the ignorant to the control and guidance of the strong and wise."[33] With that, LeConte blessed the Jim Crow oppression of the post-Reconstruction South and California's effort to obliterate its Indigenous peoples—a campaign still in full swing when he arrived in the state—as both scientifically inevitable and conforming to God's will.

In his own time LeConte enjoyed a stellar reputation. His *Principles of Geology* became a widely used textbook, and his status as scientist and scholar lifted him to the presidency of the American Association for the Advancement of Science. LeConte's presence on the faculty attracted other ambitious academics to the young, bustling, and well-endowed University of California. Still "his modesty and simplicity survived, unscathed, the applause and laudations bestowed upon him," said an academic contemporary.[34]

Muir joined in that praise. "As a teacher he stood alone on this side of the continent, and his influence no man can measure. He carried his students in his heart, and was the idol of the University," Muir remembered. More important, he considered LeConte a man of admirable gentleness. "Anything like a quarrel or hot controversy he instinctively avoided, went serenely on his way, steeping everything in philosophy, overcoming evil with good," Muir wrote. "His friends were all who knew him, and he had besides the respect of the whole community, hopefully showing that however bad the world may be, it is good enough to recognize a good man."[35]

To Muir, as to all LeConte's colleagues, family, and friends, the philosophical white supremacy he spelled out counted for nothing against him. They, too, went along with the program passed down from Morton through Agassiz and Nott to LeConte: the idea that blame for the American system of racial oppression rested with the oppressed. The once-enslaved and ever-insightful Frederick Douglass knew this playbook for what it was: "Pride and selfishness, combined with mental power, never want for a theory to justify them—and when men oppress their fellow-men, the oppressor ever finds, in the character of the oppressed, a full justification for his oppression."[36]

Not everyone who came to Yosemite boasted of the status of an Emerson or a LeConte. Each summer brought more tourists, from backcountry tyros to accomplished alpinists, to see the park's wonders. And Indigenous people worked there, too.

As Yosemite's tourist appeal grew, Miwoks, Kutzadika'as, Monaches, and descendants of Tenaya's Yosemites returned to the valley and took jobs with the rustic hotels and other businesses that served the trade. Women worked as maids and cooks and made baskets to sell to Euro-Americans shopping for authentic Native crafts. Men swung picks and axes on trail and road crews, chopped firewood, and fished to supply the hotels' restaurants with fresh trout. These Indigenous workers lived in the valley, some seasonally, some year-round.[37]

This tribal presence would continue for a full century after John Muir arrived, despite the Mariposa Battalion's hangings and shootings, the genocide that raged across California for decades, and the transformation of Ahwahnee the homeland into Yosemite the preserve. Muir wrote little about Ahwahnee's first inhabitants, however, as he looked over and past them to the valley's stone sentinels and the high country's glaciers. He adopted without question Lafayette Bunnell's version of the Mariposa Battalion's invasion of the valley and its violent campaigns against Tenaya's band, effectively saying that these people had no history before Euro-Americans set upon them.[38] Beyond that, he never inquired about or told their story. Instead, he made Yosemite into the empty, ahistorical landscape his idea of wilderness required.

Not everyone had such a blind spot about Yosemite's tribal peoples. Albert Bierstadt, the German-American painter who built a considerable reputation for his grand mountain canvasses, visited Yosemite first in 1863 and again in 1872–73, overlapping Muir's time in the valley. His painting *Indians in Council, California,* completed most likely in 1872 and housed now in the Smithsonian's American Art Museum, depicts the Yosemite Muir was looking past. Under a night sky and against the backdrop of great granite walls, Yosemites gather on the open flat of their small village in a circle illuminated by campfires. Bierstadt's Yosemite Valley is grand and majestic, yet it is also this Indigenous people's home. Some critics of the time objected to Bierstadt's inclusion of Native Americans in this painting and others, arguing that their presence marred "the impression of solitary grandeur" implicit in Yosemite's landscape. If asked, Muir likely would have agreed.[39]

Eadweard Muybridge, the eccentric and brilliant photographer who would go on to invent the first moving pictures, came to Yosemite to capture that solitary grandeur on heavy view cameras and burdensome glass negatives. Like Bierstadt, he also turned his artistic eye on the valley's Indigenous people. In fact, he and Bierstadt became friends, and he photographed the painter working at sketching a village. Muybridge's artistic photographs of Yosemite's granite monuments offered the solitary grandeur critics sought, yet his journalistic eye reported the Indigenous presence.[40]

Constance Gordon-Cumming visited the valley in 1878 after Muir had moved on. A painter and travel writer with the wealth and will to defy Victorian custom and travel the world as an independent woman, Gordon-Cumming once spent "all day sketching a most picturesque, but unspeakably filthy, Indian camp of conical bark-huts." She pronounced Native Americans only slightly more advanced than Australia's Aboriginals. "This Indian gipsy camp naturally forms a fruitful topic of conversation," she wrote, "and leads to many animated discussions between those men who consider all Indians 'a race of scoundrels—a nation who must be obliterated from the earth!' and others who see in them a race unjustly despoiled of their heritage, and whose degradation has been certainly not lessened by the invasion of the whites." Gordon-Cumming came down, softly, on the side of those humanitarians who blamed Indigenous poverty on invasion and oppression, not race. She reasoned, "One would imagine that some sense of fair-play might have induced a certain amount of sympathy with the wild tribes who saw their hunting-grounds so ruthlessly cleared, and they themselves driven out from every desirable resting-place; but this is an idea which apparently never found room in the mind of the encroaching whites." In her own gesture of fair play, Gordon-Cumming composed *Indian Camp Beside the Merced River.* Her painting places the village in a prominent foreground with the smoke of cooking fires rising over the river's flow in the direction of Half Dome. Gordon-Cumming's Yosemite was inhabited and domesticated; it was the well-tended and beloved ground these Indigenous people called home.[41]

Yosemite's tribal people complained among themselves of the poverty to which they had been reduced. In time, they carried their complaints to the White House and Congress. Identifying themselves as Yosemites, Monos, and Paiutes and drafting a petition to redress their longstanding grievances, they registered their anger at the harm done to them by invading gold miners and continued by tourists. They rightly resented being "poorly-clad paupers and unwelcome guests, silently the objects of curiosity or contemptuous pity to the throngs of strangers who yearly gather in this our own land and heritage." Euro-American encroachment degraded Yosemite with stables, corrals, hotels, barbed-wire fences, and trampled meadows. "This is not the way in which we treated this park when we had it," they declared in the petition. "Yosemite is no longer a State or National Park, but merely a hay-farm and cattle range." Destruction of the landscape broke the promise to the ancestors, for "this valley was not given us by our fathers for a day, or a year, but for all time." Signed by forty-seven Yosemites, five Mono-Yosemites, "and many others," then sent on to Washington DC, the petition drew no notice from the White House nor Congress. The grievances of Yosemite's Indigenous residents continued unaddressed.[42]

The entitlement Euro-American tourists felt toward Yosemite's tribal peoples took a turn to the ghoulish. When Indigenous residents stopped cremating the dead and their grave goods and instead began burying them, tourists dug up the exquisite blankets and tightly woven baskets interred as offerings to the departed and took them home. Abandoned by park authorities and forced to defend their lifeways themselves, tribal mourners took to cutting the blankets and baskets into tiny fragments, all to foil would-be grave robbers seeking souvenirs.[43] Not even the dead were safe.

Like the powers that were, Muir mostly ignored Yosemite's Indigenous people and focused his attention on Euro-American tourists who came "all in some measure seeing and loving wild beauty." Those who impressed him most were hardy souls who set off on their own, as Muir himself did, seeking out the park's high-altitude reaches. They were "mostly members of Alpine Clubs, sturdy Englishmen and Germans, with now and then a cannie [Scots for 'skillful'] Scotchman, all anxious to improve their opportunities to the utmost."[44] These elite climbers and explorers were the brave Nordic or Anglo-Saxon adventurers whom LeConte and Emerson placed on the top rung of America's racial ladder. Emerson even proposed to Muir how he might help their cause.

After visiting Muir, Emerson became convinced that the mountain man's life as a backcountry hermit detracted from the great good he could do for a wider audience, particularly if he were based in the populous East. Consider, Emerson suggested to Muir, what could happen if "you were to bring your ripe fruits so rare and precious into waiting society." The hermitage of the high country was sure to lose its appeal, as "there are drawbacks also to solitude, who is a sublime mistress, but an intolerable wife. So I pray you to bring to an early close your absolute contracts with any unvisited glaciers or volcanoes, roll up your drawings, herbariums, and poems, and come to the Atlantic Coast."[45]

Muir had no interest in Emerson's invitation, yet his years of solitary sauntering had left him lonely and longing. "In all God's mountain mansions I find no human sympathy, & I hunger," he confided to his journal. He longed for friendship of the sort that he enjoyed with Jeanne Carr and Joseph LeConte, both living in Oakland and connected to the cultural scene of the University of California and the wider Bay Area. So in November 1873, Muir left Yosemite to winter in the city and take a stab—temporary, he thought—at writing for a popular audience through the *Overland Monthly* and San Francisco's *Daily Evening Bulletin*. When his pieces were well received, the editors wanted more. Muir found that, although writing was for him demanding and difficult work, he could make a modest living at it. He returned to Yosemite in early fall 1874 intending to stay the winter, only to discover in the sudden solitude that his mission was changing from hermit to evangelist. "Civilization and fever and all the morbidness that has been hooted at me have not dimmed my glacial eye, and I care to live only to entice people to look at Nature's loveliness," he wrote to Jeanne Carr. When the *Evening Bulletin* offered Muir a contract to report on California's backcountry, he signed on, picked up his walking staff, and sauntered north along the stage roads.[46]

He was leaving a landscape whose Indigenous inhabitants he easily overlooked and was heading into one where recent tribal history was nothing he could ignore. About that Muir would have much to say.

6

Well Done for Wildness!

Modocs, like most other Indians, are about as unknightly as possible. The quantity of moral sentiment developed in them seems infinitely small, and though in battle they appear incapable of feeling any distinction between men and beasts, even their savageness lacks fullness and cordiality.

—JOHN MUIR, 1874

Muir walked north from Yosemite along the stagecoach roads heading up the Sacramento Valley, then climbed the Cascade foothills toward Mount Shasta. His goal was to summit the mountain even though the first snows had fallen and locals told him an ascent so late in the year was madness. An undaunted Muir stopped to prepare for his climb at Sisson's Station, a hotel-bar-restaurant operation near the base of the imposing volcanic cone. Justin Sisson readied Muir with food and blankets and deposited him in a base camp as far up the mountain as the snow would allow packhorses to climb.

Rising soon after midnight, fortifying himself with roast venison, and setting out all alone with two days' food in his pack, Muir slogged upslope through snow drifts so deep that sometimes he could plow ahead only on all fours. He made the summit a little after ten o'clock in the morning. Pressed by a fast-gathering storm, Muir took little time to enjoy the view and began his descent. The breaking weather forced Muir to bivouac in the lee of a block of red lava. He built a fire and spent two cold nights waiting for the storm to howl itself out. Meanwhile, alarmed at Muir's failure to return,

Sisson dispatched horses and riders to fetch him—"notwithstanding," a peeved Muir wrote later, "I had expressed a wish to be let alone in case it stormed." Back at Sisson's with its welcome fresh food and hot coffee, Muir watched while the storm, as sublime as any he had experienced, raged on for several snowy days more.[1]

Also sheltering at Sisson's was a hunting party of four well-to-do, adventure-seeking Europeans. Two of them, an Englishman named Brown and a fellow Scotsman, G. Buchanan Hepburn, were keen to hunt bighorns. Muir had written a glowing piece about the Sierra Nevada's wild sheep "as the noblest of animal mountaineers" for *Overland Monthly*, but he had yet to get an up-close look at these charismatic creatures. Brown and Hepburn brought along Sisson, himself an avid hunter, as a guide and invited the eager Muir to tag along when they set out for Sheep Rock, a volcanic formation due north of Mount Shasta. The sheep there proved too scarce to hunt, and the party continued northeast into the Klamath Basin toward the peak known as Mount Bremer (now called Mount Dome). It lay some seven crow-fly miles west of Tule Lake and the Lava Beds, the battleground of the Modoc War and the one and only wild landscape to give John Muir the willies.[2]

When Muir shifted his focus from Modocs to sheep, his mood lifted. Mount Bremer was, he wrote, "the most noted stronghold of wild sheep in the whole Shasta region, in which large flocks abide both winter and summer." The Van Bremers, who were local ranchers and knew the Lava Beds well, told the two hunters that it was easy to spot sheep at a distance but far harder to stalk close enough to get a shot. This caution made Brown and Hepburn even more eager to unpack their high-end, breech-loading, double-barreled rifles and head out. Soon they found that the sheep were, as the Van Bremers promised, both numerous and wary. Not until the fourth day of hard hunting did the shooters bag trophies. "Well done Scotch rifle!" Muir exclaimed at the sudden change of luck. "A ram with one barrel, a ewe with the other. The scene was wildly exciting."

For a man who was no vegetarian yet never hunted nor fished when he sauntered through the high country, that strange and rare excitement forced Muir to face his own inner wild man. "Savageness is natural; civilization, at least in this stage of the play, is strained and unnatural," Muir wrote. "It requires centuries to tame men, while they are capable of being resavagized [*sic*] in as many years. In the wild exhilaration raised by the running of game, and the firing, and the pursuit of the wounded, we could have torn and worried like mastiffs, but this all passed away, and we were Christians again." The pagan mood returned when Van Bremer slit the throat of the head-shot-but-still-breathing ewe. The life pouring from her "formed a crimson pool in a hollow of the lava," a sacrifice to the bloodlust of the hunt.

With two sheep down, Muir had his long-sought chance for that up-close look. In the natural-history style of the time, he made detailed measurements of both carcasses, then took samples from their coats with plans to give them a closer examination under better light.[3] Back in the Bay Area as 1875 began, Muir took a long look at his Klamath bighorn fleece and wrote an *Overland Monthly* article on what he found. That essay became Muir's earliest manifesto on wilderness.

"Wild Wool" opened by laying out the disregard most Americans felt for everything wild: "The barbarous notion is almost universally entertained by civilized men, that there is in all the manufactures of nature something essentially coarse which can and must be eradicated by human culture." Muir countered this commonplace sentiment with a eureka moment from the Mount Dome hunt. Examining the ram's and ewe's "beautiful wool" with a hand lens, an excited Muir shouted, "Well done for wildness! Wild wool is finer than tame!"

Muir's hunting buddies agreed. "My companions stooped down and examined the fleeces for themselves . . . each in turn paying tribute to wildness. It *was* finer, and no mistake; finer than Spanish Merino. Wild wool *is* finer than tame." The power of this evidence for wildness was that "fine wool is appreciable by everybody alike." Might it be that "all wildness is finer than tameness"?

Muir set to building the case. "Nature is a good mother, and sees well to the clothing of her many bairns—birds with smoothly imbricated feathers, beetles with shining jackets, and bears with shaggy furs." Wild wool comprised a mix of long, tough guard hairs and shorter, curly, delicate wool fibers; the fibers were about two-and-a-half times as numerous as the hairs. Muir recognized that "the wool and the hair are forms of the same thing, modified in just that way and to just that degree that renders them most perfectly subservient to the well-being of the sheep." There was nothing accidental about the attributes of the bighorn's coat; they were "inventions of God for the attainment of definite ends." Here was a perfect example of the belief both he and Joseph LeConte, his soul friend from Tenaya Lake, held. The adaptation that drove evolution's narrative proved the Creator's continuous attention in fitting wild organisms to their habitats and lifestyles.

The difference between selective breeding by humans and the natural working of the divine hand in the wild was purpose. Humans bred sheep to provide wool suited to spinning and weaving for their own uses. Nature developed "wild wool [that] was not made for men but for sheep." The fleece insulated the wild sheep with the guard hairs adding warmth and protecting the delicate wool. The result was a fabric to "wear well in mountain rough-ness and wash well in mountain storms." Wild sheep prospered because nature guided by the Creator had given them the coats they needed, not the ones humans wanted.

Muir knew that fellow Americans who viewed nature as valuable only when turned to human purpose would find his idea hard to swallow. "No dogma," he wrote, "taught by the present civilization seems to form so insuperable an obstacle in the way of a right understanding of the relations which culture sustains to wildness, as that which declares that the world was made especially for the uses of men." Such a belief was but an "enormous conceit," particularly in the absence of the least "trace of evidence that seemed to show that any one animal was ever made for another as much it was made for itself."

Lest this argument support a "selfish isolation" of one species from another, Muir added an ecological grace note. "In the making of every animal the presence of every other animal has been recognized. Indeed, every atom in creation may be said to be acquainted with and married to every other," he wrote. "No matter what the note any creature forms in the song of existence, it is made first for itself, then more and more remotely for all the world and worlds."

Small wonder, then, that plants and animals selectively bred to serve civi-lized purposes fared poorly among their wild neighbors. As Muir observed, "Give to nature every apple—codling, pippin, russet—and every sheep so laboriously compounded—muffled Southdowns, hairy Cotswolds, wrinkled Merinos—and she would throw the one to her caterpillars, the other to her wolves."

What Americans needed was not more civilization, but less. "A little pure wildness," Muir concluded, "is the one great present want, both of men and sheep."[4]

The wilderness vision that found its metaphor in wild wool proved central to Muir's writings and his public advocacy for parks and preservation over the following decades. "Wild Wool" laid out two concepts fundamental to his work as author and advocate.

The first was that wild land and wild creatures, both plant and animal, possessed inherent value and importance on their own terms. The bighorn's fleece stood in for the planet's wild places. Both served their own needs, not humankind's, and bore value in and of themselves.

Muir's sense of wildness for its own sake did not originate with him. It reached back to the eighteenth century's Enlightenment and to Romantic writers, like William Wordsworth and John Ruskin, of the early nineteenth century. It can be found, too, in the New England Transcendentalists Ralph Waldo Emerson and Henry David Thoreau, both of whom Muir admired. Emerson and Thoreau, however, offered a tame, human-sized image of nature, a cultivated countryside of woodlots, meadows, and ponds.[5] The far wilder Muir loved the West, with its vast mountains, deserts, and forests. He gave the ideal of wildness an expansive, western spin in the Klamath Basin setting of "Wild Wool" far beyond what Thoreau in his tame Walden cabin ever imagined.

Muir's second fundamental concept built on his first: humans did need wildness for something, but that something was not simply timber, clean water, fresh mutton, or stunning scenery. Wilderness fed the soul as well as the body. The wild world, unmarked by the fall from God's grace and humankind's expulsion from Eden, pulsed with the immanent presence of the deity. It offered to illuminate truths that otherwise spiritually insensitive humans could not see in their paved, overbuilt, denatured cities. Removed from civilization and transformed by wilderness, the soul might awaken to the deepest divine truth.[6]

By this time in his life Muir had thrown off the Disciples of Christ orthodoxy he inherited from his evangelical father, but he retained an essentially Christian view of the world. When humans reentered long-lost Eden by venturing into the wild, they were experiencing that unfallen world in a way impossible within the constraints and confines of civilization. Muir's brilliance as a prophet for wilderness was that he couched his message in terms sufficiently secular to appeal across a broad spectrum of belief, from atheist to evangelical. His argument that the value of wilderness lay both in itself and in its demonstration of our own species' place in the cosmic order reached beyond its Christian origins.

The bighorns of Mount Dome, with their perfect coats, signaled that the Mount Shasta region of northeastern California embodied the inspirational values Muir sought in the wild. This was a place worth preserving.

Some fifteen years after he left the Klamath Basin to return to Oakland and spend the winter writing "Wild Wool" and other essays, Muir proposed to turn the Mount Shasta region into a teachable natural space. It was wild, it was remote, and the war had cleared out those lava-hued, infernal, cave-dwelling Modocs. As for the other Indigenous nations in the area, they were nothing to be concerned about. He explained that they were "now scattered, few in numbers and miserably demoralized, though still offering some rare specimens of savage manhood." These broken peoples never had had any interest in the mountain, he claimed; in fact, they feared it. "Mount Shasta, so far as I have seen, has never been the home of Indians, not even their hunting-ground to any great extent, above the lower slopes of the base. They are said to be afraid of fire-mountains and geyser-basins as being the dwelling-places of dangerously powerful and unmanageable gods," Muir reported with seeming authority.[7]

The same claim was long made for Yellowstone with its many volcanic features, and it was as wrong there as it was for Mount Shasta. In fact, the mountain served as a sacred site for tribal peoples who lived around it: Wintus, Shastas, Ajumawis, Atsugewis, Modocs, and Karuks. To the Winnemem Wintus, the mountain's Panther Spring remains the genesis site where the Creator sent their ancestors into the world. To them it is Eden.[8]

The falsehood that Muir unknowingly repeated served a purpose, though. It portrayed the mountain as empty, pristine, pure, and useless to Indigenous people, thus making it a public property for the conquering Euro-America to do with as it saw best. To Muir this highest use was clear: "The Shasta region is still a fresh unspoiled wildness, accessible for travelers of every kind and degree. Would it not then be a fair thing to set it apart like the Yellowstone and Yosemite as a National Park for the welfare and benefit of all mankind, preserving its fountains and forests and all its glad life in primeval beauty?"[9] And with the dangerous Modocs removed and the remaining tribes too scattered and broken to pose a threat, this newly pristine land could achieve its highest spiritual purpose: a sanctuary dedicated to contemplation of the divine plan by civilized humankind.

Wherever he went in the West in those years following his excursions around Mount Shasta, the Lava Beds, and the Klamath Basin, Muir assessed whether Indigenous peoples had any claim on wild places or posed a danger to tourists and adventurers. America's tribal nations had once been a mortal threat, Muir made clear. He told how in the Oregon forests of the 1820s, Indigenous hunters repeatedly threatened and frightened David Douglas, a Scot like Muir and the botanist for whom the Douglas fir and Douglas squirrel were named, during his forest rambles. Hostile tribes, too, ambushed and killed freelance trappers who came after Oregon's beaver. By the time Muir was writing about the same forests, such danger had long vanished. "The Indians are seldom found in the woods, being confined mainly to the banks of rivers, where the greater part of their food is obtained," Muir assured his readers. "Moreover, the most of them have either been buried since the settlement of the country or civilized into comparative innocence, industry, or harmless laziness." Once the province of "oily, salmon-fed Indians," Oregon was as safe as Washington where "Indians are seldom to be met with away from the Sound, excepting about the few outlying hop-ranches, to which they resort in great numbers during the picking season." The once proud and prosperous tribal peoples of the Northwest Coast had been reduced to harvest-time fieldhands.[10]

Muir was reassuring an American public who had some good reason to fear the West's wild lands. Bad things happened. A national park as of 1872, Yellowstone became a moving battleground with the Nez Perce (Nimíipuu) nation led by Chief Joseph in late summer 1877. About 750 Nez Perces refusing forced removal from their traditional homeland along northeast Oregon's Wallowa River fled into the park after the Battle of Big Hole while being pressed in the rear by a much larger American military force. Inside Yellowstone, Nez Perce fighters ran into two groups of Montana tourists and gunfights broke out. A pair of Montanans were killed, several more wounded, and others seized as hostages. These events set the stage for the harrowing escape of yet another tourist party guided by Texas Jack Omohundro, a friend and associate of Buffalo Bill Cody and Ned Buntline as well as America's first cowboy star. Sensational press accounts of these events ran nationwide under screaming headlines. Yellowstone officials worried for a time that fears arising from such hostilities, which continued through the 1870s with several tribal nations besides the Nez Perces, might diminish tourist traffic to the new park.[11]

While the Bannock War burned across northeastern Oregon and southern Idaho in the summer of 1878, Muir was offered a chance to see the Great Basin by tagging along with a survey team from the U.S. Coast and Geodetic Survey. Muir's longtime friend Louisiana Strentzel—soon to become his mother-in-law—cautioned him against the journey. "Why do you go away and risk your life among those murderous Indians, when you might just as well remain at home in peace and comfort with your many friends. At least wait awhile until there is good prospect of the war troubles being ended," she wrote as Muir made his way to Nevada. He sent a reassuring letter back stating, "The war country lies to the north of our line of work some two or three hundred miles." As for the Native Americans he did encounter, they posed no threat. "All the Indians we meet are harmless as sage-bushes though perhaps about as bitter at heart," he explained.[12]

Muir took much the same tone in his public writings. He wanted to assure readers that Euro-Americans on a mission to behold wildness had nothing to fear from Native Americans. History and manifest destiny were on his side, clearing the path to safe solitude. "The Indians are passing away here as everywhere," he wrote.[13]

The idea that national parks were Indigenous-free zones was hardly John Muir's creation. The campaign to preserve portions of America's wilderness by dispossessing the tribal peoples who occupied them grew throughout the late nineteenth century and into the twentieth. Importantly, this movement represented a significant shift from the original proposal for national parks in the United States.

That came from George Catlin, the well-known student and painter of Native America. Traveling in the northern Great Plains in the early 1830s,

Catlin found himself appalled by the rapacious slaughter of bison for the buffalo-robe trade and the destruction of tribes of the Great Sioux Nation (Očhéthi Šakówiŋ) by rotgut alcohol. Perhaps extinction was inevitable. He conceded, "It may be that *power* is *right*, and voracity a virtue; and that these people, and these noble animals, are *righteously* doomed to an issue that *will* not be averted." Yet it didn't have to be this way, Catlin realized; the land offered a way out.

The grassy plains that stretched from Mexico to Lake Winnipeg were "useless to cultivating man. It is here, and here chiefly, that the buffaloes dwell; and with, and hovering about them, live and flourish the tribes of Indians, whom God made for the enjoyment of that fair land and its luxuries." These great prairies, with their wildlife and Indigenous peoples, could be set aside and protected to continue as they were. Then "they *might* in future be seen (by some great protecting policy of government) preserved in their pristine beauty and wildness, in a *magnificent park*, where the world could see for ages to come, the native Indian in his classic attire, galloping his wild horse, with sinewy bow, and shield and lance, amid the fleeting herds of elks and buffaloes." Catlin threw out a big idea: "What a beautiful and thrilling specimen for America to preserve and hold up to the view of her refined citizens and the world, in future ages! A *nation's Park*, containing man and beast, in all the wild and freshness of their nature's beauty!"[14]

Henry David Thoreau had a notion less ambitious than Catlin's, yet not too dissimilar. He saw wilderness as a necessity for civilization where "the poet must, from time to time, travel the logger's path and the Indian's trail, to drink at some new and more bracing fountain of the Muses, far in the recesses of the wilderness." The kings of England set aside preserves for hunting, impelled by the instinctual draw to wildness. "Why should not we, who have renounced the king's authority, have our national preserves, where no villages need be destroyed, in which the bear and panther, and some even of the hunter race, may still exist and not be 'civilized off the face of the earth?'" Such preserves would serve the purposes of "inspiration and our own true recreation."[15]

Exactly forty years after Catlin's grand awakening on the prairie, when Congress passed and Pres. Ulysses S. Grant signed the bill that made Yellowstone the first national park, even Thoreau's less expansive vision had been dimmed to but a glimmer of the original. The law aimed to set aside this huge region of nearly thirty-five hundred square miles as "a public park or pleasuring-ground for the benefit and enjoyment of the people"— meaning Euro-Americans. The law specifically excluded anyone from settling or occupying the reserve. Violators, the law declared, "shall be considered trespassers and removed therefrom."[16] That provision explicitly barred the Indigenous peoples Catlin and Thoreau considered part and parcel of their vision of "a *nation's Park.*"

The Yellowstone paradigm arose from received wisdoms unquestioned in the early 1870s. Purportedly the park was never more than thinly populated by tribal nations who had little interest in its resources. The only full-time residents were the lowly, primitive, terminally impoverished Mountain Shee-peaters (Tukudikas). Plains tribes steered clear of the place out of fear of its geysers, hot springs, and fumaroles, and the establishment of the park ended all Native interest in the Yellowstone Plateau. None of these tales was accurate. A long list of tribal nations traveled through, camped, hunted, fished, foraged, and sought visions in Yellowstone: Crow (Apsaalooke), Blackfoot Confederacy (Natsitapii), Salish (Sqelixw), Kootenai (Ktunaxa), Bannocks (Bana'kwut), Nez Perce (Nimíípuu), and Shoshone (Sosoni). As for the Mountain Sheepeaters, they practiced a vibrant culture well adapted to living on the snowy plateau all year long. Thermal displays raised no unusual fears among tribes who were as interested in Yellowstone after the park was established as they had been before. And that "before" reached back a long, long while—well over nine thousand years into the past.[17]

Native Americans' lives had changed legally just the year before the law making Yellowstone a national park was signed. The Indian Appropriation Act of 1871 declared that Native American tribes and nations were no longer political entities that had to be dealt with by treaty and ruled out all future treaty making. At the same time, the United States' reservation policy aimed to turn the tribes into slowly vanishing relics of the time before conquest. The Yellowstone law boosted this trend. It made tribal nations not a part of nature, as Caitlin and Thoreau imagined, but unworthy throwbacks who lacked histories and cultures able to withstand the all-encompassing demands of advancing Euro-America.[18]

Muir carried this idea forward. To begin with, he made it clear that Indigenous people had nothing to do with the natural world at the core of the park idea. Dirty and debased in Muir's eyes, they were no more natural than gawking tourists. In addition Muir argued that creating Yellowstone had harmed no one, a statement that completely overlooked the Indigenous nations with a stake in the plateau.[19] Then he broadened and deepened this Indigenous-free park idea. The law had described Yellowstone as a collection of "timber, mineral deposits, natural curiosities, or wonders" where wilderness was at best an afterthought. Muir, though, raised wilderness itself above Old Faithful and Half Dome within the national park idea. He saw these reserves as pristine zones of recovered Eden where tourists and adventurers might open their souls to the world as God created it. Muir wanted to preserve the land itself, freed of its tribal clutter and burden, and open it to exploration, adventure, and spiritual quest by Euro-Americans, and not to habitation, subsistence, or ceremony by Native Americans. Only then would unfettered nature achieve its greatest glory.

The flaw to this perspective was not only that it raised one race above another and worked against the dispossessed. It was also that the wilderness's historic and environmental reality was much more complicated.

Early European, Mexican, and American explorers raved about the natural, garden-like bounty of California: flower meadows and great trees, extensive prairies dotted with wild, hoofed grazers to be hunted for the cooking fires, and abundant wild fruits, seeds, and bulbs ripe for harvesting and feasting. This was nature in full bloom, and its wonder owed nothing to the Indigenous peoples who occupied California. In the explorers' thinking, the human and the natural were divided and different. The two melded only when hunting-and-gathering peoples settled down, plowed the land, and made themselves into farmers and livestock raisers. Remove hunter-gatherers from the wild scene, and what remained was God's creation—Edenic nature in its pure, primal, pristine glory.[20]

Like almost all his contemporaries, Muir held to the assumption that the human and the natural were separate realms: the less of one, the more of the other. As he saw it, subtracting tribal people from Yosemite freed the wild landscape from its human clutter and let the majestic valley's many glories emerge—not only the great cliffs and walls, granite monoliths, and stunning waterfalls, but also "the bottom [that] is level and park-like, finely

87

diversified with meadows and groves, and bright, sunny gardens." The feet of the sublime rocks rested "among beautiful groves and meadows, their brows in the sky, a thousand flowers leaning confidingly against their feet," Muir wrote. "Yosemite was all one glorious flower garden before plows and scythes and trampling, biting horses came to make its wide open spaces look like farmers' pasture fields." When still untouched, this paradise allowed trees to achieve their enormous, God-given sizes: a ponderosa pine eight feet in diameter and as much as 200 feet tall, incense cedars from six to ten feet in diameter and 150 feet in height, a gold-cup oak so massive—twenty feet in circumference—that it spanned three huge boulders near the foot of Tenaya Fall.[21]

Muir was hardly the only wilderness advocate to hold this point of view about humans and nature. Frederick Law Olmsted, father of landscape architecture and designer of Central Park, saw Yosemite Valley as the park God planned and planted. "Flowering shrubs of sweet fragrance and balmy herbs abound in the meadows, and there is everywhere a delicate odor of the prevailing foliage in the pines and cedars," he wrote. Like Muir, Olmsted was awed by the size of the valley's trees. The forest was "composed mainly of coniferous trees of great size, yet often more perfect, vigorous and luxuriant than trees of half the size ever found on the Atlantic side of the continent." Declaring Yosemite "the greatest glory of nature," Olmsted endorsed public preservation of the park for contemplation by Euro-Americans who could appreciate its grandeur. "The power of scenery to affect men is, in a large way," he was certain, "proportionate to the degree of their civilization and to the degree in which their taste has been cultivated. Among a thousand savages there will be a much smaller number who will show the least sign of being so affected than among a thousand persons taken from a civilized community."[22]

Yet what both Muir and Olmsted were missing was the reality that Native Americans shaped the environment Euro-American wilderness proponents admired as purely natural. In reality the valley was anything but pure, pristine, and primal; its Indigenous inhabitants had long managed it to their benefit. Like their predecessors and contemporaries in the colonial project of settling the continent, Muir and Olmsted assumed that Indigenous peoples had nothing to offer beyond lost Stone Age skills like flint napping and colorful myths and legends ideal for children's books. As for historical understanding or environmental wisdom, no, that came only from Europeans and Euro-Americans.

The primary tool that Yosemites, Ahwahneechees, and their ancestors used to manage the valley was fire. Burning selected areas at the right season and in the right pattern cleared out brush and saplings, benefitted sun-loving tree species over the shade-tolerant, favored plants used as food and medicines and in basketry, suppressed the pathogens that affected the staple acorn crop, and created conditions favoring such game animals as deer, quail, squirrels, and rabbits. History proved this point. After the Mariposa Battalion drove the Yosemites out and Euro-Americans took over, the valley reverted from the verdant, park-like environment Muir and Olmsted relished to something quite different.

The Indigenous people, of course, noticed the loss of the world they had known. When Maria Lebrado, granddaughter of Yosemite headman Tenaya, returned to the valley from which she and the Yosemites had been driven seventy-eight years earlier, she was repelled by the way the whole place had grown up in her forced absence. With the formerly open meadows invaded by trees and shrubs, Lebrado called them "too dirty; too much bushy," adding, "All fixed up! Ahwahnee too dirty bushy." When she came to the largest open meadow remaining in the valley, she cried out "Ahwahnee!" excitedly beholding the place as it had been when she was but a girl of ten.[23]

Some white people, too, grasped the environmental change that upset Lebrado. The Scottish painter Constance Gordon-Cumming, who included Indigenous dwellings in her renderings of the valley, was concerned that the majestic scenery drawing tourists to Yosemite would be obliterated. "So long as the Indians had it to themselves," she wrote, "their frequent fires kept down the under-wood, which is now growing up everywhere in such dense thickets, that soon all the finest views will be altogether hidden."

Galen Clark, who long lived at what is now Wawona within the park boundaries and befriended the Yosemites, had watched the valley change in front of his eyes. "My first visit to Yosemite was in the summer of 1855," he wrote almost forty years later. "At that time there was no undergrowth to obstruct clear open views in any part of the Valley from one side of the Merced River across to the base of the opposite wall." Under the traditional care of the Yosemites, meadows covered four times more area than they did four decades later. Every summer the tribe set fires to kill young trees invading the open spaces, clear the underbrush, and make hunting and acorn-gathering easier. They pulled up by hand any willows and cottonwoods that escaped the flames in moist meadows. This regimen ended when the state of California took control and knocked down all fires as threats to property and scenery. The forest encroached upon the meadows so steadily that three-fourths of the open area had disappeared, and "what there is left is becoming so thickly covered with young willows and cottonwoods of four or five years' growth that there are really not fifty acres of clear ground in Yosemite, except such as has been under very recent cultivation."[24]

The Yosemites' practice of seasonal burning at low intensity—a stewardship culture repeated up and down California, in one "wild" area after another—delivered multiple benefits to the people sustaining themselves from the land. Fire favored the growth of black oaks, the preferred acorn-producing species, making them more numerous than they would otherwise have been, and it helped eliminate pests. Fires in high-country meadows pushed encroaching trees back and promoted the deergrass, yampahs, and clovers that made excellent forage for deer fattening toward the fall hunting season. Ponderosas and sugar pines could reach the enormous sizes that so awed Muir. And since the undergrowth was gone and seasonal burns were kept low and cool, devastating, forest-destroying crown fires broke out but rarely.[25]

Muir and his allies shared the laudable urge to preserve a primal, God-created wilderness untouched by human hands or intention. But they got it wrong, unknowingly. The preservationist impulse instead set aside a garden that had been cultivated for 10,000 years. Then, by removing its Indigenous stewards, they found themselves at a loss in understanding how to nurture it.[26] This dilemma remains.

John Muir rechanneled the predominant stereotypes about Indigenous peoples from the society he lived in. His ignorance of those peoples made the social conventions about them easy to believe and convenient to further. Although he had encountered Native Americans in his tramps and travels, in only one case—Indian Tom, who carried mail on snowshoes to and from

Yosemite Valley during the winter months—did he call any Indigenous person he met by even an Americanized nickname.[27] Tribal people were less individuals than representatives of something other, something lesser, something vanishing. That was about to change. The shift came during a time when Muir traveled far off his California home range and encountered a bracingly different Indigenous reality.

7

Missionary to the Tlingits

While strolling about the streets last evening, I felt a singular interest
in the Thlinkit [*sic*] Indians I met and something like a missionary
spirit came over me. Poor fellows, I wish I could serve them.

—JOHN MUIR TO LOUIE MUIR, AUGUST 3, 1880

Muir's timing could hardly have been worse. While devoting the winter to
writing articles for money and bunking with friends in San Francisco, Muir
regularly traveled across the bay and through Carquinez Strait to the tiny
port town of Martinez. There he visited the Strentzel family. Muir found
John and Louisiana's home congenial and warm, and there was the added
attraction of their only child, Louisa Wanda, nicknamed Louie by family
and friends. Musical, cultured, and praised as kind, Louie was already into
her thirties and well past the standard marrying age for women of the time.
Muir himself was now forty-one, his beard ever longer, his style still shabby,
his manner always charming. Somehow this odd couple jelled. In early June
1879 John and Louie agreed, amid smiles, giggles, and embarrassed blushes,
to marry. At long last, John Muir had found home.

Not that the world outside ceased calling. Speaking only days later at the
National Assembly of Sunday Schools convention in Yosemite Valley's just-
completed chapel for a hundred-dollar honorarium, Muir met the Reverend
Sheldon Jackson, a pint-sized dynamo of a Presbyterian proselytizer from
Southeast Alaska. Jackson regaled Muir with tales of stunning mountains,
glaciers to outnumber and dwarf the famed ice fields of Switzerland, and

heathen souls hungering for salvation. Indeed, Jackson said, he himself would be headed back as soon as the conference ended to inspect the newest mission among the most heathen of the heathens. He invited Muir to come along.

Twelve days later Muir left fiancée Louie behind in Martinez and boarded the steamer *Dakota* bound for the Northwest. Transferring in Portland to the little Alaska mail ship *California*, Muir was on his way to the frontier outpost of Fort Wrangel. Besides Jackson, Muir shared passage with Dr. Henry Kendall, secretary of the Presbyterian Home Missions Board, and Aaron Lindsley, a Portland pastor, plus their wives. From this clerical company the ever inquisitive and endlessly conversational Muir learned that the Chilkoot (Jilkoot) and Chilkat (Jilkáat) Tlingits, the tribes the ministers were planning to visit, were Southeast Alaska's wildest unredeemed pagans. They were also the most remote, occupying a homeland at the far end of Lynn Canal, the longest, deepest fjord in North America. Converting them would extend American presence and Presbyterian leadership in this new frontier where Christian denominations had already divided up the territory and were competing to put baptized bodies in pews and saved souls in line for heaven.[1]

For the moment, Muir's role in expanding the United States' continental empire concerned him little. He relished the slow, scenic voyage north through the calm waters of the Inside Passage. "To the lover of pure wildness Alaska is one of the most wonderful countries in the world," he wrote. "No other excursion that I know of may be made into any other American wilderness where so marvelous an abundance of noble, newborn scenery is so charmingly brought to view as on the trip through the Alexander Archipelago to Fort Wrangel and Sitka." Ever an enthusiast for the scenically sublime, Muir watched in awe from the steamer's deck. "So numerous are the islands," he wrote, "that they seem to have been sown broadcast; long tapering vistas between the largest of them open in every direction."[2]

After such natural grandeur, Fort Wrangel—now called Wrangell—was a downer. "The most inhospitable place I had ever seen," Muir called it. "No mining hamlet in the placer gulches of California, nor any backwoods village I ever saw, approached it in picturesque, devil-may-care *abandon*. It was a lawless draggle of huts and houses." The ubiquitous mud was made even muddier by wandering, wallowing hogs. Tlingits, most of them Stikines

(Shtax'héen Ḵwáan) native to the area, lived at the ends of town while Euro-Americans occupied the center. Muir found it difficult, however, to tell from outward appearance which dwellings belonged to the colonized and which to the colonizers. The one giveaway was the finely carved totems some Stikines erected in front of their homes. As Muir wandered Fort Wrangel's muddy lanes, several of the village's whites warned him that the Stikines, for all their woodworking skill, were a bad lot, never to be trusted.[3]

More concerned with where he was going to spend the night in this ragged settlement that lacked a hotel or even a tavern with sleeping quarters, Muir searched until he found a temporary nest in a vacant carpenter's shop inside the fort. The U.S. Army had moved out of the stronghold two years earlier when the Rutherford B. Hayes administration redirected Alaska defense funding to the West after Custer's Little Bighorn debacle and the Nez Perce War. Now, among various enterprises and facilities, the abandoned fort housed the Presbyterian home. The three missionaries who had accompanied Muir on the *California* were bunking there with their wives and occupying the last remaining rooms. After one night on the carpenter shop's floor, Muir was taken in by John Vanderbilt, a local merchant who offered the hospitality of his fine house.[4]

Skeptical of the missionaries he had traveled with as far too similar to his own hellfire father, Muir largely kept a distance. But he discovered an unexpected affinity at first meeting with the local Presbyterian pastor, S. Hall Young. Much like Muir, Young came from a family of Calvinist persuasion and Scots-Irish ancestry. Born in Pennsylvania and spared from the Civil War draft by poor health, Young planned to study law until a sudden conversion experience ignited his religious zeal. Now, he wrote in his memoir, "The whole tide of my life flowed towards the Christian ministry and evangelization of those who 'sat in darkness'; I was a missionary from the moment of my conversion." While studying for the ministry, Young heard Sheldon Jackson speak and saw Alaska as the place where "its heathen multitudes were a reproach to Christendom," which he himself was called to remedy. Assigned to Fort Wrangel in a move the Presbyterian Board of Home Missions saw as strategic to blocking the advance of the dreaded Jesuits, Hall had landed a year earlier. As he walked away from the ship, a Hudson Bay Company agent advised him, "Don't become an Indian." Going Native tempted Hall not at all. Within days he found a proper Presbyterian wife and set about "doing what I could towards establishing the white man's civilization among the Thinglit [*sic*] Indians." He started by mandating English-only in church and school. Young wanted to "let the old tongues with their superstition and sin die," then move on to eliminating the influence of shamans.[5]

Yet there was more to Young than the hellfire Christian arrogance of, say, Sheldon Jackson. Like Muir, Young saw the divine hand at work in the natural world. When the two met, the minister recognized a sibling soul in the California naturalist. For Young, Muir became "my Master who was to lead me into enchanting regions of beauty and mystery, which without his aid must forever have remained unseen by the eyes of my soul. I sat at his feet; and at the feet of his spirit I still sit, a student, absorbed, surrendered, as this 'priest of Nature's inmost shrine' unfolds to me the secrets of his 'mountains of God.'"[6]

The purpose behind the trip to Fort Wrangel was far more orthodox than unraveling the divine mysteries of the wild: evangelizing and converting the Chilkats and Chilkoots some 250 miles further north. Since Alaska's days as a Russian colony, the two tribes had nurtured a reputation as warlike and hostile. Then the United States replaced Russia, which hungered for cash after the Crimean War and eagerly sold Alaska for a bargain-basement $7.2 million—just a bit over $135 million in today's currency—or a minuscule two cents per acre. Even as the Chilkats and neighboring Chilkoots recovered from a smallpox epidemic that killed seventy-five percent of the community, their economy was changing, English was replacing Russian, and Presbyterianism was taking over from the Orthodox Church.[7] If Jackson and his colleagues convinced the fiercely pagan Chilkats and Chilkoots to convert to Presbyterianism, they could celebrate their dominance in the race among denominations to claim Alaska's unsaved souls. The chance for a big win drew them north.

European explorers first encountered the Tlingits in the late eighteenth century, finding them to be one of the largest Indigenous nations on the long Northwest Coast. The Tlingits occupied mainland and offshore islands from Alaska's Yakutat Bay to Portland Canal just across the border in what became Canada, a crow-fly distance of some 450 miles. The Tlingits, whose name means "human beings" or "the people," trace their origins back to the fourth millennium BCE. Over all those centuries across that enormous, richly resourced landscape, they developed a complex, layered society. The Tlingits lacked centralized political authority, yet they shared territory, language, mythology, ceremonies, and awareness of themselves as a single people. Their nation was made up of smaller tribal communities called ḵwáans, which in turn contained dozens of matrilineal clans. Sometimes the ḵwáans fought among themselves, most often because of blood feuds. Other times the ḵwáans joined forces to meet common enemies.

The Russians flattered their imperial sense of themselves by seeing the Tlingits as subjects of the czarist empire. The Tlingits begged to differ; they considered themselves an independent people who served their own interests in the fur trade and demanded equal treatment. The Russians learned this the hard way in the insurrection of 1802 when most of the ḵwáans joined together to teach the Russians a painful lesson in fair trade. They burned Fort Saint Michael to the ground, wiped out a large Russian trapping expedition, and helped themselves to all the sea otter pelts they could carry.[8] Thereafter the chastened Russians treated the Tlingits with greater deference.

After 1840, when the Hudson's Bay Company (HBC) leased access to Russian-controlled ports in Southeast Alaska, the Chilkats widened their market for furs from the interior. They paid for the expansion in eulachon, or candlefish, a smelt so high in fish oil that, when dried, it could be ignited like a candle. The candlefish and furs moved back and forth between the coast and the Yukon River along a route called the Grease Trail, and the Chilkats considered it their monopoly. When HBC built Fort Selkirk on the Yukon River to bully their way into the trade, the Chilkats took the intrusion none too kindly. A fighting force descended on the fort, destroyed its inventory, and torched it without killing a soul. The point had been made. Eighty-seven years passed before HBC built another trading outpost on the Yukon.[9]

When Russia sold Alaska to the United States, the Tlingit ḵwáan headmen gathered in protest. As far as they were concerned, the Russians had no right to sell the Tlingit domain. Southeast Alaska was their land, not the Russians'.[10] And if they had to impress the very same point on the Americans that they had on Russians and Canadians, they were prepared to do so.

Long embroiled in Indian wars, the United States recognized that the new territory's Indigenous peoples might resist American control and prepared to use force. Ten years before Muir's arrival, the U.S. military had displayed its might. Tlingit resistance led to the destruction of the village of Kake by the side-wheeler *Saginaw*'s cannons. Then, in Fort Wrangel, the army shelled the Stikine village to demand the surrender of a man accused of murder. The accused was later hanged and his body left on the gallows until nightfall to teach the Stikines a lesson.[11]

Muir endorsed such military punishment as beneficial to the Tlingits. "One gunboat, first class in everything save size, would be sufficient for the whole territory because the Indians dwell in permanent villages on the edge of navigable water wedged in between the woods and deep water at the mercy of such a ship. The Indians seldom go back into the tangled woods; they live and move on the water, and have a genius for justice that is quite remarkable," he wrote in his journal. Should the Tlingits act up, the solution was collective punishment in the form of "a good thrashing, prompt, heavy and wholesale and whole-souled, discriminating only as to the offending tribes, not as to individuals." A well-applied dose of violence would work its good effects for a long while. "It is a common saying that savages respect only power; these seem literally to kiss the rod and love it, and therefore need it only once in a lifetime," Muir declared. Chastisement groomed the Tlingits for the civilization they were eager to embrace. "They are industrious, willing to give good and fair work for fair wages, and to adopt all of the benefits of the uneducated of any people under the sun. Unprincipled whisky-laden traders are their bane." The recipe for the United States to succeed in civilizing Alaska was clear to Muir: "A few good missionaries, a few good cannon [*sic*] with men behind them, and fair play, protection from whisky, is all that the Alaska Indians require. Uncle Sam has no better subjects, white, black or brown, or any more deserving his considerate care."[12]

Enlisted in the holy work central to his recipe for Alaska's colonization, Muir threw in with the Presbyterian ministers eager to gain a denominational beachhead in Lynn Canal. This fjord divided into the Chilkat and Chilkoot Rivers, with the Chilkat ḵwáan up one and the Chilkoot ḵwáan up the other. To make the journey north, Jackson chartered the little, flat-bottomed sternwheeler *Cassiar* for sixty dollars a day. The party that went aboard included Jackson and the three other visiting missionaries—whom Muir sardonically dubbed "the divines"—and their wives, Muir himself, S. Hall Young, trader John Vanderbilt and his wife, and a Christian Stikine guide and translator named Kadachan. "The legitimate object of the divines was to ascertain the spiritual wants of the warlike and conservative Chilkat Indians, with an eye to the establishment of a church and a school in their principal village," Muir wrote. "The merchant and his party were bent on business and scenery, health and wealth; while I was moved by the glaciers that are said to come grandly down into the salt water at the head of Lynn Canal."

Almost as soon as the *Cassiar* set off, the voyage went sideways. Contention between the ship's captain and engineer about boiler pressure so slowed the vessel that it covered only seventy miles on the first day. Since the ship had been chartered by the day, and since the expected four-or-five-day journey now stretched longer and costlier, the divines determined that the extra expense broke the bank. The *Cassiar* came about and headed back, leaving "unsaved Indians, beautiful islands, sunny waters reflecting God, the grand glacial revelations and all, seemingly in the midst of this solemn, deliberative financial assembly to have suddenly become mere dust in the balance," Muir noted. The missionaries' mood soured. "On the second morning of our broken-backed Chilkat excursion, everybody seemed cloudy and conscience-stricken, and ready to do any deed of redemption whatever, provided only that it not cost much."[13]

On the way back to Fort Wrangel the expedition stopped at a deserted Stikine village for a look around. Kadachan said that the settlement had been abandoned some sixty or seventy years earlier. The place stunned a disbelieving Muir: "The magnitude of the ruins and the excellence of the workmanship manifest in them was astonishing as belonging to Indians." Many of the pillars supporting the houses still stood, and life-size figures of humans and animals were carved into them. Every wall plank had been hewn straight and true from a whole log. The workmanship awed Muir, himself an expert millwright. He marveled, "With the same tools not one in a thousand of our skilled mechanics could do as good work. Compared with it the bravest work of civilized backwoodsmen is feeble and bungling." Most impressive were the totem poles, thirty to forty feet tall and carved elaborately from top to bottom. He admired how "the childish audacity displayed in the designs, combined with manly strength in their execution, was truly wonderful."

As Muir was taking notes about these miracles of workmanship, the thunking rhythm of an axe came from the other end of the village followed by a thud like a tree falling. One of the divines had ordered a deckhand to fell a totem pole, saw off the carving of a woman, and carry it to the *Cassiar* with the intention of donating it to a museum back home. Furious, Kadachan marched up to the offending minister and demanded, "How would you like to have an Indian go to a graveyard and break down and carry away a monument belonging to your family?" The question was still hanging in the air when "a few trifling presents embedded in apologies served to hush and mend the matter."[14] The minister secured his souvenir, and Kadachan suffered the indignity of seeing his heritage sold for a pittance. To his credit, Muir recognized this theft for the sacrilege it was.

A few days after their ignominious return to Fort Wrangel, the divines, Young, and Muir again chartered the *Cassiar*. The plan this time was less ambitious: steam up the Stikine River to have a look around the now largely played-out Cassiar goldfields in northwest British Columbia. While the sternwheeler was tied up at Glenora on the Canadian side of the border, Muir and Young headed off on their own after promising to be back by departure time the following morning. The pair had hatched a wild plan to summit a cluster of peaks some seven or eight miles away and seven thousand feet up, then from that high perch savor the grand Alaskan horizon at sunset. Awed by Muir's climbing ability on the steep and pathless ascent, Young fell a couple dozen yards behind. Close to the top, a stone the minister trusted as a foothold gave way. Young spilled downhill toward the cliff face, his body twisted, and both shoulders jerked out of joint, paralyzing his arms. He came to a rough stop, unable to move, with his feet dangling down the slippery slope and over the edge. Calmly and gymnastically, Muir worked Young off the cliff and back onto the ledge from which he had tumbled. Then, after resetting one shoulder and securing the other arm with his own suspenders and necktie—yes, Muir typically wore a tie in the wild—he cautiously slid Young down a glacial canyon until they reached more level ground and the missionary could walk the rest of the way on his own. The sun was rising by the time the two made it back to the *Cassiar*.[15]

Deeply bonded by this near-death experience, Muir and Young decided to pick up where the divines left off and head north to the Chilkats and Chilkoots on their own. Muir had signed on to the missionaries' Christianizing purpose, and he was drawn by the great ice rivers to be seen on the way.

Almost six weeks would pass before the two could depart; in the meantime the Stikine clan leaders in Fort Wrangel wanted to celebrate. They "got up a grand dinner and entertainment in honor of their distinguished visitors, three doctors of divinity and their wives," Muir remembered. The Stikines gave Muir a Tlingit name, Ancoutahan, which Young assured him would protect against robbery or assault by other ķwáans—likely a flattering exaggeration. Speeches followed the dances and a meal made up mostly of canned goods, in deference to white sensibilities about Indigenous foods. Presiding headman Shakes, a person of "grave dignity," thanked the Presbyterian divines for their mission: "Dear Brothers and Sisters, we have been long, long, in the dark. You have led us into strong guiding light and taught us the right way to live and the right way to die. I thank you for myself and all my people, and I give you my heart." Muir was impressed: "Altogether it was a wonderful show."[16]

In the weeks following the celebration, Young secured the canoe, a thirty-six-foot red cedar dugout, and crew: eighty-year-old Stikine clan leader and converted Presbyterian To'watte (T'aawyaatt, "Long Feather"), the canoe's owner as captain, Kadachan from the *Cassiar*, Stickeen John, and Sitka Charley. The canoe was loaded with gear and provisions; Muir and Young's food was fastidiously segregated from Tlingit fare. The expedition set off on October 14, a late start for such an ambitious northerly journey. By the time the six men returned to Fort Wrangel five weeks later, they had covered eight hundred miles of waterway.[17]

As the Tlingits paddled through the shortening days and sat around the campfire in the chilly, lengthening evenings, Muir learned about their world. Animals have souls, they assured him. Wolves were clever enough to catch salmon and seals in the water, wise enough to kill no more than they needed. They planned ahead well, too, bearing pups in the most provident season. At the villages the group visited, Muir noticed how parents governed their children tenderly. "In all my travels, I never heard a cross, fault-finding word, or anything like a scolding inflicted on an Indian child," nor did he witness even a single spanking. "I have never seen a child ill-used, even to the extent of an angry word. Scolding, so common a curse in civilization, is not known here at all. On the contrary, the young are fondly indulged without being spoiled. Crying is very rarely heard," he reported. Spending the night in a Tlingit home, Muir said that "the loving kindness bestowed on the little ones made the house glow"—how different from the family Muir himself grew up in, where his hellfire father beat him and his siblings mercilessly. It did bother Muir that the Tlingits believed in witchcraft; still, he found them "less superstitious in some respects than many of the lower classes of whites."[18]

Learning that the Chilkats were locked in a blood feud and realizing that continuing up Lynn Canal could send the canoe into a crossfire, the group turned westward and disembarked in the main village of the Hoo-nah (Xunna) kwáan. After lunch with the gathered community, a round of hymns sung by To'watte and his crew, and Young's "usual gospel sermon," the chief asked Muir to hold forth. Focusing on the brotherhood of all races and God's love for everyone, Muir thanked the Hoonahs for their hospitality and friendship and said they felt like friends he had known his whole life. He encouraged them to accept missionaries like Young who worked selflessly for their welfare. Tlingits told stories of cannibal giants, so Muir added that some tribes "killed and ate the missionaries" and he hoped the Hoonahs "would find a better use for them and put them in their hearts instead of in their stomachs." This rhetorical flourish amused the Hoonahs, who looked "into each others' faces with nods and ughs and smiles."

Muir found the Hoonahs an attractive and compelling folk. "The most striking characteristic of these people is their easy dignity under the most novel circumstances, and their willingness to abandon their usages of every kind for those of the whites," he recorded in his journal. "They are not savages in the ordinary sense of the term. I have never seen Europeans or Americans of the poorer classes who would compare favorably with them in good breeding, intelligence, and skill."[19]

When word came that the rumored feud among the Chilkats was exaggerated and posed no danger, the canoe headed back toward Lynn Canal. At one village campsite on the way, Muir and Young, fearing lice, took care to pitch their tent apart from the locals. To'watte and Kadachan were offended for their hosts. They made it clear they would feel shame if the white men tried the same thing with the fierce Chilkats. Chastened, Muir and Young promised to eat Chilkat food without complaint and to behave well.[20]

As the crew prepared to land the dugout at the village of Yandeist'akyé, Muir dressed up for the grand occasion of arriving in Chilkat country. He "found an eagle's tail feather which I stuck in my cap and found myself ready for the noble savages." This substantial community of stout log homes guarded the mouth of the Chilkat River and protected the larger upriver village of Klukwan. Stikines and white men alike were invited to the house of Daanawaák, Yandeist'akyé's headman. They were served a feast of potatoes, salmon, and candlefish oil, with berries and rose hips for dessert. Muir and Young did as they had promised and ate without complaint. Later in the evening Koh'klux—the imposing headman of Klukwan who stood over six feet tall, dressed in the robed splendor his role demanded, and wore the scars of an old gunshot wound to the face as a badge of courage—made a grand entrance with his entourage. Some 250 people dressed to the Chilkat nines crowded in close to hear Young preach, To'watte lead prayers, and Kadachan and Stickeen John sing hymns. Muir, too, stepped up for the missionary cause: "I had to deliver a sort of lecture on the fine foodful country God had given them and the brotherhood of man, along the same general lines I had followed at the other villages." He confided that he himself was drawn to abandon his world for theirs. "I felt like leaving the whites and living with them to teach them and do them good," he told the assembled Chilkats.

Later an anxious Young asked To'watte what impression he had made among the Chilkats. "They are talking about Mr. Muir's speech," To'watte said, pulling the missionary's leg more than a little. "They say he knows how to talk and beats the preacher far." Later still, when the discussion turned to sending a missionary and teacher for the village, Daanawaák said the Chilkats wanted Muir, promising not only to build him a church and school but also to provide as many wives as he liked.[21] With his fiancée Louie waiting back in Martinez to set a wedding date, Muir was flattered but unswayed.

During one of the nights Young and Muir spent in Daanawaák's house, the continual crying of a small baby disturbed their sleep. They learned that its mother had died. Since no nursing woman in the village had milk enough for an extra mouth, the orphan was sure to starve. Muir had one of the crewmen fetch the stash of Eagle Brand sweetened and condensed milk from the dugout, then mixed a can of it with warm water. He and Young fed the baby all it could hold. Muir walked with the little one in his arms until it fell asleep, wondering no doubt how this same activity might feel once he was married and cuddling his own child through a restless night. When Muir and Young left Yandeist'akyé, they gave the woman caring for the baby their remaining supply of canned milk. Muir instructed her on the way to feed and nurture the child, even bathing the little one himself to show her how, a demonstration that combined compassion for the small and vulnerable with the arrogance of teaching his perceived lessers the right way to do things.[22]

As To'watte's canoe paddled away from Yandeist'akyé, Muir carried with him an unexpected appreciation of the Chilkats. "These people are far ahead of the same class of any people in Europe," he told his journal. Their generosity, warmth, and ready acceptance of strangers awed him. He noted, "I never saw a child or servant scolded or punished, or any resentment about taking the best place at the fire, or the best bits of food. There is such abundance that this spirit of mine and thine, developed into civilized selfishness, is never apparent, if it exists at all. Many a good lesson might be learned from these wild children. They should send missionaries to the Christians."[23]

With autumn deepening into dark and stormy November, the return to Fort Wrangel proved a long, hard, perilous paddle. Muir was eager to explore every glacier along the way back, including the two ice-filled arms of Holkham Bay where icebergs charged back and forth on the tides, churning and grinding against each other. Muir wanted to push into the bay to find the source glacier, trusting that God would carry him through the danger. But To'watte, experienced in the lethal risks of paddling through calving, capsizing icebergs, refused. When Young backed To'watte, a chagrined Muir vowed to return on his own terms and find that glacier.[24]

The naturalist was not done, however, demanding that his desire to explore trump all other concerns. The tension came to a head as the dugout neared the end of the journey, and it resulted in a confrontation so embarrassing that Muir said not a word about it in his journal.

Rounding a point at the northern end of the Wrangel Narrows, the canoe ran head-on into torrential rain, heavy seas, and a wild gale. Ahead lay a rocky reef that bent out from the point in a half-curve. To'watte, seeing no clear way through, ordered everyone to stop paddling and announced that the only choice was to come about and camp until the storm passed.

Muir was having none of it. "It is getting late now, and we must get home. Go on, and make a further effort to get around this reef," he said.

To'watte gave it his all, yet the gale rose to such a howl that the canoe made no headway. Muir only became more insistent. "Keep on going," he demanded. "Cross the reef and get along."

When To'watte shook him off, Muir raised the ante: "Ah, you are all cowards. Go across, go across."

Something in To'watte snapped. "If we die, you die too," he shouted before steering the canoe headlong into the white water, nearly swamping it. As rocks looming close on both sides scraped the sides, a wave lifted the dugout up and over the reef and dropped it in the calmer water on the far side. To'watte turned the canoe into a cove and called Muir to him. It was time to have this out.

The naturalist, the elder and captain made clear, knew a great deal about the world but he was ignorant of Alaskan waters. "Many times on this trip you acted like a silly child," he declared, adopting the tone Muir admired in a Tlingit parent instructing a wayward juvenile. "If we had listened to you we would not be alive now." Maybe Muir and the younger crewmen would have survived, but the old chief and the physically challenged Young would have drowned. "Would you be happy now on the shore with us lying among the breakers? Hereafter, let me manage this canoe. Don't act like a fool anymore," To'watte demanded.

Muir, "meek as a child," did as he was told and bided his time until the dugout made it back to Fort Wrangel. Already he was planning to come back to Southeast Alaska to see what he had missed.[25]

Muir made good on that plan the following summer; his timing on the domestic front was even worse than the first time around. Now married to Louie, who soon became pregnant, he moved to the Strentzel farm and into the house Louie's parents provided, and he devoted himself to learning the orchard business as a dutiful son-in-law. Yet as summer deepened and domesticity loomed large, Muir longed for somewhere wild. Acting on impulse, he took off for Alaska after promising Louie and his in-laws to return in time for the baby's birth and the fall harvest. In mid-July he walked down the pier at Fort Wrangel, dropped in on a surprised S. Hall Young, and asked how soon he could be ready to head north again.[26]

This time To'watte could provide neither canoe nor leadership. He had been shot dead in a dispute between the Stikines and the Takus (T'aaku). Young and Muir both grieved the loss of a man they admired. To replace him, the minister turned to dugout-owner Lot Tyeen and his son-in-law Hunter Joe, who rounded the crew out with a mixed-race, bilingual man named Smart Billy Dickinson. When the canoe was provisioned and about to disembark, Young, on a whim, decided to bring along Stickeen, the aloof, multicolored mongrel his wife had received as a wedding present. The smallish dog understood his privileged position atop Fort Wrangel's caste-based society. Although the Stikines took to Stickeen as a talisman of good luck, Young's pet avoided hanging out with their dogs, refused play dates with their children, and acted friendly only toward those few "who had adopted the white man's dress and mode of living, and were devoid of the rank native smell." Muir objected to bringing the pet along. "I like dogs, but this one seemed so small and worthless that I objected to his going," he remembered. Still, Young insisted, and Stickeen took his place in the dugout. In time, Muir's tune changed. "There's more in that wee beastie than I thought," he admitted.[27]

The Tlingit crew were masters of the water, yet a conflict erupted on land when Hunter Joe hauled into camp a young mountain goat ram he had shot. It was, he boasted to Young, "the fattest and most tender of those I killed." A startled Young asked whether Hunter Joe had killed more than one. Eleven, he answered proudly. Muir's face flushed an angry red, and he started for Hunter Joe, who scrambled up the rocky hillside and came back only when assured that Muir would do him no harm. "I shared Muir's indignation," Young wrote, "and would have enjoyed seeing him administer the richly deserved thrashing."[28]

This incident consists of more than Muir and Young's reaction to killing wildlife beyond need and reason. That take, of course, fits with Muir's standing as prophet and protector of the wild. But the right to administer a "richly deserved thrashing" derived from the privilege of a master caste that saw itself as instructing unsaved, heathen Stikines in civilization's better ways. In threatening Hunter Joe without even asking him why he had done what he did, Muir was acting as much like a colonial overlord as nature's guardian—the one who had the right to set the rules and who assumed that nothing Indigenous had any lasting value. And had Hunter Joe defended himself and taken Muir on, he would have marked himself as a rebel who needed to be knocked down a peg or two. Wisely, he ran.

Despite this row, the voyage put Muir in his happy place. Since the journey started two months earlier than the prior year's excursion, he stood much better odds of beholding glaciers he had been forced to bypass before. "The care-laden commercial lives we lead close our eyes to the operations of God as a workman, though openly carried on that all who will look may see," he wrote. Indeed, following a new route to the north and west, he was soon reveling in grand glaciers that instilled in him an awareness of nature's divine and creative center. Muir's obsession with ice, which offered no promise of either gold or game, so fascinated the Stikines that they nicknamed him Dleit Aankáawu (Glate Ankow or "Ice Lord"), a moniker bestowed with no small irony.[29]

Yet it was the very ice Muir adored that nearly cost him and Stickeen their lives. Camped in Taylor Bay, off Cross Sound to the west of Glacier Bay, Muir resolved to rise early the next morning and explore the ice field now known as Brady Glacier. A fierce rainstorm that blew up overnight did nothing to forestall his plan. He reasoned that "many of Nature's finest lessons are to be found in her storms." Muir skipped breakfast and coffee, stuck a piece of bread in his pocket, grabbed an ice axe, and was off before anyone else in the camp was awake. Everyone, that is, except Stickeen, who insisted on coming along and could not be persuaded to return to camp. Soaked through but making good progress over the course of the day, man and dog crossed the glacier. Then the rain turned to cold, blinding snow, and Muir lost sight of his position in the vast field of riven ice. Leaping one by one across a series of crevasses, Muir hurried his pace in what he hoped was the right direction. He realized that spending the night on the glacier looked all too possible. He recalled, "We were hungry and wet, and the wind from the mountains was still thick with snow and bitterly cold, so of course that night would have seemed a very long one." Then a great crevasse, far too wide to leap, blocked the way. Either Muir and Stickeen could retrace their steps, which would take hours and maroon them overnight, or they could bet their lives on the sliver of an ice bridge that crossed the gaping crevasse. A fall meant certain death. "Of the many perils encountered in my years of wandering on mountains and glaciers none seemed so plain and stern and merciless as this," Muir remembered. "And it was presented when we were wet to the skin and hungry, the sky dark with quick driving snow, and the night near." For Muir and Stickeen, it was do or die. Dleit Aankáawu chose to do.

The ice bridge crossed the crevasse diagonally twenty-five or thirty feet below the glacier's main level. Swinging his ice axe, Muir cut steps down to the bridge, then edged step by slippery step along it to the opposite side where he had to cut more steps up to the glacier's surface. Muir had made it. Meanwhile, Stickeen remained on the far side, crying and whining piteously at the icy abyss separating him from his master for the day. In a sudden, agitated rush Stickeen scampered down the steps Muir had cut, crossed the bridge with precise footwork, and bounded up the far side to safety. The ecstatic dog raced back and forth, twirled, lay down, and rolled over, yipping, howling, and barking all the while. "Never before or since have I seen anything like so passionate a revulsion from the depths of despair to exultant, triumphant, uncontrollable joy," Muir wrote. The two fairly raced the whole way back to camp, arriving only a couple of hours short of midnight and too cold and tired to eat more than a few bites before collapsing into sleep.

Stickeen and the glacier enlarged Muir's sense of the oneness of being. He explained, "There is no estimating the wit and wisdom concealed and latent in our lower fellow mortals until made manifest by profound experiences; for it is through suffering that dogs as well as saints are developed and made perfect." Through Stickeen, "as through a window," he wrote, "I have ever since been looking with deeper sympathy into all my fellow mortals."[30]

Then, too, the experience made Muir realize that his rashness had endangered Stickeen needlessly. He was no longer the young man of his Yosemite days, the wild one who could take off for the high peaks on a whim and stay out as long as he wished and his bread lasted. He was a married man with a wife in Martinez, a baby on the way, and a harvest to pick, pack, and sell. Hurrying on to Sitka, Muir left the canoe, waved goodbye to Young and the crew, and took the mail steamer south toward California and the next chapter in his life.

The two dugout voyages in Southeast Alaska both confirmed and changed John Muir. He was, as ever and always, a wildlands tramper who relished the distant, precipitous, grand, and even perilous. At the same time, the experience knocked this man who avoided tribal people or looked down on them out of his habitual paradigm. The Tlingits he traveled with impressed him. The men in the dugout crews "all behaved well . . . exerted themselves under tedious hardships without flinching for days or weeks at a time; never seemed in the least nonplussed; were prompt to act in every exigency; good as servants, fellow travelers, even friends."[31]

In Muir's view, the Tlingits "differed greatly from the typical American Indian of the interior of the continent." To his eye, they had an Asian look that in the fashion of the time he called "Mongol." More important, they were "willing to work, when free of the contamination of bad whites. They manage to feed themselves well, build good substantial houses, bravely fight their enemies, love their wives and children and friends, and cherish a quick sense of honor." The Tlingits, he was saying, were of an altogether different human variety than California's dirty, degraded tribes.[32]

Muir didn't know that the Tlingit language belongs to the Na-Dene family, which includes tongues spoken by Indigenous peoples in California and Oregon and across the Southwest, including the Navajos (Dinés) and the Apaches. All Na-Dene speakers share a common origin somewhere in the deep past. Muir failed to see that history and the colonial system made the difference, not racial lineage. The slower pace and lesser pressure of Southeast Alaska's colonization gave the Tlingits the room to breathe and the time to adapt that had been denied Native Californians. They, too, had been spared a genocide of the cataclysmic sort that turned California into a killing field.

Like California, Alaska began as an exploitation colony. In the 1860s only 430 Russians represented the empire's interests among an Alaska Native population that numbered a little over thirty thousand. The colonizers' goal was to keep the colony's tribal subjects in line, exploit their labor in turning fur seals and sea otters into rubles, and ensure that their cut of the take was as small as possible. The United States picked up where the Russians left off. At the time of Muir's canoe voyages with Young, the territory remained an exploitation colony and Alaska Natives outnumbered non-Natives by more than seventy to one. The white population did grow to a little more than forty-two hundred over the next decade, but few of these immigrants came to stay. Most headed north to make a financial killing then return home, rather than settle and raise a family.[33]

An advocate for collective punishment when needed, Muir backed the Alaska colonial system that placed Euro-Americans over Tlingits and sought riches extracted from the land. He even advanced it in a roundabout way. His enthusiastic newspaper pieces about the scenic glories of Southeast Alaska prompted interest among would-be tourists to lay their own eyes on this region. Muir's writings lent Glacier Bay such a glow that, grabbing a new opportunity, veteran coastal shipmaster James Carroll piloted the *Idaho* and the first batch of paying tourists into the bay in 1883. By way of gratitude, Carroll attached the naturalist's name to Muir Inlet and Muir Glacier. That inaugural voyage prompted a steady stream of summer cruises and laid the foundation for turning the bay into a national park in 1925.[34] Muir was gone by then, but surely he would have been proud.

Not all of Muir's influence was quite so ecotouristically benign. On the way back from the first canoe journey to the Chilkats, he sent off an article entitled "Alaska Gold Fields" to the *Daily Evening Bulletin* in San Francisco. The story's tone was both sober and mildly boosterish.

"The gold of Alaska is still in the ground," he wrote in his opening line, implying that prospecting persistence might yield a major return. "Probably not one vein or placer in a thousand has yet been touched by the prospector's pick, while the interior is still a virgin wilderness—all its mineral wealth about as darkly hidden as when it was covered by the ice-mantle of the glacial period." Gold figured to be a central source of wealth in this newest American territory, Muir was certain. "Alaska will be found at least moderately rich in the precious metals, and . . . gold-mining, notwithstanding the disadvantages of climate, heavy vegetation, and beds of glacial drift, will come to be regarded as one of the most important and reliable of her resources."

As for the threat the Chilkats posed to prospectors, Muir's visit with Young had removed that risk. "The Chilkat Indians have hitherto been hostile to miners entering their country, but last summer one of their chiefs made a formal contract with parties in Wrangel to conduct them on a prospecting tour next spring to the reputed gold mines at the head of the Chilkat River."

When Muir, whose writings were beginning to develop a reputation, passed through Portland on his way back to California, local progressives lassoed him into giving three paid lectures about his trip north. The first two elaborated the naturalist's glacial gospel and were well received, but it was the third, on the potential of Alaska's undiscovered gold fields, that lit a wealth-seeking fire under the audience. Sketching on a blackboard, Muir explained how the West's gold and silver lodes reached all the way up into Alaska. In the far north, an undiscovered Sutter's Mill or Comstock strike beckoned the persistent and the industrious.

Late the following spring, as Muir promised in the *Daily Evening Bulletin,* a prospecting expedition accompanied by armed American sailors climbed from the head of Lynn Canal to the notch in the ridge known as Chilkoot Pass and entered the Yukon. More and more prospectors, many supported by Tlingit packers carrying their gear, came year by year, and slogged up the same demanding route. In 1898 some twenty thousand gold seekers climbed the pass toward the Klondike gold rush and the great colonial invasion of the Tlingits' last redoubt was on. John Muir, apostle of wilderness, had helped set the table.[35]

8

One Savage Living on Another

Thursday, October 13th—123rd day—Willow tea. Strong south
southwest winds. No news from Nindermann. We are in the hands of
God, and unless He relents, we are lost. We cannot move against the
wind, and staying here means starvation. . . . All united in saying Lord's
Prayer and Creed. After supper strong gale of wind. Horrible night.

—GEORGE W. DE LONG, ON THE LENA RIVER DELTA, 1881

The decision, about again heading far north, loomed so momentous that
Muir hesitated to make it alone. Instead, the brand-new father—first child,
Wanda, had arrived only a month earlier in April 1881—put the question to
a council of the Strentzel family. Should he accept an invitation to join the
Thomas Corwin as a naturalist on its voyage to locate, and perhaps rescue, a
well-publicized scientific expedition gone missing in the Arctic? The ship
was departing San Francisco in mere days and would be at sea until at least
October, possibly much longer if the fall freeze-up trapped the *Corwin* and
forced the crew to overwinter. Muir was torn. Ecstatic as he was over his
first child, still he longed for this chance to see the primal ice world of the
Arctic. Muir's family agreed: the opportunity was too rare to refuse. And so,
on May 4, 1881, Muir departed on the *Corwin*. Its first port of call lay almost
two weeks to the north at Unalaska on the Aleutian Islands' western tip.[1]

Muir owed his invitation to the ship's captain, Calvin L. Hooper of the
U.S. Revenue Marine, the predecessor of the modern Coast Guard. The two
had met in Alaska and trusted each other. As Hooper navigated the Revenue

Marine cutter northward, Muir both pined for the home and family he had left and relished the wildness of this voyage toward the edge of the known world. "Oh, if I could touch my baby and thee!" he wrote his wife, Louie, as the *Corwin* slogged through foaming, gale-driven storm seas. "This has been a very grand day—snow, waves, wind, mountains!"[2]

As befits a military mission, Hooper and the *Corwin* were under orders. The objective was to rescue an expedition whose still-unknown fate underscored that era's poor understanding of the Arctic. In late spring 1879 the *Jeannette* had sailed out through the Golden Gate under the command of George W. De Long, U.S. Navy lieutenant and unabashed enthusiast for polar exploration. De Long secured, equipped, overhauled, reinforced, and renamed the vessel that had begun its life as a bark-rigged steam yacht called the *Pandora*, all with financing from James Gordon Bennett. Every inch a Gilded Age tycoon, Bennett was the publisher of the *New York Herald*, then the United States' leading newspaper, and an accomplished yachtsman whose friends plumped his ego by calling him commodore. He regularly used his own wealth to generate and gin up news, like financing Henry Morton Stanley's "rescue" of David Livingstone from East Africa. Some critics dismissed the *Jeannette* as just another Bennett publicity stunt. And it was.

De Long, though, qualified as a serious explorer. He based his strategy for the voyage on the thinking of August Petermann, a respected German geographer. Petermann argued that the Arctic resembled the Antarctic: a major, unknown landmass extending northward from Greenland that reached across the pole almost to Siberia. In addition, a continuous, warm current circulating in the Arctic Ocean would allow a ship that made it through the drift ice to sail across an open polar sea and reach the North Pole. De Long was willing to bet his life, his crew's well-being, and James Gordon Bennett's investment on Petermann's untested ideas. The voyage's itinerary called for the *Jeannette* to steam north through the Bering Strait into the Chukchi Sea, then make for the recently discovered Wrangell Land, now known as Wrangel Island. Petermann thought this landmass was in fact the head of a peninsula reaching south from the nameless Arctic continent. De Long would proceed up the east coast of Wrangell Land toward the North Pole and its ice-free sea while leaving cairns and other markers along the shore to guide any following ships. After topping the globe, the ship would bear south, still following the long coast of the uncharted continent, across the Canadian High Arctic and on to Greenland. From there it could sail down the Atlantic toward New York City, where a gala return orchestrated by the publicity-conscious and ever-promotional Bennett awaited.[3]

De Long and Bennett's plan started well and then went all wrong. The *Jeannette* seemed to have vanished. It was nearly two years overdue by the time the *Corwin* was outfitted, reinforced with oak planking against the ice's crush, and provisioned. Presumably De Long's vessel had been trapped in closing pack ice, forced to overwinter twice, and remained frozen in place. The *Corwin* planned to retrace De Long's course in the hope of coming across the *Jeannette* or at least picking up news of its location and fate. Hooper also hoped to find the *Vigilant* and the *Mount Wollaston*, Arctic Ocean whaling vessels that had gone missing during the 1880 hunting season. And while the *Corwin* pursued its mission of reconnaissance and rescue, it could have a look at this little-explored corner of the world. That was why Muir had been invited aboard, along with physician-anthropologist Irving Rosse. They could take advantage of the rare scientific opportunities afforded by this journey into the largely unknown frontier of an expanding American empire.[4]

The *Corwin* first dropped anchor in the deep-water port on Unalaska, known now as Dutch Harbor and made famous by the Discovery Channel's *Deadliest Catch* series. Muir found the place fascinating: "The Aleutian chain of islands is one of the most remarkable and interesting to be found on the globe." The islands had formed "from a degraded portion of the North American coast mountains, with its foothills and connecting ridges between the summit peaks a few feet under water." Although the Aleutians are utterly treeless apart from a few spruces planted by the Russians during their occupation, they brimmed with living things, including the Aleuts (Unangax̂), who were the island chain's Indigenous nation. According to the 1880 census, Aleuts in the islands outnumbered whites and mixed-race people more than three to one, but Muir predicted that their dominance was sure to erode. "They are fading away like other Indians," Muir reported, echoing the then-widespread belief that America's Indigenous peoples were doomed. "The deaths exceed the births in nearly every one of their villages, and it is only a question of time when they will vanish from the face of the earth," he wrote, even though "the Aleuts are far more civilized and Christianized than any other tribe of Alaska Indians." Many were literate, and the men hunted sea otters for the Alaska Commercial Company, which had inherited the fur trade from the Russians. But civilization had brought the Aleuts alcohol, Muir made clear, and whisky was their undoing.[5]

The *Corwin*'s next stop, St. Paul, one of the Pribilof Islands in the Bering Sea, served up the same problem amid greater prosperity. Here some three hundred Aleuts lived amid no more than twenty whites in a neat village of framed cottages, a Russian Orthodox church, a schoolhouse, and a priest's residence. "It is interesting to find here an isolated group of Alaskan natives wholly under white influence and control, and who have in great part abandoned their own pursuits, clothing and mode of life in general, and adopted that of the whites," Muir observed. The Aleuts killed and flayed about one hundred thousand fur seals a year, bloody work that paid them forty cents per skin for hides that sold for fifteen dollars apiece on the London market. Despite their vanishingly thin slice of the fur-trade pie and the prohibition of alcohol on the island, one Aleut told an officer of the *Corwin* that he would happily give his entire $800 savings for a single bottle of whisky. Given such consumer demand, alcohol was in strong supply. Most of the island, the informant confided, was already drunk or getting there.[6]

On St. Lawrence Island Muir encountered the first of the Indigenous peoples he called E——s, but who know themselves as Yupiks (Yu'pik, plural Yupiit). Out of the depressing, bedraggled village "came a crowd of jolly, well-fed people dragging their skin canoes, which they shoved over the rim of the stranded ice that extended along the shore, and soon they were alongside the steamer, offering ivory, furs, sealskin boots, etc., for tobacco and ammunition." They also wanted rum and rifles, although American law forbade selling either to Alaska Natives. Still, these people impressed Muir with their endless sense of humor. "Always searching for something to laugh at, they are ready to stop short in the middle of the most important bargainings to get hold of some bit of fun." Four of the St. Lawrence Yupiks came aboard to guide the *Corwin* to its next stop at Plover Bay in Siberia. They traveled light: a disassembled skin boat, raw walrus for food, a rifle, and a few odds and ends, "yet they seemed more confident of their ability to earn a living than most whites on their farms."[7]

While the *Corwin* lay at anchor off a small Chukchi (Lyg″oravètļ′èt) settlement on the Siberian coast, word of the lost whaler *Vigilant* arrived with a boatload of locals. In November 1880 three seal hunters well up the coast beyond the Bering Strait had found the vessel locked in ice with its masts broken off and the crew dead on the deck. Hooper, "knowing the ability of these people to manufacture tales of this sort," dismissed the tale as exaggeration. This would hardly be the last time on the *Corwin*'s voyage that American officials rejected Indigenous news as the fiction of primitive minds. Nor would it be the last time those officials were wrong.[8]

While Muir found the Chukchis strange and exotic, he also sensed something deeply human about them. When the *Corwin* hired a local the crew nicknamed Chukchi Joe to bring his dog team along, his wife came aboard to send him off. "After taking him aside and talking with him, the tears running down her cheeks, she left the vessel and went back with some others who had come to trade deerskins, while we sailed away," Muir remembered. "One touch of nature makes all the world kin, and here were many touches among the wild Chukchis."[9]

Something more struck Muir when he watched an elder distribute hardtack to his fellow villagers: "The mannerly reserve and unhasting dignity of all these natives when food is set before them is very striking as compared with the ravenous, snatching haste of the hungry poor among whites." Still, the interiors of the stretched-skin huts were unspeakably filthy and smelly, and dogs licked out the kettles used to boil seal meat. Muir explained, "They seemed to be favored in these establishments like the pigs in Irish huts." Muir, who had a low opinion of the Irish inherited from Thomas Carlyle and Ralph Waldo Emerson, did not mean the comparison as a compliment.[10]

Chukchi mothers nursed their little ones on demand and in public as if nothing could be more natural. "When a child is to be nursed the mother merely pulls out one of her arms from the roomy sleeve of her parka and pushes it down until the breast is exposed," Muir commented. "The breasts are pendulous and cylindrical, like those of the Tlingit." He had no compunction in describing the size and shape of Tlingit and Chukchi women's breasts, something no Victorian man other than an underground pornographer would have dared do with women of his own caste. But these Indigenous women invited intimate comment that European and American travelers took as a matter of course and a proof of their own racial superiority. And, even as they admired the easy way the Chukchi mothers had with their little ones, Euro-American travelers like Muir depicted them as beings that were other and primitive. They lacked the pert, upright, firm breasts of classical Greece and Rome statuary, displaying instead the elongated teats of the racially inferior. Human, yes, yet still different from *yours, mine,* and *ours.*[11]

What utterly won the ever-fastidious Muir over to the inherent humanity of the Yupiks and Chukchis was one baby's smile. "I shall remember it as long as I live," he wrote. "When its features had subsided into perfect repose, the laugh gone from its dark eyes, and the lips closed over its two teeth, I could make its sweet smile bloom out again as often as I nodded and chirruped to it." The little boys, too, struck him as charming and modest, looking away when he turned his gaze on them. "But there was a response in their eyes which made you feel that they are your very brothers," he reported. And Muir was surprised when he encountered an orphan whose mother had been Chukchi and father European. "She is plump, red-cheeked, and in every way a picture of health. That in a Chukchi hut, nursed by a Chukchi mother-in-law, and raised on Chukchi food, a half-European girl can be so beautiful, well-behaved, happy, and healthy is very notable."[12]

The Yupiks and Chukchis contrasted with the Native Americans Muir encountered back on the U.S. side at St. Michael, a settlement northeast of the Yukon Delta that served as headquarters for fur traders across northern and central Alaska. High fur prices, he was told, had "spoiled the Indians, making them insolent, lazy, and dangerous," dissolute people who "spend their idle hours in gambling and quarreling." Their camp on the beach bothered Muir. He watched as women pitched tents and cut grass for bedding, children stared at the white men like just-landed extraterrestrials, and the "dandy warriors [were] arrayed in all the colors of the rainbow, grim, and cruel, and coldly dignified." Something about them spoke of "the far wilderness whence they came—its mountains and valleys, its broad grassy plains and far-reaching rivers, its forests and bogs. The Indians seemed to me the wildest animals of all."[13]

The *Corwin* crossed back to the Siberian side south of the Bering Strait to pick up a search party that had been dropped off earlier. After talking with Chukchi hunters along that cold coast, the searchers realized that the stories they had heard beforehand were true. Three seal hunters had indeed found the *Vigilant* locked in the pack ice, described its crushed remains in detail, and displayed a trove of objects they retrieved from the wreckage, including a marine telescope, a hand lamp, two carpenter's saws, and a pump handle. The locals had found four long-dead bodies in the ship's cabin. Whether the rest of the crew had survived a trek over the ice to the Siberian coast or died trying, there was no telling. Even though the *Corwin's* brass had earlier rejected this report of the *Vigilant's* demise as fiction because it was relayed down the coast by the Chukchi social network, it was now corroborated. The Chukchis had been telling the truth all along.[14]

Indigenous truth-telling, and Euro-Americans' assumption that they knew better, would figure big time into the most horrific incident the *Corwin* was to encounter.

Edward William Nelson was an energetic, twenty-six-year-old natural history collector who, in service to the Smithsonian Institution, had come to St. Michael, Alaska, as a U.S. Army Signal Corps private. His job was to record an unbroken series of meteorological observations, explore the eastern Bering Sea region, and collect specimens for the museum. Before heading north through the Bering Strait to look for the *Jeannette*, the *Corwin* stopped at St. Michael to take on food and coal and to bring Nelson onboard. He had been seconded to the Revenue Marine Service on orders to investigate and collect data about a reported mass die-off of Yupiks on St. Lawrence Island. The *Corwin* doubled back to St. Lawrence to give Nelson the close look his orders required.[15]

Muir found this ninety-mile-long volcanic outcrop, the largest island in the Bering Sea, wildly inhospitable. He described it as "a dreary, cheerless, mass of black lava, dotted with volcanoes, covered with snow, without a single tree, and rigidly bound in ocean ice for more than half the year." The Yupiks saw it differently. They had called it home for some twenty-five hundred years, living principally on walruses and whales as well as seals, birds, and fish that thrived in the cold, pounding, fertile seas surrounding the island. This strategy worked until the late nineteenth century when an invasion of whaling vessels, mostly American, came north each summer to kill whales for blubber oil and walruses for ivory. Those fast-falling populations, combined with unfavorable winds that turned the already bad hunting disastrous, set St. Lawrence up for famine in the winter of 1878–79. It only got worse when some unknown disease or diseases—most likely measles, dysentery, or influenza—swept through the Yupik villages. Nor did the famine end in one winter. A repeat of the same unfavorable weather the following year worsened the crisis. People weakened by hunger now had even longer to starve, be killed by the epidemic, or both. When it was all over, approximately two-thirds of St. Lawrence's two thousand or more Yupiks, including every last soul in the largest village, had died.

Muir, Hooper, Nelson, and physician-anthropologist Rosse went ashore to have an up-close look at one of the ravaged villages. "We found twelve desolate huts close to the beach with about two hundred skeletons in them or strewn about on the rocks and rubbish heaps within a few yards of the doors. The scene was indescribably ghastly and desolate," a shaken Muir wrote. "The shrunken bodies, with rotting furs on them, or white bleaching skeletons, picked bare by the crows, were lying mixed with kitchen-midden rubbish where they had been cast out by surviving relatives while they yet had strength to carry them. In the huts those who had been the last to perish were found in bed, lying evenly side by side, beneath their rotting deerskins." One hut held thirty corpses. About half were piled like cordwood in a corner, and the rest stretched out in bed "as if they had met their fate with tranquil apathy."[16]

Nelson could scarcely believe the abundance St. Lawrence's horror dropped into his collector's lap. He "went into this Golgotha with hearty enthusiasm, gathering the fine white harvest of skulls spread before him, and throwing them in heaps like a boy gathering pumpkins." Nelson collected almost a hundred crania and hauled them aboard the *Corwin*.[17]

Ghoulish as Nelson's actions are to twenty-first-century readers, they were standard operating procedure for the U.S. military in 1881. Thirteen years earlier, George Otis, assistant surgeon general of the U.S. Army, circulated an order among military physicians to require their help in building the Army Medical Museum's collection of crania that were indigenous to North America. The response among uniformed medical personnel was so enthusiastic that the collection grew more than tenfold in only five years and would eventually come to number over twenty-two hundred specimens.

The official rationale for this skull gathering was comparative study of racial differences, putatively scientific work that showed Indigenous peoples to be so lacking in mental capacity that their subjugation as inferiors by superior Euro-Americans was evolution's mandate. Otis's order marked the United States as the only national government ever to collect human skulls as an official enterprise. Nelson was doing his part to advance that work. Muir had no stomach for, and he made no effort to help.[18]

The St. Lawrence horror demanded an explanation: Why had so many Yupiks succumbed so quickly? Muir refused to believe the cause could be nature's caprice. The wild he knew from Yosemite and the Range of Light evidenced God's loving embrace, not an apocalypse of hunger worsened by disease. No, he was certain, the cause had to originate with the Yupiks themselves because "these people never lay up any considerable supply of food from one season to another." Alcohol worsened this tendency, since hunters would gladly opt for a good, long drunk at home over the hard work of taking walruses and seals from the icy sea. Improvidence and alcoholism, Muir was sure, had doomed the Yupiks.[19]

Nelson saw it the same way as Muir. "Just before the time for the walrus to reach the island that season, the E—— obtained a supply of whisky from some vessels and began a prolonged debauch, which ended only when the supply was exhausted. When this occurred the annual migration of the walrus had passed, and the people were shut in for the winter by the ice," he reported.[20]

Captain Hooper, too, laid blame on the Yupiks' failure to plan ahead and gather sufficient food before winter. "They make no provision for the future, but depend upon what they can get from day to day; of course failure means starvation," he declared. The Yupiks' slavery to alcohol only made matters worse: "So long as the rum lasts they do nothing but drink and fight." Without government intervention, alcohol was sure to kill off St. Lawrence's remaining Yupiks.[21]

In reality, Arctic peoples follow hunting-and-gathering strategies designed to lay by enough food in seasons of abundance to sustain them through seasons of scarcity. And, had Muir, Nelson, and Hooper asked the island's survivors what happened in the winter of 1878–79, they would have gotten a story different from the one they invented. Summer hunting had proved scanty, at least in part because of the toll taken by American whalers. Then heavy fall winds from the south, southeast, and east kept the pack ice away from the island and prevented walrus hunting even as untoward currents driven by those same winds made it equally impossible to net seals. Pack ice formed around the island much later than usual, and by then the migrating walruses had swum past. So the Yupiks began to starve. Hunting the following year was just as bad, and the epidemic almost certainly contracted from Euro-Americans made everything worse. Civilization, in its manifestations of industrial whaling and unaccustomed pathogens, lay at the core of the disaster, not the Yupiks' moral failure and bad planning.[22]

Ironically, the skulls taken from the island and later examined in detail by Irving Rosse at the Army Medical Museum boosted the Yupiks' credibility in a roundabout way. For one thing, it surprised Rosse that these people were laid out physically in largely the same manner as "other varieties of men." Beneath their furs, Yupiks looked pretty much like white folks. During the *Corwin*'s voyage Rosse found striking evidence of the Yupiks' quick wits. It amazed him that "a people we are accustomed to look upon as ignorant, benighted, and undeveloped can learn to talk English with a certain degree of fluency and intelligibility" from no more instruction than a few meetings every year with passing whalers. Their skulls provided corroborating evidence that the Yupiks were smarter than Euro-Americans assumed. The conventional wisdom of the time held that Yupiks had primitive skulls, much like Native Americans elsewhere on the continent or Africans, and the low-grade mental capabilities to match. Rosse begged to differ. Measuring and averaging the cranial space in Nelson's collection showed "the brain capacity to be the same as that of the French and Germans," but not quite so high as the English—and, by implication, Anglo-Saxon Americans. He observed that the Yupiks were surprisingly intelligent, remarkably kind to their children, and paragons of truthfulness and honesty who lacked quarrelsomeness, jealousy, and the least urge to warfare. "The same cannot be said, however, for their sexual morals, which, as a rule, are the contrary of good," he wrote. When it came to Indigenous peoples, there was always something.[23]

With St. Lawrence fading in its wake, the *Corwin* returned to St. Michael before pushing northward through the Bering Strait and into the Chukchi

Sea, first along the Alaskan shore in the direction of Icy Cape. The goal was to seek information about other lost whalers, then cross to the Siberian side to look for the trail of the *Jeannette* around Wrangell Land.

In Kotzebue Sound, the ship stopped to trade for caribou skins in order to make winter clothing. Muir worried over the catastrophic slaughter of these northern deer by Iñupiats using repeating rifles. Still, he found himself admiring these people, as murderous of wildlife as they seemed to him: "Though savage and sensual, they are by no means dull or apathetic like the sensual savages of civilization, who live only to eat and indulge the senses, for these E——s, without newspapers or telegraphs, know all that is going on within hundreds of miles, and are keen questioners and alive to everything that goes on before them." Their lives, though, were difficult in ways he could hardly comprehend. "Cool and breezy must be their lives, and they can have but little inducement to look up, or time to spend in contemplation," he wrote. "Theirs is one constant struggle for food, interrupted by sleep and by a few common quarrels. In winter they hibernate in noisome underground dens. In summer they come out to take breath in small conical tents, made of white drill when they can get it." And when he watched a group of sailors from the *R. B. Handy*, an American whaler, kill walruses by the dozen for nothing but their tusks, he wondered who the real savages were. "In nothing does man, with his grand notions of heaven and charity, show forth his innate, low-bred, wild animalism than in his treatment of his brother beasts. From the shepherd with his lambs to the red-handed hunter, it is the same; no recognition of rights—only murder in one form or another."

Muir's low opinion of his fellow humans fell further when the *Corwin* surprised three polar bears on the pack ice and gave chase. The crewmen shot them all down in fusillades of rifle fire. "It was prolonged, bloody agony, as clumsily and heartlessly inflicted as it could well be," he reported. "The E——s hunt and kill them for food, going out to meet them on the ice with spears and dogs. This is merely one savage living on another. But how civilized people, seeking for heavens and angels and millenniums, and the reign of universal peace and love, can enjoy this brutal amusement, is not so easily accounted for." He lamented, "Of all the animals man is at once the worst and the best."[24]

August 12, 1881, reminded Muir that the *Corwin*'s exploration served the purpose of America's manifest destiny. "A notable addition was made to the national domain when Captain Calvin L. Hooper landed on Wrangell Land, and took formal possession of it in the name of the United States," he reported in a bemused and sardonic tone. Hooper in fact had no claim by either discovery or conquest under the international law of the time, nor was any plan laid to inform the Russians of Hooper's quixotic flag raising. Czar Alexander III and his government went right on thinking of Siberia as theirs.

Having come so close to mysterious Wrangell Land, Muir, Hooper, and the other officers and scientists did make a contribution to Arctic geography. Wrangell Land, they recognized, was not the southernmost reach of some mythic Arctic continent but rather an island whose rough outline Muir sketched in his journal.[25]

After finding no sign that the *Jeannette* had passed this way and recognizing the threat the fast-closing pack ice posed, the *Corwin* came about and headed back toward Point Barrow, on the Alaskan side, to seek information about yet another lost whaler. The *Daniel Webster*, as it turned out, had been crushed between pack and shore ice, and Iñupiats from the Point Barrow village had gleefully carried off everything they could from the ruined ship, including a keg of rum. "As wreckers, traders, and drinkers these sturdy E——s are making rapid progress, notwithstanding the fortunate disadvantages they labor under, as compared with their white brethren, dwelling in so severe a climate on the confines of the frozen seas," Muir wrote.[26]

It was a reindeer-herding Chukchi family at the head of Siberia's Plover Bay that left Muir most in awe of the well-adapted Indigenous lifestyle. The family, comprising father, mother, one daughter, and two sons—"fine, strapping, elastic fellows"—managed a herd of several hundred reindeer and relied on the animals for food, transport, clothing, and shelter. The family's hide huts leaked and looked a tad shabby, but Muir took a shine to these people. "The Chukchis seem to be a good-natured, lively, chatty, brave and polite people, fond of a joke, and as far as I have seen, fair in their dealings as any people, savage or civilized. They are not savage by any means, however, but steady industrious workers, looking well ahead, providing for the future, and consequently seldom in want," he wrote. As reindeer herders, they largely escaped seasonal hunger. And the reindeer the Chukchis herded stood apart from any other domesticated animals Muir had seen: "these beautiful animals are allowed to feed at will, without herding to any great extent. They seem as smooth and clean and glossy as if they were wild. Taming does not seem to have injured them in any way. I saw no mark of man upon them." Muir and his companions headed back to the *Corwin* bearing a young, fat reindeer the Chukchis had slaughtered, skinned, and butchered for payment in tobacco, lead, gunpowder, percussion caps, calico cloth, and knives. Dinner that night featured fresh, all-natural Chukchi venison.[27]

Having taken on more coal and water, the *Corwin* again headed north in hope of returning to Wrangell Land to make a last search for the *Jeannette*'s trail. On the way, driven back by ill winds and anchored in the lee of Big Diomede Island, Muir went ashore for "a stroll through the streets and houses of the curious village there." The Iñupiat people of Big Diomede (Imaqłiq) used their strategic position athwart the Bering Strait to serve as middlemen for other Indigenous peoples trading between northwest Asia and Alaska. Muir marveled that "they can keep warm and make a living on this bleak, fog-smothered, storm-beaten rock," raise families well trained in the many necessary skills of hunting and fishing, and "still have time to be sociable, to dance, sing, gossip, and discuss ghosts, spirits, and all the nerve-racking marvels of the shaman world." It was an accomplishment that showed "how truly wild, and brave, and capable a people these island E——s are."[28]

When the wind tapered off, Hooper steamed the *Corwin* northward into the ever-advancing, ever-grinding ice pack. Soon he realized that trying to work closer to Wrangell Island so late in the year posed too great a risk. He brought his ship about and headed south. The *Corwin* had done all she could.

At almost the same moment that Hooper gave up the search and turned the *Corwin* back toward Unalaska and San Francisco, the *Jeannette*'s commander George De Long was making his last journal entry. His vessel had indeed spent two long winters locked in ice that drifted slowly clockwise around the North Pole. The end came on June 13, 1881, when the crushed hull sank some three hundred nautical miles off the Siberian coast. So far, all thirty-three men aboard remained alive. Sensing that the ship's end was near, they made ready by lowering the three small boats and offloaded sledges, firearms, food, and other equipment needed to travel first across the ice and then over the open sea toward Siberia. Setting the Lena River delta as their destination, where they expected to find refuge among Indigenous villagers, the three boats sailed together until a nighttime gale separated them. One boat disappeared, and the remaining two came ashore near the Lena many miles apart. Neither knew what had happened to the other. One crew was sheltered and fed by local Evenki and Russian political exiles. In time these survivors made it down the Lena to the city of Yakutsk, and from there traveled across Russia and back to the United States nearly a year later. As for the remaining boat, only two of its crew were still alive when rescuers arrived. The rest, including De Long, had died from starvation and exposure.[29]

All told, only thirteen of the thirty-three men aboard lived to tell the *Jeannette*'s sad tale. The Arctic had conquered manifest destiny.

Muir caught that reality in a journal sketch showing the flag the *Corwin*'s landing party raised on Wrangell Land to lay claim to the island. In the foreground, two walruses and a seal popped their heads up through the ice to have a look at a polar bear with hot lunch on its predatory mind. The flat, stony, hard-frozen island lay well back, the waving Stars and Stripes dwarfed by the icy immensity into near invisibility against a gray sky. This inhospitable, wild expanse humbled America's imperial ambitions.[30]

Muir came away from the *Corwin* with an admiration for the shared humanity of the Chukchis, Yupiks, and Iñupiats and a confidence that northern Alaska's immensity protected them. As long as the U.S. government continued its prohibition on alcohol and repeating rifles, the Indigenous peoples of the Far North could survive, even thrive. Never, though, did Muir ask himself what claim of ownership Chukchis, Yupiks, and Iñupiats, or their Indigenous neighbors to the south, could properly lay on their homelands. He accepted the United States' right to expand into new territories and rule the peoples it found there as colonial subjects. To be sure, he wanted that rule to be benevolent, even respectful. But it was rule nonetheless: a superior people subjugating inferiors.[31]

When Muir arrived home in Martinez and hugged Louie and baby daughter Wanda, it felt to him like high time to come in from the cold. This saunterer of high country and devotee of glaciers planned to fashion himself into something new, something far more domestic and businesslike than anything he had been before. After all, he needed to make some serious money.

9

The Grapes of Wealth

> Thou shalt not sow thy vineyard with diverse seeds: lest the fruit of thy
> seed which thou hast sown, and the fruit of thy vineyard, be defiled.
>
> —DEUTERONOMY 22:9

When John Muir married Louie Strentzel, he gained more than a wife.
She brought him hearth, home, family, and farm arisen from a tradition
reaching back into eastern Europe. John Strentzel, Louie's father, was born
and grew up in partitioned Poland. As a teenager, he took eager part in the
failed 1830 uprising against Russian rule and decided to leave the country,
settling on Budapest and medical school. Degree in hand, he sailed to New
Orleans in 1840 before traveling on to Texas to practice medicine, homestead, and make Louisiana Erwin his wife. When the California gold rush
offered a new, glittery promise farther west, Strentzel joined a wagon train
following the southern route to the newly American territory—a dry, hot,
murderously dangerous trek. In time Strentzel came north to have a look
around the tiny Bay Area port town of Martinez on a friend's recommendation; he had succeeded at several short-lived businesses and was seeking
something permanent. Liking what he saw, he bought twenty acres of shady,
well-watered bottomland among the oak-dotted hills of the Coast Range a
little over two miles south of town.[1]

First up, John and Louisiana Strentzel renamed the valley they would call
home for the rest of their lives. Back in Spanish times, soldiers on the trail
of escaped mission neophytes, likely from the local Karkin tribe, nicknamed

the valley Cañada del Hambre ("Hunger Gulch") when their rations ran out. Louisiana Strentzel considered the name inelegant. She and John rechristened it Alhambra, after the stunning palace and fortress complex of southern Spain, and thereby declared the land theirs.[2]

An avid horticulturist, Strentzel recognized the natural advantages of his new home: warm summers tempered by breezes coming down Carquinez Strait, abundant sunshine, few hard frosts, usually adequate winter rains, and fertile alluvial soils. Soon he was raising cattle and growing hay and wheat as well as experimenting with a capacious variety of crops: apples, pears, peaches, plums, apricots, figs, cherries, currants, blackberries, gooseberries, strawberries, sugar beets, oranges, almonds, grapes, and olives. Strentzel plowed the profits of this abundance into acquiring more land. Eventually he owned over twenty-three hundred acres as well as whole blocks of the growing town of Martinez and its waterfront.[3]

More than applied botany to Strentzel, horticulture represented a social, economic, and aesthetic movement that saw the picturesque, agrarian landscape as the foundation for building strong communities, creating a vibrant economy, and healing the environmental scars left by gold mining, logging, and other extractive enterprises. A fruit tree was more than a tree, he wrote. It was "an heirloom of future generations, it is a sign of expanded culture and civilization."[4]

When John Muir married Louie, John Strentzel welcomed his new son-in-law into the family and onto the farm, treating him as the heir he would become. The Strentzels bestowed their Dutch Colonial cottage on the new couple as a wedding present and began building a seventeen-room Italianate Victorian mansion atop a commanding knoll where they would live out the rest of their days.[5] And when Muir returned from the Arctic and the *Corwin*, Strentzel shifted more and more management responsibility onto his eager son-in-law; soon Muir was handling day-to-day farm operations. Now he was the man in charge, a role he took on with enthusiasm.

Just as Muir was focusing his attention on the Strentzel farm, California agriculture was undergoing a sea change. Under Spanish and Mexican rule, California's farms and ranches, many on mission lands, served to feed the colony and profit friars and ranchers. Hides and tallow from semi-wild herds of cattle that roamed the grasslands were the principal cash export. Fruits, vegetables, and grains were grown and consumed locally during the gold rush and into the early years of statehood. Shortly thereafter wheat replaced hides as California's principal export.[6]

Yet California's unique competitive strength lay far less in steers and grain than in a climate ideal for raising perishable, even exotic, fruits and vegetables—from wine grapes and olives to salad greens and asparagus. Although California's population was growing fast, particularly after the Civil War, local markets could absorb only so much of this abundance. Meanwhile, the distant, urban East was swelling with a rapidly expanding middle class that had money to spend. How could California's perishable produce take advantage of this alluring opportunity on the far side of the continent?

The first part of the answer came when the transcontinental railroad was completed in 1869. With the lowering of freight rates through the 1870s and 1880s and the development of the refrigerated car, those booming, distant markets in New York, Philadelphia, and Chicago moved within the reach of California growers. By the late 1880s, the weight of fresh fruit shipped east increased from a little under two million pounds annually to almost fifty-four million. The California fruit boom was on.[7]

Not only the infrastructure and production, but also the culture and strategy, of California agriculture were shifting. Horticultural utopians like John Strentzel faded into the past as quaint romantics, while younger, profit-driven agricultural capitalists took over. These new businessmen of farm and field recognized that large growers were far better positioned to benefit from rapid technological change than were small-scale growers. And they saw that specialization in the few most profitable crops would yield far better returns than horticultural diversity. California growers set about creating an industrialized agriculture unlike any seen before in the United States. The goal now was not more crop varieties but more money, always more money.[8]

Muir made this paradigm shift his own. He aimed to be a successful businessman whose vision focused on the bottom line, and his first task was to reshape the land to his purpose. Alhambra and Franklin Creeks coursed through the farm. Their banks were thick with trees and brush and prone to flood during heavy winter rains. Muir and his farmhands cut trees and shrubs in the creeks' lower stretches, fired the underbrush, planted exotic eucalyptuses and cedars higher up the flow for shade and firewood, then dug irrigation ditches to carry water from creeks into croplands. In the course of this difficult and dirty work, Muir dove into more than a few poison oak thickets. Once he developed a rash so bad that his eyes swelled shut and he had to spend several days in bed, mostly blind and itching madly.[9] It must have felt to him like Indianapolis all over again.

Several years earlier, Muir had published "Flood-Storm in the Sierra," an up-close-and-personal account of a hundred-year inundation on the Yuba and Feather Rivers that flooded towns downstream, including Marysville. He adored the watery excess of the fierce storm that fueled the flood: "How terribly downright must seem the utterances of storms and earthquakes to those accustomed to the soft hypocrisies of society. Man's control is being steadily extended over the forces of nature, but it is well, at least for the present, that storms can still make themselves heard through our thickest walls." The rising rivers swamped central Marysville, a misfortune to be sure for those in the flood's path. Still, it proved a good thing that "the easy-going apathy of many persons was broken up," Muir wrote. "True, some goods were destroyed, and a few rats and people were drowned, and some took cold on the house-tops and died, but the total loss was less than the gain." Now, just a few years later, the same man who had written those words was replumbing natural creek channels to ensure that his farm did not become a mini-Marysville.[10]

Muir's effort to control the environment extended not only to the watershed but also to the unwanted creatures that infested crops and lowered yields and profits. Ground squirrels that burrowed in and around the roots of trees and vines, fruit-eating birds like house finches and California quail, and insects from scales to cutworms had no place on the farm. The move into intensive agriculture replaced a complex, diversified, natural ecosystem with a simplified, managed landscape that invited invasion by hordes of daunting pests.

Controlling them, like stream clearing, resulted in personal injury. During the mixing of a rodent poison that contained white phosphorus, which ignites on contact with air, a sudden burst of flame set Muir's clothes afire and severely burned him. When S. Hall Young, the Presbyterian missionary with whom Muir had traveled in Southeast Alaska, dropped by for an unannounced visit, the naturalist told the parson what had happened. "I came near dying a mean, civilized death the other day. A C—— emptied a bucket of phosphorus over me and almost burned me up," he told Young. "How different that would have been from a nice white death in the crevasse of a glacier!"[11]

Yet despite the cost to body and soul, Muir kept farming even while lamenting that "I am losing the precious days. I am degenerating into a machine for making money." He focused intensively on the most popular and profitable crops to gain the business advantages of scale. Muir converted the thirty acres that John Strentzel had used for hay and grain into grapes, then added more and more acres of vineyard. Within a few years he became the state's largest supplier of fresh tokay table grapes. The pear orchard that once produced sixty varieties was converted to Bartletts alone. He made no apology for raising little besides tokays and Bartletts. "Give the people what they want," Muir said.[12]

As a formula for business success, his strategy worked. Where John Strentzel in his heyday had sold hundreds of crates of fruit and made a modest living, Muir was selling thousands and gaining a reputation as a hard-bargainer among the San Francisco wholesalers who bought his crop.[13] And, like every grower who went all in for intensive, large-scale fruit production, Muir needed on-demand labor at the cheapest possible price. That's where the Chinese came in.

As long as there has been European-style agriculture in California, there have been farm workers paid too little to toil long and hard in fields, orchards, and vineyards. It began with the missions. The friars saw their role as saving pagan souls and instilling civilization by teaching Native Californians Catholicism and fieldwork. Baptism bound tribal neophytes to the missions that provided inadequate housing and minimal food while owning their labor on farms and ranches. Never mind that neophytes died in the missions at nearly six times the mortality rate of enslaved peoples in the American South, largely from poor nutrition worsened by diseases ranging from smallpox to syphilis. As the friars saw it, there were always more Indigenous people in the hills, woods, and mountains. Recruitment consisted of sending soldiers to round them up and bring them in—for the good of their souls, of course.[14]

After Mexico secularized the missions in 1833, Spanish-speaking Californios as well as American and European immigrants picked up where the
church left off. They continued the system of debt peonage to bind Native
Californians to particular landholdings and enslave them. The most notorious
was Johann—later John—Sutter. A Swiss immigrant, Sutter settled in what is
now Sacramento and built a fortified town he called New Helvetia, after the
Roman name for Switzerland. Sutter forced the local Nisenan and Miwok
peoples to work for him, locked them up overnight in dormitories without
latrines, fed them at troughs that ran a slurry of barely cooked animal offal
and grain, and kept them working among his crops and livestock. Whenever
any of his conscripted workers ran off, Sutter's private militia—dressed like
Gilbert and Sullivan extras in surplus uniforms picked up cheap from the Fort
Ross Russians on the coast—hunted them down, tortured and killed a few for
sadistic example, then dragged the survivors in chains back to New Helvetia.[15]

The American military governors who ran California from 1846 until
the territory established civilian rule in the closing months of 1849 were
careful not to upset the debt peonage system. By then, the newly installed
legislature and the first civilian governor, Peter Burnett, were facing a new
challenge: a severe labor shortage brought on by the gold rush. Everybody
and his brother had left their jobs and lit out for the diggings. The first law
passed by the new legislature and signed by Burnett aimed to ensure a steady,
cheap supply of Indigenous workers to fill the gap. It was named, with mal-
ice aforethought, the Act for the Government and Protection of Indians.[16]

Fashioned after the Black Codes of the pre–Civil War South, the new law
effectively compelled Native Californians to work for whites. Convict leasing
was one such compulsion. A landowner could visit the local jail, pay the fines
of tribal people arrested for nothing more criminal than "loitering," and
require them to work off the debt. Growers, most notably vineyards and win-
eries around Los Angeles, turned the law into a system of repeat involuntary
servitude. Farmhands were paid on Saturday night in *aguardiente*, a potent
brandy. The resulting nocturnal merry-making invited raids by the sheriff
and his deputies, who arrested Native Californians by the dozens, often for
no good reason, and locked them up. Growers stopped by the county jail
on Sunday, paid the fines, and assembled their convict work crews for the
upcoming week. Come next Saturday, the cycle repeated.

Horace Bell, an early American Angeleno who later became a lawyer and newspaperman defending the poor, knew what he was seeing. He reported, "Los Angeles had its slave mart, as well as Constantinople and New Orleans— only the slave at Los Angeles was sold fifty-two times a year as long as he lived, which generally did not exceed one, two, or three years under the new dispensation." The system was deadly: "these thousands of honest, useful people were absolutely destroyed in this way."[17]

The Thirteenth Amendment and post–Civil War federal laws undermined the legal foundation of California's system of short-term enslavement. It might have persisted, though, except for the fatal fact Bell pointed out: Native Californians were being killed off by state-sponsored genocide that included the forced labor sanctioned by California law as well as disease, murder, and massacre. By 1870 the Native population, which numbered one hundred fifty thousand in 1846, had fallen to just thirty thousand. And it would continue to decline, reaching fifteen thousand people by 1890. Given these deadly demographics, Native Californians were diminishing as a source of abundant, low-cost farm labor. Yet California's intensifying agricultural industry needed a hands-on work force as captive and cheap as tribal people had been. It found the solution in Chinese laborers.[18]

This immigrant group, almost entirely men, began coming to California during the gold rush, largely from China's Pearl River Delta and neighboring areas of Kwangtung Province. This was a region of meager natural resources and a swelling population beset by the Opium Wars, the T'aip'ing Rebellion, and clan warfare. Add to those human catastrophes the lure of gold, and Chinese headed to California by the thousands. They paid their own passage in cash if they could or by going into debt. By 1860 the Chinese had become the largest foreign-born group in the state, making up some ten percent of California's total population.[19]

Not that they were welcome. Many Euro-Americans saw Chinese newcomers as alien competitors who took good jobs and easy gold that should have been theirs. In their eyes, the Chinese became not equal competitors but the enemies of a free-labor republic and a loathsome menace they slurred with terms used for Native Californians and Blacks.[20] Something had to be done, they demanded, and soon it was. First came the Foreign Miners' Tax Act, which was driven by anti-Chinese sentiment and did just what its title said, followed by waves of white vigilantes and mob violence, some of it under color of law. All these actions aimed at driving the Chinese off their claims and out of the mining districts. Throughout the 1850s California's legislature championed bills to prevent Chinese immigration, and local communities passed ordinances to make Chinese feel unwelcome and unwanted, from cutting their queues to banning them from the streets after dark.

As economic slowdown deepened into a nationwide depression in the 1870s, anti-Chinese agitation grew more extreme. California's Ku Klux Klan unleashed upon the Chinese the same violence that its Southern arm focused on African Americans. The western Klan enjoyed an added advantage lacking in the South until Reconstruction ended: active government and political support. Understanding that the situation of the Chinese in the state mirrored that of Blacks in the South, and wanting to keep them in their lowly place, California became the sole Free State to reject ratification of the Fourteenth and Fifteenth Amendments.[21]

The violence was still ramping up as the transcontinental railroad was completed, and most of the ten thousand Chinese who had built the section from Sacramento to Promontory Point, Utah, returned to California to look for work. They joined the fifteen thousand new immigrants from China that year. The Chinese labor force was swelling just as the state's increasingly intensive fruit farms began seeking a reliable seasonal supply of cheap workers for all the many hands-on tasks orchards required, particularly the delicate work of moving fresh fruit from trees and vines to packinghouses. Orchards and vineyards represented significant upfront investment in land, trees, vines, irrigation, and reclamation; years passed before those costs began to pay off. Cheap labor kept orchardists in business until revenues rose, and afterward it assured that the operations earned the profits their owners expected.[22]

Facing growing discrimination and legally banned from more and more lines of work, many Chinese signed on with the fruit farms—not because they relished hard work at low pay, but because discrimination and legislation left little else open to them. Chinese workers were paid less than Euro-Americans: $22 a month in the summer and $30 in the winter, without board, while whites earned $30 summers and $40 to $50 winters, plus meals. Typically they worked in gangs of six to ten men under a "China boss" who moved his crew around as needed, could speak at least some English, and took responsibility for the contract that kept the workers working and the growers paying.[23]

Just as Muir was getting into the intensive-orchard business, the movement against Chinese workers took yet another nasty turn, both locally and nationally. In May 1882 a Martinez mob set upon Chinese cannery workers, badly injuring several by throwing them out of an attic window, and sixty-four stalwart citizens formed the anti-Chinese Liberty League No. 1 of Contra Costa County. That same month, Pres. Chester A. Arthur signed the Chinese Exclusion Act of 1882. Based on a provision of the revised 1878 California constitution intended to protect the state against the foreign-born, the new law prohibited the immigration of Chinese laborers into the United States and prevented Chinese already in the country from becoming citizens. It represented the first and only U.S. immigration statute ever to target a specific ethnicity or nationality.

Paradoxically, the exclusionary law benefitted the Chinese already working California's farms and vineyards. Realizing that now they were difficult to replace, Chinese field workers—once lauded as docile as well as cheap—showed their fierce savvy in bargaining for better wages and working conditions. They even organized strikes to win their case and better their lot.[24]

Muir depended on Chinese labor, and he regularly supervised from fifteen to forty farmhands at a time, depending on seasonal needs. He found this management task so galling that he complained about it in a letter to his sister Sarah. She wrote back, hoping "that the care and oversight of those Ch—— will not upset you again." The workers who performed jobs from planting to pruning to harvesting in Muir's orchards were lodged in five small houses along Franklin Creek. They settled into these temporary quarters often and long enough that they planted and cultivated a vegetable garden to supplement their meals. Chinese farmhands were a fixture on the farm for decades, yet never is it recorded that Muir called any of them by name, even the "Ch——" who doused him in flaming phosphorus. He saw the Chinese as alien, other, even dangerous. "Don't let the children get too familiar with that Ch——," he cautioned his wife in a letter when he was away, "and keep them in sight."[25]

Muir reflected the attitudes of his time, no worse and certainly no better. Support of the Chinese and opposition to the Chinese Exclusion Act came primarily from businessmen in manufacturing and agriculture who wanted to keep wage rates low, as well as from Protestant missionaries who longed for a rich harvest of heathen souls. Principled advocacy for the Chinese on the basis of human or constitutional rights was practically nonexistent.[26] Had Muir wanted to do better than his peers toward the Chinese, he had no examples to learn from and no desire to be a pioneer.

Nor did Muir have any desire to help the Chinese become part of America. That task he saw as impossible. "Some of the best people in the world are Chinese, and we must not hate them," he wrote in a note to himself. "But we should not try to flock too closely with the Chinese, for they are birds with feathers so unlike our own they seem to have been hatched on some other planet. America can make Americans out of almost any people, but the Chinese though—."[27] There the note broke off, his thought uncompleted.

In the meantime Muir followed the agricultural business model of the era and turned cheap Chinese labor, a growing market for California fruit, and the transcontinental railroad to his profit. He developed a reputation for hard bargaining with the jobbers who bought his fruit wholesale for shipment east. They soon learned that they either took Muir's price or went without his premium product. Usually they paid up. And his reputation as a major agricultural player carried sway with local authorities. When Muir complained that the cobbled streets of Martinez leading down to the waterfront rattled the wagons carrying his crated crop and damaged it, the city fathers pulled up the cobblestones and graded the right of way smooth.[28]

Ever hard-nosed and single-minded, Muir cleared on average some $5,000 in annual profit, which is close to $150,000 in contemporary dollars. He deposited this money in interest-bearing accounts at several banks and let it compound as an inheritance for daughters Wanda and Helen and their future families. By the time Muir died, the principal had swelled to $184,000 in cash, more than $4.4 million today. Add in the real estate he owned, and his estate exceeded what would be $6.5 million now. By any measure Muir, who had arrived in Martinez with little but boxes of books, modest savings from magazine writing, his many backcountry notebooks, and a few well-worn clothes, had made himself and his family a comfortable fortune.[29]

For all the wealth the farm brought him, Muir never enjoyed the work or the place. The long, hard days felt too much like what he had known in Wisconsin under his tyrannical father. Farming was a penance to be endured only because it made money. "I am lost and choked in agricultural needs," he wrote to Millicent Shinn, editor of *The Overland Monthly*, explaining why he had no new articles to send her. "Work is coming on me from near and far and at present I cannot see how I am to escape its degrading vicious effects. Get someone to write an article on the vice of over-industry, it is greatly needed in these times of horticultural storms." He said much the same to S. Hall Young, lamenting that "I am learning nothing in this trivial world of men." After a full decade driving the industrialization of California agriculture, Muir happily turned day-to-day management over to his brother David and brother-in-law John Reid, who were now living in Martinez. In time he sold part of the farm and leased out the rest. He was ready to move on.[30]

From the time John Muir married Louie Strentzel until the end of his life, Martinez remained his home base, the center of his family, a legacy to his daughters and grandchildren, a boon to his siblings and in-laws, and the source of his wealth. Yet he never invested in Martinez and the Alhambra Valley emotionally or spiritually. Even while he was courting Louie, he dissed the Contra Costa countryside. He complained, "The ranch and the pasture hills hereabouts are not very interesting at this time of the year. In bloom-time, now approaching, the orchards look gay and Dolly Vardenish, and the home-garden does the best it can with rose bushes and so on, all good in a food and shelter way, but about as far from the forests and gardens of God's wilderness as bran-dolls are from children." For all the years he spent there, Muir never felt at home in Martinez. He was always drawn elsewhere, higher up, into the Sierra Nevada. Late in his life, he told a visiting journalist that his Martinez home was "a good place to be housed in during stormy weather, to write in, and to raise children in, but it is not my home. Up there is my home," gesturing eastward, toward Yosemite.[31]

There was the wild and wilderness, he was saying, and there was the city and civilization. The Martinez farm, for all its rural reality, belonged to the latter. Where wilderness was to be preserved at all costs as sanctuary and refuge, the city and its industrialized croplands existed for commerce's sake, not nature's.

Muir understood who buttered his Martinez bread. Almost simultaneously with the publication of Frank Norris's *The Octopus*, the classic novel that portrayed the railroad and its greedy barons as the enemy of California's farmers, Muir did a favor for the railway industry that delivered his crops to market. When the Santa Fe Railroad constructed a trestle across the Alhambra Valley just south of the farm's boundary, he donated a portion of his land for use as a station. The gesture was Muir's way of saying thanks.[32]

To this day the trestle crossing the canyon symbolizes the bright line Muir drew between wilderness that demands protection as sacred sanctuary, and cultivated land that welcomes industrialization and secular use. He was hardly the first to do this, nor the last. Indeed, this sharp divide between wild and civilized continues to underlie the way twenty-first century Americans look at wilderness and their overall responsibility to the planet.

As Muir gave up day-to-day management of the farm and freed himself to look beyond its boundaries, the nature of the wild and the need for preservation would center the closing act of his life. His timing couldn't have been better.

FIG. 1. A morning council in an Indigenous village along the Merced River in 1872. This stereograph, taken by Eadweard Muybridge before he won fame as the inventor of moving pictures, shows that Yosemite Valley was an Indigenous homeland when Muir was living and working there, a reality his writings overlook. Yosemite Archives, Historic Photo Collection, YM_05315.tif.

FIG. 2. Above: The young John Muir, photographed by San Francisco and Yosemite photographer Carlton E. Watkins. This portrait dates to 1875, a year after Muir visited the Modoc War's battleground in the upper Klamath Basin, while in the process of reinventing himself as wilderness writer and advocate. MSS 048.f23–1249, John Muir Papers, Holt-Atherton Special Collections and Archives, University of the Pacific, © 1984 Muir-Hanna Trust.

FIG. 3. Right: Bridgeport Tom, a.k.a. Indian Tom, worked for James Hutchings, the Yosemite Valley hotelier who hired John Muir to build and run his sawmill. Of the dozens of Indigenous people living and working in the valley at the time, Tom was the one and only who appears by name in Muir's writings, and even then just once and in passing. Courtesy of Yosemite Archives, Historic Photo Collection, RL_14129.tif.

FIG. 4. Joseph C. LeConte at a lectern festooned by his University of California students to mark the scientist's seventy-sixth birthday in 1899. A one-time Confederate and slave owner who became a public apologist for "scientific" racism, LeConte connected with Muir through their shared love for wild places. The two remained fast friends until LeConte's sudden death in 1901. Courtesy of University of California at Berkeley [negative], Oliver Family Photograph Collections, BANC PIC 1960.010 ser. 1:0096–NEG (4x5), Bancroft Library, University of California, Berkeley.

FIG. 5. As a Kutzadika'a family prepares acorn mush west of Mono Lake, Muir looks past them toward C. Hart Merriam, who took this photograph in summer 1900. This is the only known image showing Muir in the presence of Indigenous people. Courtesy of C. Hart Merriam Collection of Native American Photographs, BANC PIC 1978.008 x\23a\P26\no.1–PIC, Bancroft Library, University of California, Berkeley.

FIG. 6. Muir (*left*) with Charles Fletcher Lummis at California's Mission San Luis Rey, around 1902. The editor of *Out West* magazine, which featured Muir's writings, Lummis founded the Sequoyah League to procure a new homeland for two dispossessed tribes. Muir contributed to Lummis's effort and thanked him for this "noble work." MSS048.f25–1368, John Muir Papers, Holt-Atherton Special Collections and Archives, University of the Pacific, © 1984 Muir-Hanna Trust.

FIG. 7. From Glacier Point in 1903 President Theodore Roosevelt and John Muir behold the granite majesty of Yosemite Valley. On this historic camping trip Muir convinced a sympathetic Roosevelt that the valley, then under the control of the State of California, should be added to Yosemite National Park to ensure its preservation. Yosemite Archives, Historic Photo Collection, RL_13238.tif.

FIG. 8. The Muir family at home in Martinez, about 1905: daughters Wanda (*left*) and Helen, with Louie and John. MSS048.f24–1349, John Muir Papers, Holt-Atherton Special Collections and Archives, University of the Pacific, © 1984 Muir-Hanna Trust.

FIG. 9. John Muir with Henry Fairfield Osborn, most likely in Yosemite Valley in 1910. Osborn made his scientific reputation as a paleontologist—he named *Tyrannosaurus rex*, among other accomplishments—and used that foundation to advocate for eugenics and "scientific" racism. MSS048.f26–1444, John Muir Papers, Holt-Atherton Special Collections and Archives, University of the Pacific, © 1984 Muir-Hanna Trust.

FIG. 10. John Muir with C. Hart Merriam in the study of Muir's Martinez home in 1914, the year Muir died. Originally a physician and then a field zoologist, Merriam became fascinated by Native Californians. He spent more than two decades studying them firsthand and advocated for their fair and equitable treatment. MSS048.f26–1457, John Muir Papers, Holt-Atherton Special Collections and Archives, University of the Pacific, © 1984 Muir-Hanna Trust.

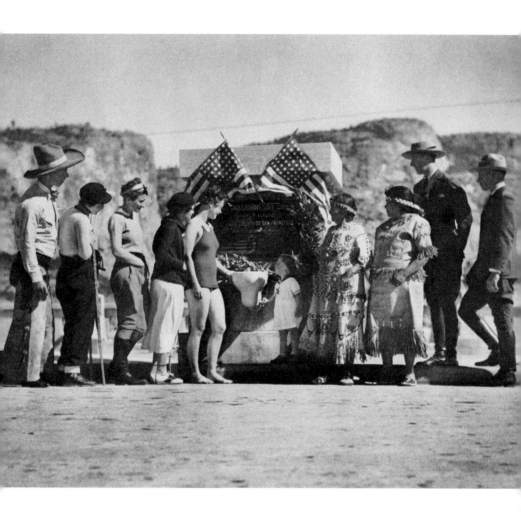

FIG. 11. When the O'Shaughnessy Dam that turned Hetch Hetchy into a reservoir—a project Muir opposed fiercely—was dedicated in July 1923, the San Francisco Public Utilities Commission posed this group photo to convey wide acceptance of the project, even among the tribes whose homeland was flooded. In fact, no one ever asked them. The Native woman on the right is Tabuce, a.k.a. Maggie Howard, longtime and well-known resident of Yosemite Valley; the woman next to her remains unidentified. Courtesy of San Francisco Public Utilities Commission (PUC) Digital Collection, San Francisco Public Library.

FIG. 12. Tiana Williams-Claussen, who directs the Yurok Tribe's Wildlife Department, shows the right way to handle a California condor and its nine-foot wingspan. The tribe's condor restoration program grew from an elder council's vision for bringing the world back into balance. It is built on a partnership with the National Park Service and the U.S. Fish and Wildlife Service and is returning the long-missing birds to their historic range across northwest California, southwest Oregon, and beyond. Courtesy of Yurok Tribe, Klamath, California.

FIG. 13. Tara Fouch-Moore (*left*), secretary, and Sandra Chapman, chair, help lead the Southern Sierra Miwuk Nation in their decades-long effort to obtain tribal acknowledgment from the federal government. Courtesy of Jeannie Tyrell, *Mariposa Gazette*.

PART **3**

One Last Time

I will lift up mine eyes unto the hills, from whence cometh my help.
My help cometh from the Lord, which made heaven and earth.

—PSALM 121:1–2

10

Wilderness Influencer

I suppose we need not go mourning the buffaloes. In the nature of things they had to give place to better cattle, though the change might have been made without barbarous wickedness.

—JOHN MUIR, 1901

As associate editor of *The Century Magazine*, Robert Underwood Johnson prided himself on sensing the quickening pulse of emerging social and political trends and making the acquaintance of the people who shaped them. His formula worked. *The Century* grew into a high-circulation, high-end success by publishing the fiction of such Gilded Age luminaries as Mark Twain, Kate Chopin, and Bret Harte and curating pictorially rich nonfiction series, including reminiscences by decorated generals on both sides of the Civil War.[1]

The success of those Civil War features brought Johnson to San Francisco; he had sold editor-in-chief Richard Gilder on a similar series focused on California gold rush pioneers. While he was in town, he wanted to meet one of *The Century*'s now-and-again writers in person and encourage him to submit more articles. John Muir, glad to get away from managing his Martinez orchard, joined Johnson for dinner at downtown San Francisco's Palace Hotel. The two men, who shared a love for mountains and woods, took to each other immediately. Soon they hatched a plan. Once Johnson wrapped up his gold rush interviews, he and Muir would take off for Yosemite Valley and the Sierra Nevada high country.

With a wrangler-cum-cook named Pike and three anonymous burros carrying their food and gear, Johnson and Muir hiked out of the valley up to Tuolomne Meadows and camped at Soda Springs. They swapped stories around the fire in the evenings and sauntered among peaks and meadows through the days.

Johnson admired Muir's easy way of skimming over smooth terrain and leaping from rock to rock with a bighorn's springy certainty. "A trick of easy locomotion learned from the Indians," Johnson declared, though it surely wasn't. Still, the journalist saw something else in Muir that convinced him of the workability of the plan he was forming. "In the wilderness Muir looked like John the Baptist, as portrayed by Donatello," Johnson declared.

In a campfire's dancing light, he revealed what he had in mind. Like Muir, Johnson was an advocate for saving spectacular wild lands from exploitation for profit. He backed a legislative proposal to create a Yellowstone-like Yosemite National Park that would encompass the state reserve in Yosemite Valley and protect a significant reach of the Sierra Nevada. Soda Springs offered graphic evidence for why such a solution was needed. Numerous flocks of sheep driven—by Portuguese herders, Johnson made clear—into the once chest-high meadows each summer ate everything green down to the roots. Muir despised sheep as "hoofed locusts" and like Johnson wanted them gone. Knowing that stock grazing would be banned in a national park, Johnson made Muir an offer he couldn't refuse: if Muir would write two articles, one describing the valley's wonders as "treasures," and the other outlining the reserve's boundaries and explaining its rationale as a national park, Johnson would convince his editor-in-chief to run them. Then he himself would put the published pieces before the U.S. Congress's Committee on Public Lands to help push the Yosemite National Park proposal forward. Johnson enjoyed personal relationships with key politicians in Congress, and he felt certain that a national park was politically possible. Muir signed on.[2]

He completed the articles, as ever a painfully slow process of writing and revising again and again over several months, and *The Century* ran them with its characteristic, finely detailed illustrations. "The Treasures of the Yosemite" appeared first, in August 1890. Muir spelled out the core threat: "In Yosemite, even under the protection of the Government, all that is perishable is vanishing apace." Two illustrations, one of a meadow plowed up to grow hay and another of a forest of young pines cut to stumps, underscored that destruction. Losing the valley to such rapacity would be unimaginable, Muir wrote, holding that "no temple made with hands can compare with Yosemite." The valley stirred visitors deeply, "as if into this one mountain mansion Nature had gathered her choicest treasures, whether great or small, to draw her lovers into close and confiding communion with her." The tourist sauntering the valley's meadows and taking in its enlarging vistas of monumental granite was in fact a worshipper seeking a deeper truth within the wild world.

Muir enlarged his praise song and plea with "Features of the Proposed Yosemite National Park" in the September issue. Yosemite was more than just the valley; it belonged to a wider region of wonder. "Most people who visit Yosemite are apt to regard it as an exceptional creation, the only valley of its kind in the world," he wrote. "But nothing in Nature stands alone. She is not so poor as to have only one of anything." The less-known Hetch Hetchy Valley rivaled Yosemite for granite monoliths and spectacular waterfalls. And it was but one of many miracles to be savored within the proposed park, from the sauntering grounds of Tuolomne Meadows to the tourist-friendly ascent of Mount Dana, from the scenic descent of Bloody Canyon toward Mono Lake to the icy minarets of the Lyell Glacier. The entire landscape, outlined in detail by a map that showed how the national park would embrace the valley, deserved federal attention. "Unless reserved or protected, the whole region will soon or late be devastated by lumbermen or sheepmen, and so of course made unfit for use as a pleasure ground." The threat was clear: "Ax and plow, hogs and horses, have long been and are still busy in Yosemite's gardens and groves. All that is accessible and destructible is being destroyed."

As for the Indigenous peoples who once lived here, they drew but slight attention from Muir. The Tuolomnes had inhabited the Hetch Hetchy Valley, he wrote, much as Yosemite Valley had been the haunt of the Yosemites. Muir dropped in a few of their place names to add local color, but he was making the tribes relics of a fast-fading past. Manifest destiny had conquered them, lumbermen and sheepmen filled the void, and now was the time to chase out the loggers and the herders and raise Yosemite to its highest, best, and most appropriate use: as a contemplative pleasure ground for Euro-American tourists and nature lovers.[3]

With Muir's articles in hand, Johnson appeared before the House committee overseeing the Yosemite National Park bill. His timing was fortuitous. Even though the committee's members had no idea who John Muir himself was, they had heard about Muir Glacier in Glacier Bay. Remarkably, landmark status proved endorsement enough. With surprising unanimity, the committee agreed to the national park idea and moved it forward. Within months the proposal and the amount of land it preserved grew to the capacious boundaries Muir had proposed. Once the bill passed both houses of Congress, Pres. Benjamin Harrison signed it into law on October 1, 1890.

Johnson and Muir had started something: after two decades of debate about the destruction of public resources for private profit, Congress was embarking on a wild-lands tear. Just a few days before Harrison's signing of the Yosemite bill, he put his signature on another law that established Sequoia National Park in the Southern Sierra. The Yosemite law contained provisions that set aside General Grant National Park, which protected many of the giant sequoia groves and would be enlarged into Kings Canyon National Park in 1940. The following spring, President Harrison signed the Forest Reserve Act of 1891 that granted the president executive authority to protect watersheds and timber. Muir's prophetic appearance on the wild-lands scene at Johnson's prompting had scored success farther and faster than either would have thought possible back at their Soda Springs campfire.[4]

Politicians, like magazine editors, pride themselves on knowing the direction of public opinion's variable winds and raising their sails at the right moment. John Muir's appearance as a reluctant wilderness prophet and public voice came at a propitious time shaped by growing anxiety.

The year 1890, when Yosemite became a national park, stands as the marker for one era's end and another's beginning. Late in the year, the Seventh Cavalry surrounded some 350 Minneconjou (Mnikowoju) and Hunkpapa (Húŋkpapȟa) Lakotas at Wounded Knee, South Dakota, and killed most of them for no good reason—except, perhaps, to avenge Custer's disaster at Little Bighorn. That massacre signaled the end of the United States' western Indian wars and closed the extermination phase of America's conquest of the West. Now the challenge was to keep the tribal nations on their reservations, shrink the boundaries of those reserves as fast as possible, and finish the work of stealing Native American land under color of assimilation.

As a step toward that strategy, the 1890 United States census was the first to enumerate all classes of Indians, both those paying taxes and those not. That same year, the Census Bureau also declared that the American frontier— defined as fewer than two people per square mile, with untaxed Native Americans left uncounted—was over and done with. No longer, the Census Bureau said, was there an ongoing westward movement of Euro-Americans. Soon thereafter, Frederick Jackson Turner, a University of Wisconsin historian who had grown up close to the Muir homestead in Portage, turned this demographic event into his classic essay "The Significance of the Frontier in American History." Turner concluded that "now, four centuries from the discovery of America, at the end of a hundred years of life under the Constitution, the frontier has gone, and with its going has closed the first period of American history."[5]

For some Americans, particularly those who considered themselves descended in body and spirit from early European pioneers, the new United States taking shape behind the closed frontier looked dark and menacing. Cities fueled by America's industrialization were growing rapidly. New York City, as one example, expanded from just under 814,000 residents in 1860 to over 3.4 million by 1900. Demographics were changing as well. Black Americans escaping the South's Jim Crow oppression settled into northern cities like Detroit, Chicago, and New York. And swelling immigration from southern and eastern Europe was changing urban populations at a rate some commentators took to be a threat to "real" Americans.[6]

Francis Amasa Walker was one of those commentators. Formerly head of the Office of Indian Affairs, superintendent of the 1870 census, and at the time the president of the Massachusetts Institute of Technology, Walker sounded a warning about the quantity and the quality of immigration. These weren't the people the United States was built from, he argued. In prior decades, immigrants from southern Italy, Hungary, Austria, and Russia made up perhaps one percent of each year's influx, and they were far outnumbered by immigrants from England, Ireland, Scotland, and Germany. But through the 1880s southern and eastern Europeans had risen to forty percent of new immigrants and looked likely to hit fifty or even sixty percent. "The entrance into our political, social, and industrial life of such vast masses of peasantry, degraded below our utmost conceptions, is a matter which no intelligent patriot can look upon without the gravest apprehension and alarm," Walker wrote in *The Atlantic*. "They are beaten men from beaten races, representing the worst failures in the struggle for existence."[7]

Theodore Roosevelt was less concerned than Walker about where immigrants came from than with a fear that the frontier's loss threatened American manliness. The nation had been forged in righteous struggle against both a dangerous landscape and an Indigenous foe. "It was a war waged by savages against armed settlers, whose families followed them into the wilderness," Roosevelt asserted. "Such a war is inevitably bloody and cruel; but the inhuman love of cruelty for cruelty's sake, which marks the r—— Indian above all other savages, rendered these wars more terrible than any others." Yet for all the avenging horror that settlers turned back on the tribes, they remained ever and always in the right in Roosevelt's telling. "The settler and pioneer have at bottom had justice on their side; this great continent could not have been kept as nothing but a game preserve for squalid savages," he maintained. America needed struggle to become the vigorous, manly republic that it was. Now, Roosevelt worried, with the frontier gone and the vanquished tribes confined to reservations and slow extinction, what would become of the Euro-American manly men on whom our nation's civilization depended?[8]

Roosevelt proposed a solution to keep America virile: big-game hunting. Not for food, the way immigrants and Natives killed to turn noble beasts like buffalo and elk into meat in the locker, but for trophy, sport, and the thrill of the chase—the adrenaline rush of facing down the big and bad on its own wild ground. The 1870s and 1880s made it increasingly clear that unrestrained killing of game—particularly by market hunters who supplied butcher shops with wild meat, immigrants who hunted even songbirds for the table, and tribal people who killed to eat—was threatening one species after another. If nothing was done, wildlife was sure to disappear. Several states stepped in with game laws regulating hunting, establishing wildlife commissions, and appointing game wardens. The conservation movement was rising.

As an enthusiastic conservationist and a rifleman with the funds to pursue big game in remote areas, Roosevelt saw hunting as a pursuit that benefitted both individual and nation. "The free, self-reliant, adventurous life, with its rugged and stalwart democracy, the wild surroundings, the grand beauty of the scenery, the chance to study the ways and habits of the woodland creatures—all these unite to give the career of the wilderness hunter its peculiar charm," Roosevelt wrote. "The chase is among the best of all national pastimes; it cultivates that vigorous manliness for the lack of which in a nation, as in an individual, the possession of no other qualities can atone." The hunters Roosevelt praised were as much naturalists as sportsmen who made themselves into new American natives with every right to the wild lands they hunted. The civilized had replaced the primitive and barbarian, Roosevelt was saying, as evolutionary progress demanded.[9]

Where Roosevelt personified the elite male made vigorously manly by the hunt, George Bird Grinnell brought scientific bona fides to the sport-hunting movement and the conservation effort it birthed. Like Roosevelt, Grinnell was a New Yorker of aristocratic background and considerable means. The son of Cornelius Vanderbilt's principal Wall Street broker and the grandson of a ten-term member of the House of Representatives, he traced his ancestry to the *Mayflower*. Grinnell was hammering away at a doctorate in osteology and vertebrate paleontology at Yale while also working at the Peabody Museum of Natural History when he joined the magazine *Forest and Stream*, then only three years old, as natural history editor for ten dollars a week (about $250 today). At almost the same time, George Armstrong Custer, whom Grinnell knew from working as a field naturalist during the Black Hills expedition, invited him to come along on the Seventh Cavalry's campaign into Dakota Territory. Grinnell reluctantly begged off, concerned that a fast-moving cavalry operation would leave too little time for scientific work. The decision likely saved Grinnell from premature death at Little Bighorn, and it confirmed his career choice. He devoted the next thirty-five years to *Forest and Stream*. He became the top editor five years into his tenure and built an audience that grew into the leading political force advocating for conservation and promoting sport hunting and fishing.

Grinnell was high on the list of close friends and associates Teddy Roosevelt invited to a dinner party at his sister's Madison Avenue home in mid-December 1887. Besides knowing Roosevelt, all the guests belonged to the moneyed Eastern elite and were avid hunters who pursued trophies in remote, wild places. Roosevelt, ever the organizer, had an idea: an elite sportsmen's club of rifle hunters that would be called the Boone and Crockett Club. By summoning the images of two mythic frontiersmen, hunters, and Indian fighters, the club would connect modern sportsmen with the noble violence and self-reliant woodcraft of a soon-to-disappear American frontier threatened by population growth and immigration from all the wrong countries.

The following month, the group met again, this time at Pinard's Restaurant on Fifteenth Street, to adopt a constitution and elect Roosevelt its first president. Among the Boone and Crockett Club's goals were promoting "manly sport with the rifle," advocating for "the preservation of the large game of this country," and lobbying for legislation to advance the club's purposes. Boone and Crockett was picky about its membership. It limited the total to one hundred men, all of whom had proven their hunting chops in killing at least one variety of North American big game by sportsmanlike "fair chase." They also created a committee to decide on potential new members. The committee included Roosevelt and Grinnell, and among the first new members they tapped were several notables: retired Commanding General of the U.S. Army William Tecumseh Sherman, who after the Civil War went on to lead wars against tribal nations and make the West safe for big-game hunters; George Vest, a U.S. senator from Missouri and defender of the Confederacy's Lost Cause who also protected Yellowstone against monopolistic concessions driven by the Northern Pacific Railroad; and Edward F. Beale, a prominent Washingtonian who owned Decatur House, the preferred hotel for luminaries on political business in the capital. Clearly, the Boone and Crockett Club meant to play insider pool.[10]

The club stood out for its built-in, well-moneyed elitism, but it was hardly the only organization of like-minded, mostly urban, well-to-do people advocating for protecting America's vanishing wildlife. Grinnell himself had organized the first iteration of the Audubon Society only a year before that meeting at Roosevelt's home to address the massive decline in bird populations, in part because of market hunting for the millinery trade. Ever the editor and publisher, Grinnell set up *Audubon Magazine* to keep society members informed and committed to their shared effort to protect birds. The publication went under in early 1889, however, when the society had achieved a membership of 48,862—impressive, but not big enough to pay for producing the magazine. Despite this seeming failure, Grinnell, Roosevelt, and their Boone and Crockett comrades had seen grassroots conservation's power. They knew they were on to something.[11]

Other organizations besides the Audubon Society were embraced by urbanites who looked to the wild and natural for recreation and spiritual sustenance beyond the city. The earliest was the Alpine Club of Williamstown in 1863, followed by the White Mountain Club, the Rocky Mountain Club, the Appalachian Mountain Club, and the American Ornithological Union. With those predecessors in mind, Joachim Henry Senger, professor of German at the University of California, proposed in 1886 that Yosemite Valley should feature a library of mountaineering resources for climbers and hikers. By the early 1890s Senger's suggestion grew into a rough plan for a Sierra Club, an idea popular among Berkeley faculty and students. Senger found an ally in English lecturer William Armes, and the two academics discussed the notion with San Francisco attorney Warren Olney.[12]

Soon John Muir came onboard, writing to Senger that "you may count on me as a member and as willing to do all in my power to further the interests of such a club." This would be an organization devoted to preserving scenic wild land for its aesthetic beauty, spiritual import, and opportunities for mountaineering—think Boone and Crockett without all the bloodletting. Following various meetings and discussions, Olney drew up articles of incorporation for the new Sierra Club. Twenty-seven men came together in his San Francisco law office on June 4, 1892, to sign the papers and elect the first slate of officers. Muir became president, a position he would hold for the rest of his life. The group comprised an A-list of Bay Area professionals besides Senger, Armes, Olney, and Muir. Among them were newly installed Stanford University president David Starr Jordan, scenic photographer William Keith, and University of California professor—and one-time slave owner and current philosopher of scientific racism—Joseph C. LeConte.[13]

Like Boone and Crockett, the Sierra Club didn't admit just anybody. The articles of incorporation created a thirteen-member admissions committee that voted would-be members up or down. That structure helped ensure that the club remained middle-and upper-class, professional, exclusively Euro-American, and predominantly male. The 182 charter members represented what the Sierra Club was and wanted to be: 177 men and five women, twenty-five university professors, one university president, twelve physicians, and four men carrying the honorific "honorable." Twenty-eight of the charter members were affiliated with the University of California, nine with Stanford University, six with the California Academy of Sciences, and two each with the San Francisco Stock Exchange and the U.S. Geological Survey. The club radiated an urban and professional energy, mostly male and Protestant.[14]

The first public meeting of the Sierra Club on September 16, 1892, welcomed 250 members and friends to the California Academy of Sciences in San Francisco to hear featured speaker John Wesley Powell talk about exploring the Grand Canyon. Powell personified the manly explorer of the West. A veteran of the Civil War who lost his right arm to a Minié ball at the Battle of Shiloh, Powell led the first government-sponsored expedition down the Green and Colorado Rivers in 1869, an area then little known to Euro-Americans. Although he would later go on to lead both the U.S. Geological Survey and the Smithsonian's Bureau of Ethnology, he made remarkably few notes during the expedition about Indigenous peoples along the Colorado and its side canyons. Despite Powell's inattention, they were there. Other members of the party made far more extensive journal entries about the Indigenous presence, and modern archaeology has revealed thirty-seven occupied sites along the route Powell and his men followed. Powell's omission made the canyon seem far more uncharted and "pristine" than it was and boosted his reputation as a daring explorer of the uncharted.

Like most people in his Sierra Club audience, Powell arranged societies on an evolutionary ladder from savagery through barbarism to civilization. "In savagery, the beasts are gods; in barbarism, the gods are men; in civilization, men are *as gods*, knowing good from evil," he wrote. Civilization was a rare human achievement. It applied only "to one great stock of people—the Aryan race—together with the other stocks, as the Egyptian, the Semitic, and Turanian [Turkic] races, whose history is involved in that of the Aryan, and with whom they were inextricably mixed." The best path for Native Americans to rise above their inborn barbarism and share in Euro-American civilization was to accept the loss of their lands, cultures, and mother tongues. He asserted that "the most important thing is to teach them the English language." Indigenous languages were so charged with myth and sorcery that "the ideas and thoughts of civilized life cannot be communicated to them in their own tongues." Intrepid, daring, and brave as he was, Powell signed onto the settler-colonialist agenda: declare the land empty, invalidate its Indigenous inhabitants as mere barbarians, and tell them that becoming civilized meant rejecting who they were and becoming what Euro-Americans wished them to be.[15]

Powell so impressed the Sierra Club audience that he and several other prominent men—among them Robert Underwood Johnson—were elected honorary lifetime members of the Sierra Club two months later. Wilderness preservation and settler colonialism were working hand in glove.[16]

As president, Muir had little to do with the day-to-day operations of the Sierra Club. Rather, he was becoming what Robert Underwood Johnson had envisioned at Soda Springs: a John the Baptist crying out for wilderness, the prophetic voice for a growing movement.

Meanwhile, the U.S. Army was getting down to work. In April 1891 Troops I and K of the Fourth Cavalry stationed at San Francisco's Presidio under Captains A. E. Wood and John Dorst received orders to protect the new Yosemite, Sequoia, and General Grant reserves. Wood drew Yosemite and established headquarters at Wawona, inside the boundaries of the months-old Yosemite National Park. Dorst headed south with his troopers to Sequoia and General Grant.

A military man to the core who became Yosemite's acting superintendent, Wood envisioned the park as a fortress under siege. At the top of the enemies list were the herders. "The sheep have been the curse of these mountains," Wood reported, blaming the animals for eroding soils and upending game populations, particularly bear, deer, quail, and grouse. He had a low opinion of the men who made a scant living driving sheep into the summer mountains; they were "foreigners—Chilians [*sic*] . . . Portuguese, French, and Mexicans." He came up with an ingenious method for dealing with them. Any cavalry patrol that caught a trespassing flock separated sheep from shepherd, then escorted the herder to one side of the park and drove the flock to the other. It took days for the herder to make his way back across the wilderness and round up what remained of the flock, which had typically dwindled in number owing to predators with a taste for lamb and mutton. Rather than accept this financial loss, more and more herders steered clear of the park and its cavalry. "I have effectively stopped such vandalism," Wood reported with clear pride and predicted that the park "would be alive with game" in but a few years.[17]

Muir applauded the cavalry's fast and focused work in turning Yosemite into a defended fortress. Understanding in hindsight the significance of his long talk with Robert Underwood Johnson at their Soda Springs camp-site, Muir exulted that "in a little over a year from the time of our first talk beside that Tuolomne camp-fire the bill organizing the park passed, and a troop of cavalry was guarding it." No longer did the region look "broken and wasted, like a beautiful countenance destroyed by some dreadful disease. Now it is blooming again as one general garden, in which beauty for ashes has been granted in fine wild measure. The flowers and grasses are back again in their places as if they had never been away, and every tree in the park is waving its arms for joy." The cause of all this restored glory was "protection from the sheep scourge," a struggle that figured into a cosmic combat. "The battle we have fought, and are still fighting, for the forests is a part of the eternal conflict between right and wrong, and we cannot expect to see the end of it," Muir declared. "The smallest forest reserve, and the first I ever heard of, was in the Garden of Eden; and though its boundaries were drawn by the Lord, and embraced only one tree, yet even so modest a reserve as this was attacked."[18] Muir was making park protection the holy act of restoring Eden itself.

The cavalry cut no slack for tribal nations on the hunting ban within national parks. During the 1890s, cavalry patrols put an end to Indigenous deer hunting in the Tuolomne and Merced watersheds, which had been fully legal until those areas fell within the new park. Muir stood firmly behind this effort. "It is when the deer are coming down that the Indians set out on their grand fall hunt," he remembered. "Too lazy to go into the recesses of the mountains away from trails, they wait for the deer to come out, and then waylay them." Muir never hunted, yet he was voicing the aesthetic judgment of Teddy Roosevelt and every other Boone and Crockett Club charter member. Trophy hunting in the high country was the noble pursuit of manly outdoorsmen, but hunting for food through ambush, the way Native Americans did, was a slothful crime against nature. "Central camps are made on the well-known highways of the deer, which are soon red with blood," Muir explained. "Each hunter comes in laden, old crones as well as maidens smiling on the luckiest. All grow fat and merry." These hunts, with a little forceful urging from the cavalry, were vanishing as surely as the tribal nations, "and their red camps on the mountains are fewer every year."[19]

Since the cavalry worked the Yosemite backcountry and the valley remained under the control of the state of California, the troopers rode their patrols well away from the areas most tourists frequented. Muir approved, pleased that "the soldiers do their duty so quietly that the traveler is scarce aware of their presence."[20]

During Muir's early days in Yosemite, he saw tourists as comical. "All sorts of human stuff is being poured into our valley this year, and the blank, fleshly apathy with which most of it comes in contact with the rock and water spirits of the place is most amazing," he had written to friend Jeanne Carr back in 1870. Sitting in their saddles "like overgrown frogs," the tourists only feel "comfortable when they have 'done it all,' and long for the safety and flatness of their proper homes." Fortunately, "the tide of visitors will float slowly about the *bottom* of the valley as a harmless scum, collecting in hotel and saloon eddies" while never learning that "the top of the valley is more than half way to real heaven."[21]

By the 1890s Muir was singing from a more welcoming hymnal. His growing warmth toward tourists came at the urging of Robert Underwood Johnson, who realized that American wilderness could be saved only if it appealed to Eastern urban professionals like himself. Hard-core mountaineers on the order of the young Muir were few and far between, so for the parks to succeed they also had to appeal to tourists seeking a less strenuous experience. The increasingly domesticated Muir came to describe Yosemite and Sequoia as "the wildest health and pleasure grounds accessible and available to tourists seeking escape from care and dust and early death."[22]

Muir wanted to convert his readers into park tourists, in part by persuading them that nothing untoward would come their way. Native Americans, Muir assured his readers, posed no risk at all: As to Indians, most of them are dead or civilized into useless innocence." In Yellowstone, the nation's first park, "no scalping Indians will you see. The Blackfeet and Bannocks that once roamed here are gone." Likewise, the fearsome and once-dangerous

Yosemites had been cleared out of the park that carried their name four decades earlier. Frontier justice had been done, conquest completed, and the park rendered safe. The cavalry kept it secure against inroads and threats, quietly and out of tourists' sight, preventing vanishing tribal remnants from hunting deer and foreign-born shepherds from grazing their flocks inside the park. The line had been drawn, the wall surrounding the sanctuary built, the defense mounted.[23]

This well-defended temple sanctified a vision of wilderness centered on Euro-American perceptions, values, and desires. It was, in a word, white. Yosemite could be contemplated, not lived in; the benefits of this wild space accrued to the soul, not the body, so it only made sense to ban all hunting and gathering, even by Indigenous peoples who had taken their sustenance from the landscape for millennia. Given their lower status on the racial evolutionary hierarchy of the late nineteenth century, forcing them out of the park and banning all hunting and gathering rededicated their former homelands to the purpose God intended: contemplation of the Divine amid sublime manifestations of granite and glacier. Better Euro-American visitors than Native American residents. Settler colonialism required it. Wilderness required it as well.[24]

Muir was on a roll with ongoing help from Robert Underwood Johnson. Behind *The Century Magazine* stood The Century Company, a book publisher that brought out Muir's first hardcover, *The Mountains of California*, in 1894. Muir cobbled the volume together by revising and updating earlier magazine and newspaper pieces as well as adding two new essays and building on the two original *Century* articles about Yosemite. As in those pieces, Muir promoted soul healing in the wild, especially for the casual tourist. He wrote, "Fear not, therefore, to try the mountain-passes. They will kill care, save you from deadly apathy, set you free, and call forth every faculty into vigorous, enthusiastic action." As to Native Americans, they did little more in these pages than collect and feast on pine nuts, hunt rabbits, beg whisky and tobacco, threaten woodlands by setting fires for deer hunting, and, annoyingly, clutter up the grand vistas Euro-American tourists had every right to. Muir's genial accounts of his saunters helped readers vicariously experience his mountain adventures, and they came to trust him as a guide to nature's backcountry wonders. As they read his paeans to the Range of Light, they came to share his conviction that the Sierra Nevada, secured by conquest and dispossession, must be preserved as pristine and Indigenous-free.[25]

Besides swelling Muir's devoted audience, Johnson gave him access to influential people who read and valued his books and subscribed to his vision of wilderness and national parks. Through Johnson, Muir made the acquaintance of Nikola Tesla, inventor of the alternating-current system that allowed widespread electrification; the naturalist and writer John Burroughs; Henry Fairfield Osborn, director of mammalian paleontology at the American Museum of Paleontology and later the museum's director; Charles Sprague Sargent, Harvard professor of botany and director of the university's Arnold Arboretum; historian Francis Parkman of *Oregon Trail* fame; Josiah Royce, transplanted Californian and Harvard philosopher; New York *Sun* editor Charles Anderson Dana; and writers Mark Twain, Sarah Orne Jewett, George Washington Cable, and Rudyard Kipling. When Johnson and Muir visited Concord, Massachusetts, to see the haunts of Ralph Waldo Emerson and Henry David Thoreau, Emerson's son greeted Muir like a long-lost relative, proclaiming his name a household word. Muir, whose sense of humor tended to wry self-depreciation, deadpanned, "I had no idea that I was so well known considering how little I have written."[26]

Friends in high places became Muir's companions, confidantes, and allies. With Henry Fairfield Osborn alongside, he took his fifth trip to Alaska in the summer of 1896. Before he left for the Far North, he joined Charles Sprague Sargent and the U.S. Forest Commission on a survey of woodlands in the West. There he met Gifford Pinchot, the gifted forester who would later lead the Department of the Interior. Then, seemingly out of nowhere, came an invitation from a nearly forgotten connection. It led Muir to gain a new and most surprising friend, both a looming public figure and a backroom wielder of enormous influence who proved crucial to the wilderness prophet's next big success. The connection came from someone Muir had guided around Yosemite Valley back in the day. Even over the distance of an entire generation, the naturalist had made a lasting impression.

11

On Top of the World

Perhaps for awhile a few may save themselves by retreating to the Arctic to escape the contaminating touch of the civilized, and thus the extinction of the Alaska E—— may be postponed. But there is an inevitable conflict between civilization and savagery, and wherever the two touch each other, the weaker people must be destroyed.

—GEORGE BIRD GRINNELL, 1902

In the summer of 1871, John Muir was a 33-year-old living in Yosemite and supplementing his sawmill wages by showing the valley's sights to tourists, including Clinton L. Merriam. The naturalist soon learned that Merriam was a man of some standing as a former Wall Street broker who had turned his financial success into a seat in the House of Representatives. Merriam's political career interested Muir far less than the New Yorker's enthusiasm for geology, however. He took time to explain in detail how glaciers had shaped the extraordinary valley whose scenic wonders they were now taking in. After Merriam went back east, he and Muir kept up a correspondence. Impressed with the naturalist's self-taught expertise, Merriam asked whether Muir would consider a scientific posting to the Smithsonian or some similar institution. After years of study on his own and taking practically any job that came his way, Muir was ready for a change from his patchwork life. "I answer, Yes," he wrote back. "If I could give my whole time to science, I should be happy indeed, and no amount of hardship and labor could crush or outweary me. I should like to collect plants or minerals or insects or to prepare a work upon the trees of this coast, or to take part in any exploring expedition in which there was work that I was capable of doing."[1]

That opportunity never materialized, but twenty-eight years later Merriam's son, C. Hart Merriam, recalled what his father had to say about meeting Muir back in the day. Merriam was finishing up an unusual task that had come to him as head of the Department of Agriculture's Division of Biological Survey. Into his office one day, utterly uninvited, walked a middle-aged man who cut a less than impressive figure: short, with thinning hair, a dark and expressionless face atop a pugnacious chin, and a drooping mustache described by a friend "as unkempt as if it had been worn by a Skye terrier." It surprised Merriam to learn that this was railroad magnate E. H. Harriman, who had just succeeded in his epic takeover of the Union Pacific Railroad. Worn out from boardroom battles and corporate infighting, Harriman wanted to kick back for a time, someplace far away. A dedicated outdoorsman and hunter, he decided that hunting Kodiak bear, the largest ursine on the planet, would give his manly soul the reboot it needed. Merriam had authored the scientific paper identifying the Kodiak as a subspecies of the Alaskan brown bear, and so it was that Harriman dropped in on him unannounced. Harriman made the astonished Merriam an offer too good to refuse: the railroad baron wanted to invite along a select group of senior scientists—all expenses paid, of course—as a way of transforming his bear-hunting outing into a grand scientific expedition. Would Merriam join the effort and choose the scientists?[2]

And so it was that Merriam invited Muir as the expedition's glaciologist. Uncertain about the notorious Harriman, Muir accepted at the last minute only because the trip would give him a chance to see stretches of the Alaskan coastline he had yet to visit. It helped Muir's decision that he was joining an elite scientific company including, among others, George Bird Grinnell; William H. Dall, United States Geological Survey scientist and namesake of the Dall's sheep; Charles Keeler, museum director for the California Academy of Sciences; and various Cornell, Yale, Harvard, and Berkeley professors. Merriam wanted to include an artistic perspective as well. He invited, among others, Edward S. Curtis, then a young and unknown photographer yet already a proven mountaineer, and painter Frederick Dellenbaugh, who had demonstrated his explorer's skills as a member of John Wesley Powell's second Colorado River expedition.

The group assembled in Seattle at the end of May 1899 and boarded the *George W. Elder*, a one-time Inside Passage tourist ship overhauled and elegantly refitted by Harriman's Oregon Railroad and Navigation Company. With the Harriman family and friends, assembled scientists and artists, a squad of professional scouts and packers, and captain and crew, the *Elder* headed north carrying 126 people. John Muir, legendary saunterer of high mountain solitude, numbered now as but one among a crowd of early, elite ecotourists and their myriad minions.[3]

The *Elder*'s first stop on the voyage north, apart from a couple of hours here and there for collecting plant specimens, came soon after the ship entered Alaskan waters. It landed on a Sunday morning at New Metlakatla, a transplanted evangelical community founded by William Duncan. A Scot by birth and a lay missionary by training, Duncan had come to Port Simpson on the northern British Columbia coast to proselytize the local Tsimshian (Ts'msyan) First Nation. Convinced that the trading post's easy alcohol and casual prostitution would erode his converts' tender faith, Duncan moved his flock farther up the coast to a new settlement called Metlakatla, north of what is now Prince Rupert. There he set out to create an evangelical utopia governed firmly by his own autocratic hand and defended by a British gunboat, a tribal police force, and his legal status as civil magistrate. Duncan argued that whites tempted the Tsimshians, already weakened by their culture of magic and superstition, into immoral ways. The gunboat and the police made sure no Euro-Canadians got within four miles of the new town.

S. Hall Young, Muir's canoe companion among glaciers and Tlingits in 1879 and 1880, visited Metlakatla and came away impressed with his fellow missionary's work. "That was where SUCCESS was spelled in large letters. Metlakatla was a great town, built after a style evolved in Father Duncan's fertile brain," Young reported. "The town was a marvel, compared with the physical and moral wilderness of that Northern country."[4]

Such success, however, did not protect Duncan from a struggle with Canada's Anglican establishment over who ultimately controlled Metlakatla. When the escalating conflict drew in British Columbia's provincial government, the missionary resolved to pull up stakes and escape north over the border to Alaska. With some six hundred Tsimshian converts in tow, Duncan headed for Annette Island, where the Alaska territorial government provided a land grant.[5]

Alaska's New Metlakatla made a big impression on the *Elder*'s passengers during their day-long visit. Nature writer John Burroughs, who authored the expedition's official memoir, called the settlement "one of the best object lessons on the coast, showing what can be done with the Alaska Indians." As he saw it, under the "wonderful tutelage of William Duncan," these Indigenous people have "been brought from a low state of savagery to a really fair state of industrial civilization." Evangelical dictatorship worked: "Mr. Duncan is really the father of his people. He stands to them notably for the gospel but for the civil law as well. He supervises their business enterprises and composes their family quarrels." It helped, Burroughs argued, that Alaska's Native Americans differed from those elsewhere—smaller, lighter-skinned, "with none of that look of rocks and mountains, austere and relentless."[6]

George Bird Grinnell, who focused his observations on Alaska Natives along the *Elder*'s course, shared Burroughs's enthusiasm. "Except for their color, and for the peculiar gait, which seems common to all these fishing Indians, these people and their wives and children could hardly be told from any civilized community of a thousand souls anywhere in the country," Grinnell reported. "It took many years for Mr. Duncan to change these Indians from the wild men that they were when he first met them to the respectable and civilized people that they now are." Liquor was banned, and since white people were kept at a distance, New Metlakatla's Tsimshians faced little temptation to abandon Duncan's rigid rules. Six days a week they worked on the community's fishing boats, in the salmon cannery and sawmill, at trades ranging from carpentry to blacksmithing, and in the four stores. Then, on Sunday, the day the *Elder* arrived, they worshiped and rested.

The town reminded Grinnell of "an old-fashioned New England hamlet in its quiet." The streets were deserted until the church bell rang and congregants spilled from their own well-kept houses onto the board sidewalks and gathered in the sanctuary. "It would be hard to imagine a more attentive and decorous audience," Grinnell wrote. Men, women, and children alike focused on the service and sermon—Duncan preached in the Tsimshian tongue—and paid no attention to the visitors from the *Elder* gathered in the back of the nave. They were self-sufficient, and "they govern themselves in town-meeting fashion, consulting Mr. Duncan frequently as to what they ought to do."[7]

Grinnell had seen firsthand the reservation misery of the Blackfeet (Piegans, Piikani), Pawnees (Chaticks si Chaticks), and Northern Cheyennes (Tsetsêhesêstâhase, So'taahe), and he worked long and hard to defend and protect the tribes. He argued that Euro-Americans who took the time to meet Indigenous people on their own ground came to demand "for the race the consideration which it ought to have." Still, as the prevailing ethnological wisdom of the time dictated, Grinnell saw Native nations as no better than barbarians halfway along the evolutionary path to civilization. "The Indian," he wrote in the *Atlantic Monthly*, compressing all the continent's Indigenous peoples into one lump, has "the stature of a man with the experiences and reasoning powers of a child." The only path to survival, he held, was for Indigenous nations to give up the old ways and accept Euro-American civilization as the future. New Metlakatla proved to Grinnell that this transformation was possible.[8]

Muir came away less sanguine with Duncan's utopia. He listened to what the missionary had to say about why he left British Columbia for Alaska, yet he shared none of his shipmates' enthusiasm for this Christian autocracy. Likely Duncan came across as an unpleasant replay of his father's evangelical intensity and dictatorial manner. As to whether Duncan's experiment was benefitting the Tsimshians, Muir said nothing.[9]

From Annette Island the *Elder* continued northward toward Wrangell and Juneau, then up the long fjord of Lynn Canal for a landing at Skagway, a boomtown born of gold fever only two years earlier. The passengers took a railroad excursion to the top of White Pass, which served as an entry to the Klondike and its dreams of easy riches. Then it was on to Glacier Bay and Muir Glacier, where the *Elder* dropped anchor abreast of a small shoreside cabin the namesake naturalist had built on a trip to the area nine years earlier. While a number of the passengers went ashore to look around, Muir camped out once more in this place he loved and knew well.

There he met a Tlingit father and son duo as they brought their canoe ashore, berthing it prudently above the tide line and carefully wetting bow and stern to keep the wood from splitting. The two offered Muir gull eggs gathered from an immense rookery nearby, hard-boiled and served up alongside wild celery peeled and dipped in candlefish oil "brown like molasses." He delighted in the pair's hospitality and the celery's bright, crisp taste, reminded no doubt of the hospitality he had known twenty years earlier among the Tlingits.[10]

Muir's focus during the Harriman Expedition was glaciers, so he filled his journals with sketches and notes about the many rivers of ice that came out of the mountains and down to the sea the *Elder* was steaming through. And when the expedition encountered an unnamed glacier at the head of a fjord in Prince William Sound, Muir proposed that it be dubbed the Harriman Glacier. That idea raised a cheer from the scientific party, and Harriman thanked Muir for gracing the glacier with his name. To this day it is known as the Harriman Glacier.[11]

This gesture was not simply sucking up to Mr. Money Bags. Muir tended to distrust magnates and tycoons, and that had been his attitude about Harriman before he came aboard the *Elder*. But as the ship bore north and west and Muir befriended Harriman's children, his initial skepticism gave way to respect that over time grew into affection.

Meanwhile, the *Elder* steamed up Yakutat Bay and became the first large vessel to push past the ice and enter Disenchantment Bay. On the way in, a number of Tlingits paddled alongside the ship to sell furs. Harriman invited them aboard. One of the visitors wore a red patch over his empty left eye socket and a braid-brimmed felt hat that, to Harriman, gave him the romantic look of a pirate. This man, whom Harriman nicknamed Indian Jim, displayed an intimate knowledge of the local terrain, so the tycoon took him onboard to advise the ship's pilot. The choice proved wise. The *Elder* was unable to find an anchorage in the fjord's deep waters until Indian Jim pointed out just the spot. The dropped anchor hit bottom and held.[12]

A party of Tlingit hunters was camped nearby on Haenke Island, killing seals for skins to sell. Shots rang out continually, and the targeted seals kept barking and half-howling in "a strange earnest voice" that troubled Muir. One seal came close alongside, moving oddly, as if it were wounded and blind. It was a distressing sight, and Muir found the "stinks of decaying seals awful." A nearby salmon cannery did not help matters. Like all the Alaska canneries of the time, the workforce was made up of "unutterably dirty, frowsy Chinamen. Men in this business are themselves canned," Muir wrote.[13]

No less than fifty-five canneries operated along the Alaskan coast at the time, netting all the salmon they could for tinned profit in defiance of unenforced laws meant to save at least some fish for the Tlingits. Rather than soften the blow by employing local people, the canneries recruited Chinese men from San Francisco, transported them north for the season, and paid them their pittance only after they were returned home. Like the Chinese field hands who worked for Muir in his Martinez orchard, cannery workers took these grinding, filthy jobs because they had no better choice.[14]

A few days after departing Glacier Bay, the *Elder* arrived where Harriman wanted most to be: Kodiak Island, home to the biggest bear in Alaska and the world. The eager tycoon went ashore with a supporting cast of trackers, hunters, and packers and returned the next day with his trophies: a sow and her small cub. It had hardly been a hunt bathed in the Boone and Crockett glory of fair chase. Beaters drove the sow into a narrow gorge where Harriman, flanked and backed by riflemen just in case, lay in ambush. He took the sow down with one shot; Luther "Yellowstone" Kelly dispatched the now-motherless cub. The bears were skinned on the spot, and the green hides were transported to the *Elder*, bound for the trophy room back home.[15]

Privately Muir ridiculed Harriman and Kelly's destruction of wildlife in the name of sport and the paltry size of the "trophy" bear. The back foot was just eight inches long, Muir wrote in his journal; he himself had spotted tracks that measured a full five inches longer. The sow was but a middling specimen of her gigantic kind, yet Harriman was pleased at killing the beast he came for. Muir scoffed at "the pleasure of making the hole in the animals, shedding the blood, satisfying the savage instincts that should be kept down rather after civilization has gone far enough for trousers and prayers."[16]

With his bear bagged, Harriman returned to acting like the railroad titan that he was. As Russia's Trans-Siberian Railway neared completion, Harriman was nursing the grand dream of a rail link between North America and Eurasia either through an undersea tunnel below the Bering Strait or over a fifty-mile-long suspension bridge above it. To decide which option it would be, he wanted a look at the strait for himself.

The *Elder* set a course for Plover Bay, south of the Bering Strait on the Siberian side. It was a long, churning slog over enormous, wind-torn swells in open sea that demonstrated why the crew had nicknamed the vessel the *George W. Roller.* As soon as the ship reached a welcome anchorage off a small village of a dozen walrus-hide huts on a windy Siberian spit, some of the local Chukchis paddled out for a visit. The men "with shaven or sheared crowns" reminded Muir of his visit on the *Corwin* eighteen years earlier. Things had changed in the meantime, though, and not for the better. "The contact with civilization of whaler seamen sort has of course spoiled them," he wrote, noting how they flooded villages with bad whiskey, targeted Chukchi women and girls for sexual violence, and spread disease. C. Hart Merriam, who had graduated from Columbia University's medical school and practiced medicine before following his bliss into natural history, recognized the sores and scars on the Chukchi men's bared scalps for what they were: syphilis. Still, tainted though the Chukchis were by civilization's maladies, Muir continued to admire these tough people: "In spite of all this they make a living in this seemingly desolate land of frost and barren stone."[17]

Once Harriman decided he understood the engineering challenges of a Bering Strait railroad connector, the *Elder* headed back across the rough and rolling swells to the Alaskan shore. Next up was Port Clarence, a rendezvous for American whalers working in the Arctic Sea and for local Indigenous peoples eager to trade. Some fifteen long, swift umiaks, each loaded with up to thirty Iñupiats, paddled alongside the *Elder*—"a merry, gypsy crowd" in Muir's eyes. He admired their sleek, seaworthy vessels: "Very fine walrus and sealskin canoes propelled by oars, paddles and sails, extremely buoyant and fast sailers." The locals wanted to sell walrus tusks, some of them carved, as well as caribou hides and boots, and the visitors were hot for souvenirs and mementos. When the shopping spree ended, with sellers heading one way and buyers another, some of the *Elder*'s passengers, including the women and children, went ashore through heavy swells that made offloading and onloading wet and cold. Several made it back into the launches for the return trip only because crewmen carried them through the pounding waves. Muir found it "a sight to see demolishment of dignity and neat propriety," a comment on civilized people ill-suited to the wild, rough place the Iñupiats called home. Harriman invited several whaling captains anchored nearby onto the *Elder* for whisky and cigars, but he refused permission to the Iñupiats to come aboard. Even here, caste and race mattered.[18]

From Port Clarence, the expedition's most northerly point, the *Elder* came about, aiming to make it back to Seattle inside two weeks' sailing time. Among the few stops on the return leg was Kodiak Island once again. Harriman harbored hopes of taking down a bigger bear than the middling sow and small cub he had already killed, and so he set out once again with his armed support staff into the day's fog and rain. "Baffled and disgusted, they returned at 10," Muir recorded in his journal with great glee. "No bears, no bears, Oh Lord, no bears shot, what hast thy servants done?"[19]

Harriman had one more stop in mind: a place painter and explorer Frederick Dellenbaugh had told him about. The artist had learned from an old gold miner on Kodiak Island about a deserted Tlingit village featuring magnificent totem poles. A penciled map the old-timer had roughed out for Dellenbaugh put the village about fifty miles southeast of Ketchikan in a small bay north of Cape Fox and within easy reach of the *Elder*'s course south. Harriman had the captain steam toward the cape and anchor a little offshore once the village came into sight. A dozen houses lined the beach, and nineteen totem poles reached into the ever-overcast sky.

The story quickly went round the ship that the Tlingits who once lived here had nearly all died of smallpox several years earlier. The few survivors, it was said, abandoned the place as cursed and vowed never to return. Why not, they wondered, turn the Tlingits' misfortune into the *Elder*'s opportunity?

Crew and energetic passengers fell to, digging, hauling, and towing several totem poles to the ship. They were massive; one measured sixty feet long and five feet across. The passengers also collected ceremonial masks, carvings, large boxes, house screens, and baskets. The spoils were later divided among the California Academy of Sciences, Cornell University, the Field Museum in Chicago, and the University of Michigan. Harriman kept for his own collection two large bears carved in ferocious poses to serve as grave guardians, and C. Hart Merriam, following his boss's lead, took for himself a blanket draped over a grave. Neither considered their actions a desecration of the dead. Rather, the bears and the blanket were relics from a fast-vanishing Indigenous nation sure to melt in the American pot and disappear as a distinct people and culture.[20]

Reality, however, differed from what the *Elder's* eager collectors imagined. The Saanya Kwáan Tlingits who inhabited Cape Fox called their village Gaash. They had indeed fled during a smallpox outbreak about seven years earlier and settled some fifty miles northwest in the missionary community of Saxman, close to Ketchikan. Despite the wholesale move, the Saanyas never thought of Gaash as abandoned in the way the Harriman expedition's passengers did. Traditional Tlingit law holds that ḵwáan property remains the ḵwáan's forever—whether the people are present or not—continues to demand respect and reverence, and never becomes free for the taking. The Saanyas knew the appropriation of the totem poles and other objects as the theft that it was. Years later, the Saanyas returned to Gaash to retrieve the poles that survived the looting and transport them to Saxman, where they carved new versions of the poles Harriman and his fellow thieves had made off with.[21]

As John Muir watched the totems and other objects being gathered and hauled to the *Elder*, he must have been going through *déjà vu* all over again. On his first trip to Alaska twenty years earlier, he had witnessed Kadachan's indignity over the felling and theft of totem images by missionaries led by Sheldon Jackson, the Presbyterian dean of the territory. Kadachan accused Jackson of grave robbing, and although he accepted money for his ḵwáan's property, the act remained a sacrilege. Muir had to have that scene in mind as he watched the plunder of Gaash by the Harriman Alaska Expedition. Yet his response this time differed. Back then, he made clear his disgust at what he called sacrilege in the account he wrote for San Francisco's *Daily Evening Bulletin* and included in *Travels in Alaska*. At Gaash he recorded nothing about the looting in his journal, except to note that two half-grown Douglas squirrels, a favorite species, were discovered in one of the totems, then "caught and made into specimens, of course." Muir kept his protest to himself: when Edward Curtis gathered the *Elder's* trophy takers for a triumphant group portrait, the naturalist made sure he was well outside the camera's field of view. He was *not*, he made clear, one of them.[22]

The Harriman expedition's members saw nothing wrong in the liberties they were taking at Gaash. Carrying off totem poles, cultural artifacts, and grave goods was the enlightened action of forward-looking men and women who grasped evolution's inevitable trend and helped it along—and in the process added to personal collections and bolstered academic careers. Nostalgia coupled with manifest destiny to yield an arrogant exceptionalism that turned Indigenous cultures into nothing more than lifeless artifacts in a museum.

Feeling ebullient after Cape Fox, the passengers gathered for evening drinks and, according to Muir, a "mighty lively & merry, witty time." Luther "Yellowstone" Kelly, veteran army scout and one-time hunting companion to Theodore Roosevelt, entertained with his rendition of a "Sioux war dance" that Muir found "very effective." Kelly had hung out with Lakotas years earlier and even met Sitting Bull (Thatȟáŋka Íyotake) in person. He once tangled with two warriors, killing both but losing a finger and taking an arrow to the knee in the fight. Perhaps Kelly danced in a way faithful to the Lakota original. More likely, though, this transplanted New Yorker appropriated what he had seen in his days riding the northern plains and turned it to his own purpose to give these elite whites the savage display they expected. Kelly's dance caught the mood and purpose of the Harriman Alaska Expedition's totem-taking: what once belonged to Tlingits and Lakotas was now the property of Euro-America. Conquest was complete.[23]

Muir dutifully wrote up his observations of the glaciers he had explored and included them in the Harriman Alaska Expedition's official publications. Yet the more important legacy for Muir from the trip was the friendships he built aboard the *Elder*. The following year, he and C. Hart Merriam revisited the naturalist's formerly solitary haunts in the headwaters of the Tuolomne and Mokelumne Rivers, where Muir awed Merriam with his detailed knowledge of the region's glaciers and their history. Some years later he joined John Burroughs at the Grand Canyon for an excursion, then the two met up again in Yosemite Valley.[24] Yet the most important and seemingly surprising relationship to come from the expedition centered on E. H. Harriman himself, a connection that proved central to Muir's next big-time conservation victory.

While the mountain region surrounding Yosemite had been incorporated into Yosemite National Park in 1890, the valley itself remained under state control, as it had since 1864. California was a far more permissive proprietor than the U.S. government, friendly to profit-oriented vendors, and little troubled by overgrazing, timber cutting, garish hucksterism, and eyesore development. Year upon year, the valley was being trashed. Muir and his many supporters in the Sierra Club argued that the only way to save it from further desecration was for California to cede the valley to the federal government and then expand the national park to include the addition. When Muir and Theodore Roosevelt camped together for three days in Yosemite in May 1903, the naturalist had little trouble persuading the sportsman president that the spectacular valley belonged inside the magnificent park. That was the easy part. Both knew it would be much harder to convince the California legislature to give up the valley and the U.S. Congress to accept it. Working always in the background, E. H. Harriman—now head of Southern Pacific, California's dominant line, and the most powerful railroad man in the nation—played a central role in winning victory on both fronts.

Lacking the railroads, with their transcontinental routes and refrigerator cars, Muir never would have amassed the fortune he did from his Martinez orchard, so he was favorably disposed to the industry. Still, the alliance Muir made with the railroads reached much deeper than his own business success. The railroads and early proponents of national parks like Muir recognized that they sought some of the same outcomes. Park proponents wanted scenic wild lands preserved for the enjoyment of tourists looking to deepen their attachment to nature. The railroads wanted more passengers and freight to keep their revenues growing. Early preservationists and captains of the railroad industry agreed on another strategic point: all along the right of way and inside the park boundaries, Indigenous peoples had to go.

The rapid expansion of the West's rail system after the Civil War built on a massive giveaway of tribal lands granted by the Pacific Railway Act of 1862. In addition to eventually transferring 183 million acres to railroad control, lines of track sliced and diced what had been expansive tribal ranges into smaller and smaller pieces, often cutting Indigenous nations off from their homelands and hunting grounds. In addition, the railroads played a key role in the near extermination of the Great Plains bison herds and the resulting starvation of the peoples who depended upon them. Hungry Native Americans were forced onto reservations as their only way to survive, confining them to bad lands and hardscrabble leftovers. By the federal census of 1890—the same one that announced the end of the frontier—the Native

American population in the United States had fallen to fewer than a quarter million from a likely original of some five million people. Both popular and scholarly opinion held that it would fall further, as the assimilated survivors of the many wars shed their tribal identity.[25]

Muir, the Sierra Club, and the other preservationist proponents of national parks bought into the same belief. Yosemite Valley, as but one example, had been the realm of the Ahwahneechees and the Yosemites, but no longer. Driven out by the Mariposa Battalion in 1850s, the valley became the sacred possession of those Euro-Americans with the spiritual sensitivity to grasp its magnificence—something no "savage" or "barbarian" could do. The narrative of vanishing Native Americans served to erase their presence within parks that could now be managed in the enlightened way only civilized Euro-Americans understood.

These shared beliefs and interests drew preservationists and railroads into a common cause. And there was an additional reason for the alliance between Muir and Harriman: the two men held a deep and genuine affection for each other. Harriman was a hunter, a pursuit Muir abhorred, yet he shared the naturalist's abiding wonder at the wild world. And Harriman knew something of preservation; he had saved the extensive forests of his estate from axe and bandsaw and planned to bequeath them to his home state of New York. Muir saw Harriman as a transformative force of nature, comparing him to "glaciers making landscapes, cutting canyons through ridges, carrying off hills, laying rails and bridges over lakes and rivers, mountains and plains, making the nation's ways straight and smooth and safe, bringing everybody nearer to one another." He praised Harriman as an industrial patriarch who paid his employees well, invested in their safety, and demanded that they exercise the focus and discipline on the job he demanded of himself. Harriman was, Muir felt certain, "one of the rare souls Heaven sends into the world once in centuries."[26]

It hardly hurt Muir's enthusiasm for Harriman that the magnate had a knack for making big things happen. Besides building enormous cash reserves, he had mastered the railroads of the West by controlling the Union Pacific, Southern Pacific, Pacific Mail, and Northern Pacific and influencing the Santa Fe to his own benefit. This well-funded dominance made him the behind-the-scenes power source of the Republican Party apparatus throughout

California and the virtual political master of the entire state through what was popularly known as Southern Pacific's Political Bureau, a corruption-friendly lobbying machine that dominated the state as Tammany Hall did New York. Harriman exercised that considerable power through William F. Herrin, the railroad's chief counsel. Muir knew Herrin as well as Harriman, and the trio came together to end the state's control of Yosemite Valley.[27]

The bill put before the California legislature in 1905 to turn the valley over to the federal government had been written by William Colby, lawyer and charter Sierra Club member, and William H. Mills, part owner of the Sacramento *Record-Union* and Southern Pacific land agent. It passed the state assembly easily, but the senate offered a greater hurdle. Business interests that were profiting from doing as they pleased in Yosemite Valley fiercely opposed turning their operations over to the federal government's stricter scrutiny. Mills and Colby canvassed the senators, counted noses, and realized the bill was sure to fail. Hoping to find a last-minute path to victory, Muir appealed to Harriman about the bill: "If you are like-minded and could help us secure its passage, I wish you would."[28]

The railroader promptly telegraphed his support and then directed Herrin and his crack lobbying team to pull out all the stops. As the bill landed on the senate floor, a number of pro-railroad senators in Herrin's back pocket switched sides and passed it by a single vote. Colby, rejoicing, let Muir know of the victory and thanked the hand of providence. Muir knew better; he shot off thank-you letters to Harriman and Herrin. Later he told *Century* editor Robert Underwood Johnson how the final battle played out: "though most everybody was with us, so active was opposition of those pecuniarily and politically interested, we might have failed to get the bill through the Senate but for the help of Mr. H., though of course his name or his company were never in sight through all the fight."[29]

The following year, the fight shifted to Washington DC. Yosemite Concessionaires, ranchers, and lumbermen lobbied to stop or delay the bill that would incorporate the valley into the national park. When the cause once again looked no better than doubtful, Muir went back to the well. Again Harriman agreed to help. The railroad magnate interceded through his many lobbyists in both the House and the Senate, and the bill passed. On June 11, 1906, Pres. Theodore Roosevelt signed the Yosemite Valley law.

Muir had saved his happiest place from desecration and destruction. No doubt remembering the marvels of his Yosemite camping trip with Muir three years earlier, Roosevelt agreed. And he understood the law's significance in furthering his own global dream "that America, Australia, and Siberia should pass out of the hands of their red, black, and yellow aboriginal owners, and become the heritage of the dominant world races."[30]

More than allies, Muir and Harriman were friends and companions. In the summer of 1908 Harriman invited Muir to come and stay with him and his family at their recently acquired lodge on Pelican Bay in Upper Klamath Lake. Harriman had purchased the place as a wilderness getaway, and it offered him a strategic perch to oversee the Southern Pacific's expansion into south-central Oregon and leave no money on the table. When Harriman's invitation came, Muir at first begged off, explaining that he was too bogged down in a so far fruitless attempt to write his autobiography to leave the vexing project behind. Phooey, said Harriman, "you come up to the Lodge and I will show you how to write books." Muir did go, and when his writer's block continued, Harriman ordered his personal secretary to follow the naturalist around, capture his musings in shorthand, then type them for review. The process worked so well that Muir stayed most of the summer. He had a serviceable first draft in his bag when he and Harriman left Upper Klamath Lake to travel together to Portland—by rail of course. "At the stations along the road," Muir wrote of Harriman's triumphal progress across Oregon, "he was hailed by enthusiastic crowds assembled to pay their respects, recognizing the good he had done and was doing in developing the country and laying broad and deep the foundations of prosperity."[31]

Early the next year, during a trip to Arizona and Southern California, Muir detoured to consult with Harriman over the Colorado River flood that had inundated much of the Imperial Valley, wiped out the town of Mexicali just across the border with Mexico, and created the Salton Sea.[32] As they walked and talked about the engineering challenge of returning the great river to its original course, Muir surely noticed that Harriman was looking unwell. The railroad baron complained of an ever-worsening upset stomach that dulled appetite and drained energy. Soon the malady was diagnosed as stomach cancer too far along to treat. Harriman died before the year was out.

The death hit Muir hard; his circle of friends and family was shrinking fast. Longtime close friend Joseph C. LeConte—one-time slave owner, popular apologist for white supremacy, University of California professor, and wilderness enthusiast—had died of a sudden heart attack on the first Sierra Club summer campout in Yosemite Valley. Next, he stayed at the bedside while his wife, Louie, sickened and died from lung cancer at age fifty-eight. Her passing left Muir unmoored, devastated, and bereft. Daughter Wanda had married and moved away, and daughter Helen was about to. Now Muir bumped about the Martinez mansion on the knoll alone but for a handful of anonymous Chinese servants. Harriman's passing at age sixty-one capped Muir's string of losses. "I feel very lonesome now my friend Harriman is gone," he confided in John Burroughs. "At first rather repelled, I at last learned to love him."[33]

In the years following Harriman's death, Muir continued a close relationship with Harriman's widow, Mary, who remained his friend and patron for the rest of his life. She centered a network of powerful, preservation-minded friends, acquaintances, and allies drawn together by a city-leveling earthquake, America's changing face, and the rediscovered heredity experiments of an Austrian monk. Drawn by his vision for protecting wilderness, Muir soon found a central place within this emerging coalition.

12

River Out of Eden

And a river went out of Eden to water the garden; and from thence it was parted.

—GENESIS 2:10

In the fall of 1872, late enough in the year that the first snow could fall any day, a young John Muir trussed up wool blankets, coffee, three loaves of bread, and a popular tinned beef-extract spread from the pampas of Uruguay. Hefting the bundle onto his back, Muir sauntered from Yosemite Valley toward another glacial valley some twenty miles to the northwest. He climbed the divide between the Merced and Tuolumne Rivers, then followed the downhill track left by a family of grizzlies. Muir was careful to make noise as he walked; he didn't want to stumble into a startled sow defending her cubs. Still, the unseen animals' path took him where he wanted to go, into the wide, deep canyon called Hetch Hetchy.

Muir likely did not know that the valley's name came from a still-unidentified grass with edible seeds that the Central Sierra Me-Wuks cooked into a mush and named *hetch-hetch-e* or *hatchatchie*. On that first visit, Muir encountered recent evidence of an Indigenous presence that dates back some 10,000 years. "A group of Indian huts," he noticed, sat near the rushing Tuolumne River. The valley was "diversified with groves and meadows in the same manner as Yosemite," he reported, taking special note of "fine groves of the black oak" and their delectable acorns. That staple food source drew the tribes to Hetch Hetchy and led them to steward the trees with controlled

170

burns that removed invasive brush and saplings and tamped down pest infestations. Add the well-maintained "berry gardens and acorn orchards" to the *hetch-hetch-e* seeds and other edible plants, throw in abundant black-tailed deer with their savory venison, and it's easy to see why Indigenous tribes—particularly the ancestors of the Central Sierra Me-Wuks and Southern Sierra Miwuks from the western Sierra and the Kutzadika'as from the eastern side—had been making their way into Hetch Hetchy for ten millennia. And these Indigenous residents left marks besides controlled burns: seasonal villages, hunting camps, sacred sites, gathering fields and groves, and petroglyphs. The Central Sierra Me-Wuks even set one of their creation myths in Hetch Hetchy, clear sign of the place's centrality to their worldview.

Besides the "Indian huts," Muir spotted summer shelters used by sheep herders whose search for pasture first brought Euro-Americans into Hetch Hetchy. As early as 1850, the wonderfully surnamed Screech brothers—Joseph, Nathan, and William—led their ever-hungry animals into the valley's meadows "when the D—— Indians held possession of it as an acorn orchard." In Muir's retelling, it was an abundance the Indigenous people were willing to share. Nathan Screech married a tribal woman and learned the Central Sierra Me-Wuk dialect, a sign that his and his brothers' sojourn was friendly, not hostile.

Above all else, Hetch Hetchy stood as a place in thrall to water. Great glaciers had carved the Tuolumne's valleys and waterfalls, much as they had the similarly sculpted Yosemite Valley along the Merced. The river and its many tributaries that formed in the glacier's retreat created a fertile corridor through which Indigenous peoples moved, hunted, gathered, settled, and traded along and across the Sierra Nevada spine. "Please communicate that the whole river is used," a tribal elder told contemporary researcher Shelly Davis-King. "The Tuolomne is the silver thread that connects our places. The whole river is important. What do you hold sacred if it is broken up?"[1]

Indeed, the silver thread would be broken up for the very reason that Hetch Hetchy is all about water. San Francisco, you see, is a thirsty place.

For all its natural advantage as one of the planet's finest harbors, San Francisco lacks a reliable local water source. The climate is Mediterranean, with adequate rain only in the winter, and even then the sandy soil absorbs too little to keep streams running through the dry months. Right from the city's beginnings as a gold-rush boomtown in the late 1840s, water offered a profit opportunity for peddlers who filled up tank wagons elsewhere and hawked their wet wares on the city's streets. The peddlers gathered into several companies that consolidated in the 1870s to form the monopolistic Spring Valley Water Company. Thinking ahead, the company's leaders had bought up almost all water sources and watersheds around the Bay Area to monopolize the supply. Fights over water rates became a perennial fact of life in the city.

Small wonder, then, that San Francisco's leaders began casting about for a way to develop their own water supply and undercut Spring Valley Water's greed. In 1900 the California legislature passed a new city charter that required San Francisco to own its utilities. Rather than buy Spring Valley Water and reward its owners, Mayor James D. Phelan wanted to find alternative water sources, even at a distance.[2]

For Phelan, public works were essential to urban grandeur. A wealthy Democrat whose political power came from San Francisco's large, working-class Irish Catholic community, the mayor wanted to build a refined, beautiful city to rival ancient Rome. And since the capital of the Caesars boasted aqueducts delivering water from far away, Phelan's San Francisco needed the best equivalent modern civil engineering could deliver.

There was American precedent as well. New York City had tapped the Catskills to water its growth, and Los Angeles was reaching into Owens Valley on the eastern side of the Sierra Nevada. San Francisco could follow the same strategy of pulling distant sources in as close as dams, pumps, and aqueducts would bring them. This was, after all, the new Progressive Era of enlightened resource management serving the needs of a fast-growing nation.[3]

Phelan solicited reports on possible water sources from various engineers in the federal government and San Francisco's Public Works Commission. Most of them liked the looks of Hetch Hetchy. It lay an unappealing 150 miles away, but the valley's flat floor, copious river flow, and narrow opening on the downstream end made what Muir had taken to calling the Yosemite of the Tuolomne a prime reservoir site. When Phelan learned that the dam, reservoir, and aqueduct system could be built for $38 million, about the price to buy Spring Valley Water outright, he set his sights on Hetch Hetchy. Yes, it did fall within the boundaries of Yosemite National Park, but that was an advantage: Hetch Hetchy had only one landlord, the federal government, a legal reality that simplified the sticky spider's web of California water law. Given the apparent ease of engineering, distance from Yosemite Valley's tourist buzz, and legal simplicity, damming Hetch Hetchy became the apple of James D. Phelan's urbanizing eye.[4]

At first the effort went Phelan's way. Pres. Theodore Roosevelt signed the Right of Way Act in 1901, giving the Secretary of the Interior the power to route aqueducts through California's national parks. San Francisco applied for a permit to dam Hetch Hetchy and nearby Lake Eleanor under that law, which said nothing about permitting reservoirs and required that the parks' scenery and beauty be preserved. Ethan Hitchcock, then Secretary of the Interior, denied San Francisco's application on the grounds that the Hetch Hetchy project violated Yosemite's wild integrity as a national park. Phelan and the city came back twice, and each time Hitchcock said no.[5] Hetch Hetchy looked to be dead.

On April 18, 1906, the San Francisco earthquake brought it back to life. When hydrants went dry as firefighters tried to knock down blazes consuming the shattered city, public anger rose over the water system's sorry shape. Soon Phelan's dream of an imperial city watered by Sierra Nevada snows was reborn. Less than a year after the earthquake, Hitchcock resigned as Interior secretary and was replaced by James Garfield, who was well connected to San Francisco's political leaders and enjoyed direct access to the Oval Office. In May 1908, Garfield reversed Hitchcock's decision and allowed work to go forward on limited parts of the Hetch Hetchy project. The dam was yet to be fully approved, but the idea was once again on the table, much to the displeasure of John Muir and the Sierra Club.[6]

The struggle between pro- and anti-dam forces turned on a core disagreement about the nature and purpose of wilderness. Personified by Chief U.S. Forester Gifford Pinchot, the son of a timber magnate and a one-time Muir confidante and ally, the conservationists held that a civilized society required the enlightened management of natural resources to fuel growth and prosperity. National forests provided timber, water, and pasture. Their utility lay in the social benefit they delivered—lumber to build houses, water to drink, hydroelectricity to power trolleys and light homes, range to fatten cattle and sheep. Hetch Hetchy made sense as dam and reservoir because this remote, little-visited valley could serve the greater good of San Francisco's many citizens.

Not so fast, countered Muir and his preservationist allies. Wilderness had value in and of itself; mountains, valleys, and wild rivers were literally priceless, beyond economic valuation. Wild spaces provided both physical recreation and spiritual renewal for urbanized people frazzled and worn by the demands of their increasingly technological world. The national park boundary represented a temple wall separating the sacred within from the secular outside. Violate Hetch Hetchy, as the dam would, and the wild's virginal holiness was sullied. Muir held Hetch Hetchy to be irreplaceable, "as if into this glorious mountain temple Nature had gathered her choicest treasures, whether great or small, to draw her lovers into close, confiding communion with her." Muir meant to sound religious. The fight over Hetch Hetchy figured as "part of the universal battle between right and wrong," he wrote. Against the dam's proponents he directed the righteous fervor of an enraged Jeremiah: "These temple destroyers, devotees of ravaging commercialism, seem to have a perfect contempt for Nature, and instead of lifting their eyes to the mountains, lift them to dollars and dams. Dam Hetch Hetchy! As well dam for water-tanks the people's cathedrals and churches, for no holier temple has ever been consecrated by the heart of man."[7]

The dam's proponents launched their own war of words. William Kent, the wealthy California congressman who, ironically, donated the redwood grove that became Muir Woods National Monument, said that his one-time ally "is a man entirely without social sense. With him, it is me and God and the rock where God put it, and that is the end of the story." San Francisco's city engineer Marsden Manson assailed the dam's opponents as lacking the stones to proceed with so daring a project as Hetch Hetchy, proclaiming them "short-haired women and long-haired men." James Phelan laced social class with gender. Real men, like the Irish Catholic workers who had formed the backbone of Phelan's political movement, labored hard to produce real wealth. In the national effort to create the greatest good for the greatest number, "wilderness must yield to civilization," Phelan argued. Those who opposed the dam came from the same stock as England's well-heeled and well-mounted fox hunters, who could pursue their sport on reserves set aside for their exclusive use and closed to proletarian underlings. Noble as the pursuit of game was, "the hunter is the forerunner of the pioneer; but we cannot maintain the conditions of the wilderness when the pioneer wants to build a home." Muir's wilderness contemplation must yield to urban thirst.[8]

As stinging as the name-calling was and as great as the divide between the two sides gaped, neither disagreed that it was up to Euro-Americans to decide Hetch Hetchy's future. The struggle between reservoir and preserve fell well within manifest destiny's mandate. No one ever thought to ask the Central Sierra Me-Wuks and the Kutzadika'as about their concerns for the valley within their home territories, nor to consult with the five other Yosemite tribes over the national park's future. Not a chance: Hetch Hetchy was a political fight among Euro-Americans over the best use of their conquered continent, not over the conquest itself.

When Phelan called Hetch Hetchy's opponents fox hunters, he was arguing that the struggle was all about rich people preserving a playground for their own pleasure. That's where Mary W. Harriman entered the picture.

When railroad magnate E. H. Harriman died in September 1909, his entire fortune became the property of his wife, Mary, as sole beneficiary. Into her widowed and well-bred hands passed an estate that included some 64,000 miles of rail lines and was valued at between $70 million and $200 million—$2 billion and $5.8 billion in today's currency. Upon becoming the richest woman in America, Harriman continued to direct the business. Rail operations ran in her blood; her father had headed up the old Ogdensburg and Lake Champlain Railroad. Her soul work, though, was philanthropy. Within six months of her husband's death, she was flooded with charitable requests totaling $250 million. Harriman was picky; she chose to finance only those causes she felt deeply about and wished to promote. That was why she helped fund her friend Muir's nationwide campaign against Hetch Hetchy. It was also why she provided the start-up funds to launch the eugenics movement in the United States.[9]

Harriman's commitment to helping the best breed and the worst fade away began with her daughter, also named Mary, who was described as captivating and vivacious. The younger Mary studied sociology at Barnard and, after graduating, took a summer internship in a laboratory established with Carnegie Institute money only a year earlier at Cold Spring Harbor on Long Island's North Shore. Set up to study evolution experimentally, the lab was headed by Charles Davenport. A conservative, well-born, ambitious, Harvard-trained zoologist, Davenport often wore white to signal his commitment to eugenics' purity. His project aimed to study how "defective" individuals, particularly those from lower and immigrant classes, passed on debilitating physical and mental characteristics that consigned their offspring to bordellos, prisons, and asylums. Excited by the promise of this work, daughter Mary introduced mother Mary to Davenport. Soon the elder Harriman and the eugenics scientist were meeting—in Harriman's brownstone on Manhattan's Fifth Avenue, on her 186-foot yacht *Sultana*, at Davenport's lab office, over lunch at the Ladies Annex to New York City's Metropolitan Club. In 1910 Harriman made a donation to found the Eugenics Record Office (ERO) and seventy-five acres of Cold Spring Harbor real estate to build it on. Harriman also established an annual maintenance fund to keep the ERO humming. Over time the yearly grants rose into the hundreds of thousands of dollars—millions by today's measure—and were augmented by funding from John D. Rockefeller, Jr. The investment paid off right from the beginning. In 1911, the ERO published its first bulletin: *Heredity of Feeble-mindedness* by Henry H. Goddard. Other such publications and a program of public-policy advocacy would follow. Davenport was nothing if not an evangelist.[10]

The term *eugenics* had been coined by biologist and statistician Francis Galton, a cousin to Charles Darwin, almost three decades earlier. He combined the Greek roots -*eu* (good) and -*genēs* (born) to create a term describing policies and actions taken to favor reproduction of the fittest and prevent breeding by the unfit. Galton's interest in applying evolutionary theory to race got a shot in the arm when he, as well as other turn-of-the-century biologists, rediscovered Gregor Mendel's mid-century research on inheritance. An Austrian monk who studied sweet peas he bred experimentally in the monastery garden, Mendel demonstrated that certain characteristics, such as flower color and overall height, were passed down from generation to generation in a predictable pattern of dominants and recessives. For researchers like Galton and his disciple Davenport, Mendel's genetics lent racial theorists the evolutionary mechanism they had been looking for. In the received Western wisdom of the time, individuals, cultures, races, and nations could be arrayed on a ladder from lower to higher, savage to civilized. Surely heredity was the key to this hierarchy, and science could elucidate and manage its workings to benefit society. That was what Davenport set out to do at the ERO. Geneticists couldn't control human breeding the way Mendel manipulated his sweet peas' sex lives. Still, they could gather the pedigrees of individuals under study and identify the characteristics these subjects had inherited and were sure to pass on to their offspring for good or ill. Enlightened public policy would follow science's revelations and offer the best and longest-lasting solutions to vexing social issues.

This all made obvious sense to science-minded Progressives in the early twentieth century. Almost no one questioned eugenics researchers who declared that complex human characteristics, such as sexual appetite, feeble-mindedness, and intelligence, were inherited in the same, simple way as flower color in Mendel's sweet peas. Davenport, as well as other research-ers, equated nationality with race and declared that the two determined how individuals from those groups looked, fared, and behaved. He noted that Germans and Scandinavians tended toward thrift, intelligence, and chastity that contributed to "good manners, high culture, and the ability to lead in all social affairs." The Irish, by contrast, tipped toward "alcoholism, considerable mental defectiveness, and a tendency to tuberculosis." Even the Irish penchant for machine politics—think of their decades-long role in New York City's Tammany Hall—arose from a racial characteristic favor-ing graft. Italians displayed "a tendency for crimes of personal violence," inherited of course, and Jews, owing to their defective genes, fell on the "opposite extreme from the early English and more recent Scandinavian immigration."[11]

Eugenics caught on because it fed fear and loathing among Anglo-Saxon Protestant Americans even as it offered them pseudo-scientific solace. Eugen-ics made them feel special, selected by evolutionary genetics to reign and rule. It played, too, into their dread of an apocalypse brought on by immi-grant hordes from southern and eastern Europe determined to outbreed and push them aside. This feared future was dubbed race suicide—that era's version of today's great replacement theory. The anti-Semitism and racism implicit in eugenics appealed to its supporters not as an atavistic impulse to bigotry and hate so much as beneficent, enlightened science brought to bear on the hard facts of social reality. This was a time when one could believe simultaneously in social reform to improve the human condition and in an inherited racial hierarchy verified by science. The Progressive Era held both ideas to be true at the same time.[12]

Conservation and preservation each offered a similar appeal, and eugenics proponents lined up on both sides of the Hetch Hetchy fight. Some saw the reservoir as advanced, science-based management of natural resources for the greater public good. An example was David Starr Jordan. The first president of Stanford University and a one-time Sierra Club director, Jordan walked away from the organization after splitting with Muir over Hetch Hetchy. More eugenicists, however, particularly the most ardent, took Muir's preservationist side because they valued spectacular scenery over urban utility. They saw wilderness as the hard-yet-sacred environment that had transformed Anglo-Saxons a.k.a. Nordics or Aryans—into the dominant and domineering race that built America. Allowing Hetch Hetchy to be dammed and flooded not only swamped irreplaceable scenery but also sapped the strength of the supreme race. Muir drew active support from several prominent and powerful eugenicists, notably Charles Eliot, Harvard University president; Vernon Kellogg, Stanford biologist and Sierra Club director; and Luther Burbank, famed horticulturalist and plant breeder. Towering above them all was Henry Fairfield Osborn.[13]

Osborn, a friend to both Mary W. Harriman and John Muir, was his era's version of public intellectual on the order of Anthony Fauci or Neil deGrasse Tyson. Born to wealth in a family that included kingpin financier J. Pierpont Morgan, Osborn considered eminence his due. After all, he was the Princeton-trained vertebrate paleontologist who had named *Tyrannosaurus rex* as a species and went on to head the American Museum of Natural History. When he was elected secretary of the Smithsonian Institution, the highest scientific position in the country, Osborn turned the honor down. His research and leadership calendar was too packed to take on the added responsibility that came with the accolade.[14]

Osborn and Muir became fast friends after being introduced by *The Century* editor Robert Underwood Johnson. They spent time together as often as residents on opposite sides of the continent could. Muir and the

Osborn family cruised together through Alaska's Inside Passage in 1896. And whenever Muir was in the East, particularly after Louie Muir's death, he was a frequent house guest at Castle Rock, Osborn's grand country manse up the Hudson River from New York City. Whenever distance separated the two, correspondence flowed between them.

Although Muir and Osborn came from different social classes and educational backgrounds, they shared similar views on science and religion. Muir saw evolution not as the bloody survival of the fittest but as the unfolding of the Divine's loving creation. Osborn similarly understood evolution as a spiritual force joining science and religion. He wrote that "from the earliest times Nature has been regarded as the work of God, full of moral beauty, truth, and splendor." It made sense that the naturalist was a religious individual; after all, "primitive religion issues out of the heart of Nature in reverence for the powers of the unseen." Science all by its lonesome fell short: "Here nature, religion, and beauty, kept apart by the superficial vision of man in science, theology, and aesthetics, are one in the eternal vision and purpose of the Creator."[15]

This unity became incarnate in John Muir. The naturalist, Osborn wrote, felt deeply that "all the works of nature are directly the works of God. In this sense I have never known anyone whose nature-philosophy was more thoroughly theistic; at the same time he was a thorough-going evolutionist and always delighted in my own evolutionary studies, which I described to him from time to time in the course of our journeyings and conversations." Osborn was sure that Muir's point of view arose from both nature and nurture. He explained, "I learned through correspondence and through long and intimate conversations thoroughly to understand his Scotch soul, which had a strong Norse element in it and a moral fervor drawn from the Bible of the Covenanters."[16]

Long years of study in the field and the laboratory led Osborn to claim for himself a deep "penetration into the sources of human character and personality . . . due to my studies in heredity and my observations on the difference in races and racial characteristics." Race was all important, for "distinctive spiritual and intellectual powers originate along lines of slow racial evolution in climate and surroundings of distinct kinds," Osborn argued. He divided "*Homo sapiens* into three absolutely distinct stocks, which in zoology would be given the rank of species, if not genera; these stocks are popularly known as the Caucasian, the Mongolian, and the Negroid." The biological divisions among these three varieties of human were, according to Osborn, as deep-rooted and absolute as those dividing domestic dogs from foxes and jackals. As he saw it, "The spiritual, intellectual, moral, and physical characters which separate these three human stocks are very profound and ancient." We humans were not all one, not by a long shot.

As Osborn saw the matter, not even all Caucasians were equal white people. Rather, Europe's nations fell into three races distinguished by characteristics so stark "that if we encountered them among birds or mammals we should certainly call them *species* rather than *races*." The most highly evolved, a race bred to conquer and rule, were the Nordics: a tall, fair-haired people that included not only Scandinavians but also Anglo-Saxons, northern Germans, and Lowland Scots like Muir. Nordics were "fond of the open, curious and inquisitive about the causes of things; deliberate in spiritual development," and "very gradually they reached the greatest intellectual heights and depths." Then there were the broad-headed and broad-faced Alpines, a.k.a. Celts. They arose in Central Europe, a talented race but "neither adventurous nor sea-loving." Last and lowest came the dark-eyed Mediterraneans; think Italians, southern French, and Greeks. Great sailors and artists for sure, yet they mistook nature for God, lacked any aptitude for study and contemplation, and could never rise as high as Nordics or Alpines in conquest or intellect.

Muir's genius turned on his being a Scot, according to Osborn. Evolutionary racial reality gave him the nature-penetrating heart of a Norse sea-rover. And Muir proved to be a warrior renowned for his Viking-style "fearlessness of attack, well illustrated in his assault on the despoilers of the Hetch Hetchy Valley of the Yosemite, whom he loved to characterize as 'thieves and robbers.' It was a great privilege to be associated with him in this campaign."[17]

It only made sense for Osborn to join Muir in the fight to stop the dam. "It appears," he wrote, "that the finest races of man, like the finest races of lower animals, arose when Nature had full control, and that civilized man is upsetting the divine order of human origin and progress." What could be more civilized than the wilderness-violating Hetch Hetchy dam, reservoir, and aqueduct? Small wonder that "in America the original pioneer stock is dying out; the foreign element is in the ascendency." Osborn made clear what had to happen: "Care for the race, even if the individual must suffer—this must be the keynote of the future."[18]

The men Osborn recruited into the save-Hetch-Hetchy campaign shared his white-supremacist views. The most prominent, and notorious, among them was long-time friend Madison Grant. Like Osborn, Grant came from ancestral lines privileged by power and wealth since colonial times. Sent to Germany in adolescence to study with private tutors, Grant returned to the United States to graduate from Yale and earn a law degree at Columbia. He passed the bar and for a time maintained a law office, but, with no need to earn money beyond his massive inheritance, Grant turned into a professional joiner, founder, and leader of elite WASP clubs, most of them alarmed by the surge in immigration. An avid and accomplished hunter, he was a founding member of the Boone and Crockett Club and a cofounder of the New York Zoological Society, known now as the Wildlife Conservation Society. Grant led Osborn to see that wilderness preservation and eugenics were two sides of the same coin: pure wilderness, pure race.[19]

While the Hetch Hetchy fight boiled, Grant was working on a book manuscript that built on the pseudo-scientific white supremacy Osborn championed. Entitled *The Passing of the Great Race: or, The Racial Basis of European History*, the draft so impressed Osborn that he served as one of Grant's early readers, proposed revisions, wrote a laudatory preface, and put the manuscript in front of Charles Scribner, his publisher and old Princeton friend. The conservative, patrician Scribner liked what he read. He signed a publishing contract with Grant and handled the project himself before passing it on to famed editor Maxwell Perkins. The first printing of what would be four editions rolled off the press and into bookstores in 1916, then posted modest but steady sales based on praise-filled reviews. Theodore Roosevelt lauded *The Passing of the Great Race* as "a capital book; in purpose, in vision, in grasp of the facts our people most need to realize." The *New York Herald* praised it as "a profound study of world history from the ethnological standpoint." *The Nation* pointed to Grant's "originality, conviction, and courage." Scholarly journals, like *Science* and the *Journal of Heredity*, groused about the lack of footnotes and Grant's partisan tone yet largely agreed with the book's premises and conclusions. The principal dissenter was the "father" of American anthropology, Franz Boas. Boas advocated strongly for the importance of culture over race, and he was moving to distance his academic discipline from pseudo-scientific eugenics. He rejected Grant's racial hierarchy and saw the book as ideological screed rather than scientific analysis. Most general readers, however, didn't care what an academic like Boas thought. They bought the book anyway.[20]

Boas was stating the obvious: practically nothing in *The Passing of the Great Race* was original. The book amounted to a gathering of other authors on hot topics, from anti-Semitism and Christ's Nordic heritage to mixed-race breeding as the fast track to cultural decline. Because Grant argued for these borrowed racist ideas in a clear, entertaining style that non-scholars could grasp, the book worked commercially. With *The Passing of the Great Race* making its way to libraries, bookshelves, and coffee tables, the biological threat that inferior races, including the swelling floods of eastern and southern European immigrants, posed to old-stock Americans moved from private speculation to public fact.

The time for action had come, Grant declared: "Neither the black, nor the brown, nor the yellow, nor the red will conquer the white in battle. But if the valuable elements in the Nordic race mix with inferior strains or die out through race suicide, then the citadel of civilization will fall for mere lack of defenders." Nordic Euro-America had its back against the racial wall, and the slow slide toward the bottom had already begun. "If the Melting Pot is allowed to boil without control and we continue to follow our national motto and deliberately blind ourselves to all 'distinctions of race, creed, or color,'" he wrote, "the type of native American of Colonial descent will become as extinct as the Athenian of the age of Pericles, and the Viking of the days of Rollo."[21]

Despite its singular focus on race, Grant's masterwork, like Henry Fairfield Osborn's later *Man Rises to Parnassus*, largely skipped over the Indigenous peoples of the Americas. Defeated and dispossessed, felled by violence, disease, and poverty, they mattered to Osborn only as Stone Age relics and to Grant as inferior gene pools. In their alliance with Muir over Hetch Hetchy, Grant and Osborn did not care that the Indigenous peoples of the Tuolumne and Merced drainages were never consulted about the fate of their homelands. History's inexorable racial forces had already pushed them aside, the two authors reasoned. The region's original residents could hope for nothing beyond physical survival, and even that was no guarantee.[22]

Grant's impassioned screed won him admirers not only in the United States but also in Europe, where a fierce blood-and-soil nationalism was rising. The German translation of Grant's book, *Der Untergang der Grossen Rasse*, won many admirers, among them an up-and-coming political star who penned an admiring fan letter to Grant. "The book is my Bible," wrote Adolf Hitler.[23]

The final acts of this transoceanic ideological drama played out well after the Hetch Hetchy saga had come to its sour end and Muir had departed the scene. And while he surely knew Osborn's racist thinking in detail from their many conversations, and Grant's as well, Muir never commented one way or another about either. Likely he more or less agreed with them. As a Lowland Scot and thereby a birthright Anglo-Saxon, Muir had little reason to dispute the white supremacy of the era and the privilege it lent him. In addition, its pseudo-scientific, evolutionary wrapping further convinced him, as it persuaded many of his peers. Still, the scientific glitter eugenic thinking gave American racism wasn't the point for Muir. What mattered was that Osborn, Grant, and their many powerful, well-placed associates and colleagues joined him as comrades in the fight to preserve wilderness. The rest, as far as Muir was concerned, was simply by the by.

As of the spring and summer of 1911, the Hetch Hetchy struggle looked to be heading in the direction Muir, Osborn, Grant, and their allies hoped for. A year earlier, Muir had guided Pres. William Howard Taft around Yosemite Valley, then took Interior Secretary Richard Ballinger to see Hetch Hetchy's grandeur firsthand. The experience left both skeptical about the viability of San Francisco's dam ambitions.

There was more good news. The wild-lands system—which had grown during Theodore Roosevelt's presidency to four national reserves, five national parks, eighteen national monuments, fifty-one bird reserves, and 150 national forests—grew yet again when Montana's Glacier National Park was added after a decades-long campaign led by George Bird Grinnell. The new park came at a price: it cut the Blackfeet (Piegans) off from what had been the western half of their homeland. Further, it denied them hunting, fishing, and gathering rights granted under an 1895 treaty negotiated by Grinnell himself when the tribe desperately needed money to fend off starvation. But it didn't matter to preservationists or conservationists that the Blackfeet had been disadvantaged under color of law, an injustice that continues to this day. Rather, they felt triumph in setting aside a spectacular landscape that embodied Euro-America's notion of pristine, Indigenous-free wilderness.[24]

Given breathing room by these victories, the aging Muir resurrected a dream from his young manhood. Back then he had planned to follow his walk to the Gulf of Mexico with a saunter through South America in the footsteps of the great naturalist-explorer Alexander von Humboldt, only to be stopped by malaria and prevented from getting farther south than Cuba. Muir never lost his youthful ambition to go all the way. In the spring of 1911 he wrote a friend, "Have I forgotten the Amazon, Earth's greatest river? Never, never, never. It has been burning in me half a century, and will burn forever." Always the long-range traveler and enthusiastic admirer of great trees, Muir hatched a new plan to travel far. He would see the great river of his dreams and seek out the wondrously remote and rare monkey puzzle tree of the Andes, then cross the Atlantic to southern Africa, where the equally wondrous baobab called to him.

Before he could leave, Muir had to hit his deadlines on the manuscript for *My Boyhood and Youth* and the page proofs of *The Yosemite*. The book on the park was timely, for its long praise song ended on a chorus to Hetch Hetchy "as a grand landscape garden, one of Nature's rarest and most precious mountain temples." To get the book just right, the endlessly word-fussy Muir holed up at Mary W. Harriman's Manhattan townhouse and at Osborn's Castle Rock mansion. "I'm now pretty well hidden up here on Professor Osborn's place in a cabin in a grove of hickory finishing the Yosemite book," he wrote to daughter Helen. After weeks of doing work that he found endlessly tedious, Muir sent the proofs off to Robert Underwood Johnson and the manuscript to the Houghton Mifflin Company. Then he made his way to the Brooklyn harbor to await a ship bound for South America. On August 12, 1911, seventy-three-year-old John Muir sailed away.[25]

This last big trip of his life swelled into an eight-month, forty-thousand-mile odyssey. He made his way a thousand miles up the Amazon, then crossed South America to Chile before looping back to Montevideo, where he found passage to the other side of the Atlantic. He sailed down the west coast of Africa and around the Cape of Good Hope to explore the continent's southernmost reaches by railroad. He continued on to the Swahili coast of East Africa and traveled overland to the north shore of Lake Victoria and back. Heading home, Muir sailed around the Horn of Africa and up the Red Sea through the Suez Canal into the Mediterranean and then the Atlantic. He landed back in New York in late March 1912.[26]

Muir did lay eyes on the trees he so much wanted to see, thanks in both cases to Indigenous people. The botanical museum in Santiago, Chile, gave him only general directions to where he might find the unusual monkey puzzle tree—so named because its interlocking spines keep even a deft monkey from scaling the trunk—hundreds of miles to the south. There he connected with the English-speaking ranchers and lumbermen Messrs. Smith, Hunter, and Williams, whose Indigenous workers, most likely Mapuches, knew right where to find this amazing, rare, and characteristically Chilean tree in their exquisitely green Patagonian homeland.

Much the same happened at Africa's Victoria Falls, on the border between Zambia and Zimbabwe, then known as Northern and Southern Rhodesia. The European hotel owner hadn't the least idea where Muir could find a baobab and wasn't even sure what the strikingly unusual tree looked like. Anxious that he might miss his chance, Muir asked around until he turned up a "plump n—— boy guide" who took him directly to a stand of baobabs only a mile and half from the falls. In neither South America nor Africa did Muir pen names for the Indigenous people who pointed him toward his pilgrim heart's desire. The trees registered as major events; the Indigenous people who got him there did not.[27]

What stands out about Muir's last great journey is not only what he saw but what he looked right past. The Amazon was, and remains, the planet's greatest wilderness, yet by the time Muir arrived, extractive industries rooted in colonialism had been plundering this wild world and its Indigenous peoples for four centuries. Rubber was the hot commodity of the moment, and the Brazilian city of Manaus had grown almost overnight into a boomtown flaunting every vice and excess of sudden wealth. The rubber rush pushed rainforest tribes to the margins where they scraped along as peons in small, poor, riverside villages. Muir lamented the rapacious clear-cutting and burning that was devastating old-growth rainforest, yet he had nothing to say about the human toll taken among that same forest's Indigenous peoples.[28]

The same held true for Africa. The Berlin Conference of 1884–85 had divided nearly the entire continent into zones for European colonial powers to conquer and exploit at will. No one in Berlin asked the continent's Indigenous peoples about this arrangement; Europeans simply barged in, almost always by force, and took what they wanted. Many Africans resisted their mandated subjection in various uprisings, rebellions, insurgencies, and wars that flared throughout the late nineteenth and early twentieth centuries. Yet, as Muir coasted along what had recently been battlefronts and killing fields, he never mentioned these struggles.

Muir's journal recorded the ship's stop at Swakopmund in German South West Africa, known now as Namibia, to pick up passengers he described as "a large number, 100 or more, third class, a curious assortment of n——s chiefly." At the next stop, Lüderitz Bay, the landscape caught his eye. "The harbor is quite extensive and picturesque," he wrote in his journal. "The rocks very resisting but extremely barren. Not a tree in sight. Charmingly sculptured like those of Alaska bays. Grand mountains about a hundred miles inland." As to the atrocities that just a few years earlier had killed most of the colony's Herero and Nama people in a rebellion, Muir said not a word. The Germans had done nothing to hide the slaughter, and American newspapers covered it regularly. Muir must have known what had happened here, yet his journal recorded nothing about it.[29]

Further evidence of imperial colonialism lay all about him. The streetcars in Mozambique were hauled "by a span of n——s instead of a span of mules." In Kampala, Uganda, Muir traveled in a rickshaw "hauled and pushed by three lusty n——s, two pushing and the other in the shafts." The trio kept rhythm by singing a work chant whose chorus sounded to Muir like "Harry Trunk! Harry Trunk!" Making the acquaintance of several fellow Europeans on the train from Mombasa to Entebbe, Muir recorded each man's name and address, unlike the Africans who faded into the nameless background at the port of Chinde: a "large tender came out over the bar, bringing many passengers, mostly colored, and also discharging many, a hundred or more, of the same mixed races."[30]

As was his wont, Muir drank in the landscape and not the colonial horror that had conquered it nor the Indigenous people whose blood had been spilled and homelands exploited. In the case of Yosemite, he justified the Mariposa Battalion's theft of the valley from its Indigenous inhabitants by retelling, without question, the standard tale of savage banditry and murder suppressed by a brave militia of pioneering, civilizing Euro-Americans. Saving the valley and its Sierra Nevada environs by creating the national park completed that conquest by turning this former Indigenous homeland into a contemplative wonderland. In the case of Hetch Hetchy, tribal nations that had long stewarded the valley likely would have supported Muir's efforts to keep the dam out, but not for the same reasons. In opposing the dam, he wasn't standing against the settler colonialism that had deprived them of their land. Rather, Muir hoped to rescue settler colonialism from its own worst impulse: destroying magnificent wild land divinely intended to serve as a pristine sanctuary for contemplating Creation's miracle.

When Muir sailed out of Brooklyn in 1911, the campaign to save settler colonialism from itself was headed in the right direction. By the time he returned in 1912, everything was going sideways.

President Taft and the two men who headed the Department of the Interior during his administration, first Richard A. Ballinger then Walter R. Fisher, harbored major doubts about Hetch Hetchy. They demanded that San Francisco prove the valley inside the national park to be the only viable source for the city's water needs. That report, created under the direction of renowned hydrological engineer John R. Freeman, became a masterpiece of technical dazzle and public relations sizzle. It reassured readers that a flooded Hetch Hetchy would be far more scenic than the valley *au naturel,* that it would meet the water and electricity needs of the entire Bay Area for the next century, and that no other water source could come close to delivering all this benefit at the same low cost. San Francisco spread the good word by mailing copies of Freeman's slick, well-produced report to every member of Congress in the autumn of 1912, just before the presidential election.

It helped San Francisco's cause that the city had already passed a $45 million bond measure to fund the first phase of dam construction, thus demonstrating popular support and willingness to foot the bill. It didn't help Muir and the preservationists that Taft and his Hetch Hetchy doubters were nearing the last days of their political lives. With Theodore Roosevelt again seeking the presidential limelight and splitting the Republican vote between himself and Taft, the Democrat Woodrow Wilson easily won. Just before Wilson's new Secretary of the Interior, Franklin K. Lane—a former San Francisco city and county attorney under James D. Phelan, the father of the Hetch Hetchy dam—was to take over the department, Secretary Fisher issued an order that Interior not approve the project without Congressional authorization.

The city was ready. It rolled out draft legislation, a sponsor in the person of California Representative John E. Raker, and a well-paid phalanx of skilled lobbyists. Against all that firepower, the preservationists began to crumble. Muir was too ill to travel to Washington DC and testify against the legislation in person. Instead, he wrote to friends and allies like Henry Fairfield Osborn, Mary W. Harriman, and Robert Underwood Johnson to write letters of protest to their senators and get their friends to do the same. Harriman responded optimistically: "people in the East are well aroused & I do not believe the danger is very near, so . . . you may yet win out." She invited the exhausted Muir to vacation at her Idaho ranch west of Yellowstone, and he took her up on the offer. Muir came back from the visit to woods and mountains refreshed, but his new energy made no difference to the course of events. When the Raker Bill passed both the House and the Senate, Muir and the preservationists appealed to Woodrow Wilson to veto it. The president ignored them. He and signed the bill into law on December 19, 1913, and the Hetch Hetchy fight was over.[31]

Sick and spent, Muir tried to put the best face he could on the defeat. "As to the loss of the Sierra park valley it's hard to bear," he wrote to the family of Sierra Club director, Stanford biologist, and eugenicist Vernon Kellogg. "The destruction of the charming groves & gardens, the finest in all California, goes to my heart. But in spite of Satan & Co., some sort of compensation must surely come out of even this dark damn-dam-damnation." Still, the defeat stung. "The battle has lasted twelve years, from Pinchot & Co. to President Wilson, and the wrong has prevailed over the best aroused sentiment of the whole country," he wrote Osborn. "That a lane lined with lies could be forced through the middle of the U.S. Congress is truly wonderful even in these confused political days—a devil's masterpiece of log-rolling road-making." Still, Muir had faith that this loss was not the last word on wilderness: "Fortunately wrong cannot last; soon or late it must fall back home to Hades, while some compensating good must surely follow."[32]

Almost a year to the day after mailing that letter, John Muir died. Urban legend has it that the Hetch Hetchy defeat killed him. In fact, the last of a series of bouts of influenza bloomed into pneumonia that took his breath and life, alone in a Los Angeles hospital room on Christmas Eve. Beside him on the bed lay the unfinished manuscript for what would become *Travels in Alaska*. Even in his closing hours, Muir was longing for mountains, glaciers, and tall trees and working to get his wild word out, hoping to prevent another Hetch Hetchy. That battle he would win.

13

Leave Only Footprints, Take Only Pictures

A wilderness, in contrast with those areas where man and his works
dominate the landscape, is hereby recognized as an area where the
earth and its community of life are untrammeled by man, where
man himself is a visitor who does not remain.

—WILDERNESS ACT, 1964

The Hetch Hetchy struggle left a bad taste in many mouths, even among
those who won and got their dam. Resolving to limit further projects in the
new and growing national park system, Congress passed, and Pres. Woodrow Wilson signed, the National Park Service Organic Act in 1916. Besides
founding the National Park Service (NPS), the law clarified just what national
parks were all about: "to conserve the scenery and the natural and historic
objects and the wild life therein and to provide for the enjoyment of the
same in such manner and by such means that will leave them unimpaired
for the enjoyment of future generations." The Hetch Hetchy system surely
qualified as an impairment, and no project of similar sort would ever again
be built inside a national park. Even though he wasn't there to see it, John
Muir had won the long game.[1]

Still, Hetch Hetchy's modifications remained legal, and work moved forward. Nearly nine years after Muir's death in 1914, a milestone of the Hetch
Hetchy water system was marked with curious irony. The official photograph
commemorating the 1923 dedication of O'Shaughnessy Dam featured a
line of national park officials, a cowboy, a child, a bathing beauty, a hiker,

an equestrian, a summer tourist, and two Native American women posed in front of a backdrop of crisscrossed American flags. The picture left the impression that tribal nations were condoning their dispossession by dam, reservoir, and national park. In fact, no one had asked them.[2]

That image did make one thing clear: in 1923, Yosemite's Indigenous peoples remained a presence in the park. In fact, they had become a tourist attraction.

By the time the federal government turned control of Yosemite Valley over to the state of California in 1864, some of the Yosemites were once again living year-round in the valley, settling back into village sites they had been expelled from a little over a decade earlier. Men built wagon roads, cut fence rails and firewood, fished and hunted for hotel dining rooms, and wrangled horses and mules. Women cleaned guests' rooms, washed their linens, and cooked and served their meals. These workers became so woven into the valley's economy that they remained the principal source of wage labor after the valley was added to the national park in 1906.[3]

In 1916 the newly formed NPS turned the park's tribal people into the summer spectacular known as Yosemite Indian Field Days. The event featured a rodeo, bareback horse races with painted riders, and an arts and crafts fair. Tourists did come, eager to see "authentic" Native Americans in a scenic setting and buy souvenirs. Still, the event didn't draw enough spectators and buyers to make up for the decline in visitors and revenue Yosemite experienced in late summer when waterfalls dwindled to an unimpressive trickle or dried up altogether. To draw more paying end-of-season customers, Chief Ranger Forest S. Townsley decided to refashion the Field Days along the lines of Buffalo Bill's Wild West Show, which he remembered with fond nostalgia from his Oklahoma childhood. Townsley recruited dozens upon dozens of Indigenous people, dressed them up in buckskins and feather headdresses, and erected canvas teepees. It hardly mattered that the local tribes had never lived in teepees nor worn feather headdresses. Those props said "Indian" to Euro-Americans, and Townsley wanted to give white folks what they came for. In the process, the Field Days transformed from a rough-and-tumble rodeo into a major exhibition of Indigenous crafts, particularly finely woven baskets. Crowds of Euro-American consumers came to buy their bit of Native American exoticism before it vanished from the earth. By the mid-1920s the craft fair was drawing more tourists than the rodeo.

The NPS's emphasis on manufactured authenticity hit a comic high when Hazel Hogan, crowned Miss Yosemite and dubbed White Fawn for the event, swapped her dark, tight braids for a stylish marcel. NPS official Herbert Wilson threatened to fire Hogan if she didn't dump the marcel and go back to the braids. He knew that the last thing incoming tourists were interested in seeing was a thoroughly modern Indigenous maiden.

There was a problem, too, with the cars Yosemite's Indigenous workers were buying with wages boosted by Field Days earnings and prize money. Seeing a tribal person driving an automobile, even a Pontiac with its Indian-head logo, rudely pricked the bubble of throwback, befeathered authenticity tourists craved. To keep reality from puncturing fantasy, the NPS told Indigenous drivers to park on a back lot and keep their vehicles out of tourists' sight.

Housing posed another branding challenge. At the turn of the century, the valley's tribal residents lived in six small villages. The year after Yosemite Valley was added to the national park, the newly arrived U.S. Cavalry forced the residents out of Koomine village at the base of Yosemite Falls and burned their shelters to clear the site for the first military outpost in the valley. By 1910, the five remaining villages had consolidated into one—partly by force, partly to take better advantage of job opportunities in the growing tourist business. The community came together in the long-occupied village of Yawokachi (Yó-watch-ke), a sunny location at the mouth of Indian Canyon that offered the valley's warmest winter days. NPS called the place Indian Village. Some families lived in *umuchas*, traditional, conical structures built of cedar bark. Others occupied shelters constructed from cast-off military tents and makeshift shacks cobbled together from scraps and discards. Nobody had electricity or heat apart from firewood, so they didn't pay utilities, and NPS charged no rent. The *umuchas* clashed stylistically with the NPS-constructed teepees on the fairgrounds, puncturing yet again authenticity's bubble. NPS brass saw the tent-cabins and shacks as seedy and rundown, more hillbilly than Noble Savage.

Yawokachi became an issue demanding solution with the 1927 opening of the luxurious Ahwahnee Hotel, located just down the road. NPS first planned to let surrounding vegetation grow into a visual barrier that shielded high-paying guests' eyes from the village. Then, encouraged by the Yosemite Park and Curry Company, which owned and operated the hotel, NPS decided it would be better to tear Yawokachi down and move its people to another location, one well away and out of sight. Once that decision was incorporated into the park's master plan and Yawokachi's un-consulted residents caught wind of it, the NPS lost the grassroots support and cooperation it needed to keep Yosemite Indian Field Days alive. The last event was held in 1929, the same year that Hazel Hogan had to change her hairstyle and Indigenous car owners were told to park out back.

By then, NPS had also decided it was time to move on. Horse races, rodeos, and craft fairs were unknown among the Yosemites before Euro-Americans took control, the institutional reasoning ran, so Indian Field Days hardly qualified as authentic. Indeed, authenticity was coming to mean ridding Yosemite Valley of the Yosemites.[4]

Claiming that the new medical center to be built in the valley needed Yawokachi's spacious, sunny site, NPS again told the village's residents they had to move. They were consigned to a site west of the Camp Four campground, out of sight and out of mind in a former village site they called Wahhoga (Wa-hó-ga). NPS entertained the notion of erecting faux teepees, but that bad idea soon died. In the end, the government settled on a three-room cabin that measured only 429 square feet, with no plumbing except a kitchen sink and a wood stove for heat and cooking. These fifteen tiny homes crammed families of six to eight adults and children into far too little space. That was part of the plan: cramped quarters would keep what park officials considered tribal riffraff from slipping into the valley and settling.

Moving the Yosemites was just the opening move. Pushing them out of the park, Park Superintendent Charles Thomson told his superiors, "would remove the final influence operating against a *pure status* for Yosemite." Since the federal government owned Wahhoga's cabins, it now completely controlled the housing situation. For the first time residents had to pay rent and utilities, and NPS limited residence to people employed by NPS or a concessionaire in a job eligible for retirement. And, should residents fall behind in the rent, lose employment, or retire, they forfeited any right to remain in the valley and had to move out.

The situation worsened after World War II when NPS tripled rents without boosting wages. This cash crunch did little to soothe the growing antagonism

between bureaucrats and residents. Bad feelings worsened when the quali-
fication for residence in Wahhoga was further limited to only a permanent
government job. Those who did not qualify were given four weeks to clear
out, then their vacated cabin was torn down. That way, neither they nor any
other Yosemite family had a home to come back to. Year by year the attri-
tion continued, helped along by occasional chicanery. One Wahhoga elder
told of NPS assigning her husband to a work detail in the backcountry, then
evicting her and their children while he was away. The man returned to find
them gone, like so many others before and after. By 1960 only three cabins
remained. Nine years later, the few remaining residents were relocated to a
government housing project, and the last Wahhoga cabins went up in flames
to provide a practice session for the park's firefighters.[5]

Yosemite had been cleansed. Wildland purity, the preservation of the
pristine, required no less.

Had he been alive, John Muir likely would have approved. From growing up
in frontier Wisconsin through his time in the Sierra Nevada, Muir carried
an unflattering opinion of Native Americans as lowly, brutish, savage, and
dirty. That belief tempered somewhat during his trips to Alaska. The Yupiks,
Iñupiats, and Chukchis impressed him as joyful, good-humored, and gentle
people despite the unrelieved hardships of Arctic life. Muir had his most up-
close-and-personal experiences with the Tlingits. It surprised him to discover
a Native American people as upright, kind to children, self-determined, and
open to Christian salvation as they were. He expressed genuine grief on
learning that the unarmed headman To'watte, who once dressed Muir down
for behaving like an impetuous child, was killed in a gunfight. When the
Presbyterian missionaries on his first trip north cut down and made off with
a totem pole, Muir sided, at least in his mind, with Tlingit leader Kadachan,
who charged these unholy men of the cloth with grave robbing. And when the
Harriman Alaska Expedition's passengers helped themselves to totems from
the Tlingit village of Gaash and justified the theft as collecting for university
museums, Muir kept a disapproving distance from such "scientific" looting.

As age mellowed Muir, his attitude toward Native Americans did soften,
but only a little. He saw the Tlingits as exceptions to the racial rule and kept
his low opinion of other tribal peoples even in his later years, as evidenced

in the books recounting his early days in the wild. Take the Bloody Canyon story as a case in point, one that he told and retold over the course of his life. This tale mattered to him.[6]

The incident occurred during the summer of 1869, when Muir took a couple days off from herding sheep near Tuolomne Meadows to descend the canyon to Mono Lake. On the way down he ran into a group of Kutzadika'as heading up, and their out-of-nowhere appearance startled him: "a drove of beings, hairy and gray . . . progressing with a boneless wallowing motion, like bears." Muir found the people he called Monos "mostly ugly, and some altogether hideous," as well as unspeakably filthy. "Viewed at a little distance, they formed mere dirt-specks in the landscape," he wrote on his first telling, five years after it happened. When the Kutzadika'as camped too close for comfort, Muir spent a worried night, then bolted down the canyon. His mood had settled enough by the time he reached the lake shore that he paused to watch Kutzadika'a women harvesting wild rye and enjoying themselves. He found the scene so picturesque that he was reminded of the well-known song by Robert Burns, the poet and fellow Scot, titled "Comin' Thro' the Rye."[7]

Just before he set out for Alaska in 1879 and his first encounters with the Tlingits, Muir recounted the incident again for *Scribner's Monthly*. This telling began much the same way as the original, except that the Kutzadika'as, who knew little English, hit Muir up for whisky and tobacco and refused to believe he had none to share. These people of the second version were just as dirty as the first time around, and Muir was again happy for them to keep on going and disappear into "mere dirt specks in the landscape." When night fell, Muir was once more unsettled by the nearness of the "furred Monos," and he "welcomed the morning." Again he paused by the lake shore to watch the Kutzadika'a women at their joyous harvest "coming through the rye."[8]

Nine years later, after his travels with the Tlingits, he told the tale for a third time. In this version Muir decided that the offending Kutzadika'as weren't simply disappearing dirt specks. Rather, they "had no right place in the landscape." After encountering the women gathering wild rye, he described their campsite of "fragile willow huts . . . broken and abandoned." Family groups were "seen lying at their ease, pictures of thoughtless contentment, their wild animal eyes glowering at you as you pass, their black shocks of hair perchance bedecked with red castellias and their bent, bulky stomachs filled with no white man knows what." The Kutzadika'as, Muir reported as if this reality was unbelievable, had a taste for insect larvae washed up by waves in Mono Lake. "This 'diet of worms' is further enriched by a large, fat caterpillar, a species of silk-worm found on the yellow pines to the south of the lake; and as they also gather the seeds of this pine, they get a double crop from it—meat and bread from the same tree."[9]

Another six years further on, well after he had encountered the peoples of the Arctic on the *Corwin*, he detailed the Bloody Canyon story for the fourth time. This account follows the previous one almost word for word. The Kutzadika'as were pelt-covered and dirty, they begged for whisky and tobacco, and their presence proved so disquieting that Muir had trouble sleeping and couldn't wait to see them gone. Again he declared, "Somehow they seemed to have no right place in the landscape, and I was glad to see them fading out of sight down the pass." The Kutzadika'a women remained joyous in the rye field, but this time Muir dropped the warm memory of Burns's apt verse and he had nothing to say about the tribe's eating habits.[10]

The last telling appeared in print toward the end of Muir's life, when he was 73 years old and writing his recollections of his first summer in the Sierra Nevada. The Kutzadika'as in this version were again as boneless and wallowing as bears, and every bit as filthy: "the dirt on some of the faces seemed almost old enough and thick enough to have a geological significance." Again, the Monos encircled him to beg whisky and tobacco until he convinced them he had nothing to offer: "how glad I was to get away from the gray, grim crowd and see them vanish down the trail!" But this time, instead of passing a fitful night of dread at the Kutzadika'as' closeness, Muir reflected on the meanness of his response. "To prefer the society of squirrels and woodchucks to that of our own species must surely be unnatural," he noted. Then he sauntered off, wishing the Kutzadika'as Godspeed and summoning the famously compassionate lines from Burns: "'It's coming yet, for a' that, / That man to man, the warld o'er, / Shall brothers be for a' that.'"

Muir's warm and fuzzy feeling soon cooled and coarsened, however. After he descended the canyon the next morning and emerged onto the valley floor, he once more stopped to watch Kutzadika'a women gathering wild rye. They bent large handfuls of the ripe grass over, beat the grains free from the stalks, and fanned them in the wind to separate the chaff. "A fine squirrelish employment this wild grain gathering seems, and the women were evidently enjoying it, laughing and chattering and looking almost natural," Muir wrote, underscoring the "almost." He had a point to make: "Most Indians I have seen are not a whit more natural in their lives than we civilized whites. Perhaps if I knew them better I should like them better. The worst thing about them is their uncleanliness. Nothing truly wild is unclean."

Muir kept going, at pains to further depict the Kutzadika'as as unnatural. They lived, after all, in "mere brush tents where they lie and eat at their ease" and made their women pack unchivalrously heavy loads over the Sierra Nevada. Even worse, they ate insects, just as in his third retelling. Indeed, of all the foods offered by the Kutzadika'as' home range, "strange to say, they seem to like the lake larvae best of all," Muir made clear.[11]

His dietary squeamishness stands out, for, like all Scots, Muir knew his native land's national dish to be haggis, a sheep's stomach stuffed with chopped animal offal, oatmeal, suet, and spices and then boiled. It is a concoction that takes more than a little getting used to, and it is so quintessentially Scottish that Burns addressed a praise poem to the dish as "Great Chieftain of the Puddin'-race." Muir could have recognized that Kutzadika'as relishing insect larvae were no stranger than Scots savoring haggis, but no. He painted them as neither natural nor civilized, pushing them beyond the bounds of Burns's worldwide brotherhood. The Kutzadika'as were irredeemably other.[12]

Although Muir worked hard to free himself from his father's rabid religiosity, he drew still on his Calvinist upbringing and its insistence on Original Sin. That perspective made it easy to lay responsibility for terrible conditions on the people they most affected and overlook the uncontrollable social, political, and economic horrors that stoked the Kutzadika'as' particular hell.

The 1848 discovery of gold in California brought the first prospectors over the Sierra and into the Mono Lake basin. That influx widened from tentative trickle to roaring torrent when gold deposits were unearthed north of the lake near Bodie, now a ghost town and state historic park, and across the state line at Aurora, Nevada. Enterprising merchants ferried wagonloads of supplies from Southern California to the mines, and ranchers launched the first cattle drive to deliver beef on the hoof to Aurora in 1861. The 300-mile journey north became much easier in 1862 with the passage of the

Homestead Act that allowed Euro-American citizens to file claims on public lands. Because they were not citizens in the eyes of the law, Native Americans were excluded from homesteading. Southern California ranchers moved their herds north to the basin and staked claims, pushing the Kutzadika'as out of their villages and off their gathering grounds. Overgrazing reduced native grasses, and since the antelope that had supplied meat to the Kutzadika'as competed with cattle for grazing, settlers shot them as pests. They made matters worse by turning the pinyon groves where the Kutzadika'as collected pine nuts into firewood. The destruction of their food sources turned a people that had long sustained themselves from their homeland into a dependent and impoverished population that clustered around Euro-American settlements hoping for handouts and leftovers. Many of the Kutzadika'as adapted as they could, working on ranches and in mines and lumber mills. Others joined into bandit bands that stole, rustled, and killed to feed themselves and defend their tribal nation from further outrage.[13]

These, then, were the people Muir encountered in Bloody Canyon, once self-sufficient but now reduced to begging by settler colonialism. Yet Muir blamed them for their plight and made them responsible for the disheveled poverty American society forced them into.

In this instance and many others, Muir was expressing Euro-American superiority during an era that was often far more racist and white supremacist than he personally ever was. Still, he could have chosen to see Indigenous peoples in a more favorable light, as others of his time did, including men he knew and respected. Yet he did not.

Even though Muir lived close among the Tlingits during his trips to southeast Alaska, he pleaded ignorance of Native American ways closer to home. "Perhaps if I knew them better I should like them better," he lamented about the women near Mono Lake gathering wild rye, yet he never invested the time or emotional energy to grasp the lives Native Californians lived. Perhaps he thought he didn't need to. After all, tribal nations were fast fading away, many anthropologists argued, so why bother? But not everybody else was quite so sure.

One of those dissenters had attended Muir's alma mater, the University of Wisconsin. C. E. Kelsey earned his law degree in Madison and then came west, settling in San Jose, California, in 1901 and opening a law practice. San Jose was the home of the Northern California Indian Association (NCIA), a nondenominational Christian organization that focused on the state's landless tribes. Kelsey had experience with tribal issues from working as a clerk at the Green Bay Indian Agency before he went to law school. Becoming a leader soon after joining NCIA, Kelsey led its campaign to lobby Congress for laws supporting Native Californians who lived off-reservation.

The land situation in Northern California was particularly desperate. The region had only three reservations—Tule River, Round Valley, and Hoopa—to accommodate an area that once contained the densest Native American population in the United States. Kelsey discovered just why California's situation was so extreme: the secret deep-sixing of eighteen treaties with 119 tribal signatories negotiated by federal commissioners in the early 1850s that traded land for money, funded subsistence, and set up a reservation system. California politicians who hated the idea of giving valuable real estate back to the state's original inhabitants lobbied so fiercely that the Senate buried the treaties in a secret archive. More than fifty years later, with the help of a clerk who stumbled across the documents, Kelsey exposed the unratified agreements. He was appalled by what he found. "Nowhere else in the United States have the Indian lands been taken without payment," Kelsey wrote. "Nevertheless the national government has gone ahead exactly as if it had acquired title, and has sold the land to settlers and others."[14]

To demonstrate just how bad the predicament of Native Californians left landless by the treaty debacle was, Kelsey, now working for the Office of Indian Affairs as a special agent, set out to count all the state's tribal people living off-reservation. His 1906 report showed that the state contained at least twenty thousand Native Californians, not the fifteen thousand the Census Bureau totted up in 1900. And many of these uncounted people lived in horrific conditions. Kelsey wrote that "the Indian in the northern part of this State has little to look forward to" and could expect only "a life of privation, ill usage, neglect, discomfort, without opportunity to rise or hope for better conditions."[15]

The NCIA sought to remedy this injustice by acquiring land for landless tribes. Using federal funds, Kelsey purchased forty-five sites, all but a dozen in Northern California, and more were added after Kelsey left the Office of

Indian Affairs. Known as rancherias to distinguish them from reservations, these small tracts served specific tribal groups. In addition, Kelsey helped Native Californians apply for land allotments in the public domain, including national forests, and advocated for tribal children to gain access to the public schools long denied them.

Unlike so many of his contemporaries, including Muir, Kelsey understood how Native Californians had come to such desperation. They didn't choose lives of landless, hungry poverty on white society's ragged edges, nor did they suffer from some evolutionary deficit that made their decline and extinction inevitable. Their population was, in fact, increasing, despite the deck stacked against them. "The evils which the Indians suffer from the various forms of prejudice and neglect are for the most part beyond the reach of legislation. They are a reflection of public sentiment among white people," Kelsey told a meeting of San Francisco's Commonwealth Club of California, the nation's oldest public-affairs forum. Euro-Americans had made this mess; now they needed to clean it up.[16]

John Muir never met nor talked with Kelsey, who could have told him that he was utterly misreading the Kootzaduka'as and other Native Americans he disparaged. But Muir did have a longstanding connection to two friends who largely shared Kelsey's take.

The first was Charles Fletcher Lummis. Like Muir, Lummis began his career by walking a long way, then writing a book about it. Muir hoofed it from Kentucky to the Gulf of Mexico and told the story in *Thousand-Mile Walk to the Gulf.* Lummis hiked a loopy route from Chillicothe, Ohio, to Los Angeles—approximately thirty-five hundred miles—to take up the job he'd been offered as the *Los Angeles Times'* first city editor, a journey he detailed in *A Tramp Across the Continent.* The two men came to know each other when Lummis took over a Southern California-based promotional magazine that grew into *Out West.* He steered the publication in a new, literary direction by soliciting articles from notable western writers, including Muir. In addition to magazine work, the two men shared an ongoing correspondence about their children, Hetch Hetchy, and backcountry excursions.

Lummis and Muir also shared a connection with Theodore Roosevelt. Lummis had been Roosevelt's classmate at Harvard before he dropped out of college, and he maintained the friendship for years after. Muir and Roosevelt camped together in Yosemite and corresponded until the politics of Hetch Hetchy drove a wedge between them. Muir, Lummis, and Roosevelt thought somewhat alike. All three saw civilization as a force that drained men of their virility and had to be countered by manly pursuits like hunting, wilderness camping, and long-range saunters. None of them welcomed the surge of immigrants pouring into the United States from southern and eastern Europe, and they were all concerned that the Anglo-Saxon, or Nordic, root stock of the American people would be swamped out by fertile foreigners. None ever became as extreme in their thinking as Henry Fairfield Osborn and Madison Grant, yet they did sing from a harmonious hymnal.

Lummis, though, differed on an important issue: Native Americans. He saw them as a significant element in the West's complex cultural mosaic, recognized the injustice they had been subjected to, and took steps to remedy it.

This revelation came to Lummis when he was residing in the Pueblo of Isleta (Shiewhibak), a Tiwa community in the Rio Grande Valley south of Albuquerque. He had retreated from Los Angeles to New Mexico to recover from partial paralysis brought on by a stroke at the age of only twenty-nine. The move proved salutary. "I have lived now in Isleta for four years, with its Indians my only neighbors; and better neighbors I never had and never want," he wrote. "They are unmeddlesome but kindly, thoughtful, and loyal, and wonderfully interesting." He praised "their endless and beautiful folklore, their quaint and astonishing costumes, and their startling ceremonials." Lummis later invited his Tiwa neighbors to perform at fiestas he organized in Los Angeles, and he advocated for two nearby tribes when they were forced off their homeland.[17]

San Diego's Warner Ranch, known now as Warner Springs, had been the territory of the Cupeños (Kuupangaxwichem) and Diegueños (Kumeyaay) peoples for centuries. When two prominent Californians acquired much of the land, they saw the tribal people as squatters and wanted them gone. After a decade-long legal battle that climbed the judicial ladder, the U.S. Supreme Court ruled that Cupeños and Diegueños had no legal right to the land and forced them to give up their homes. Responding to the ruling, which he saw as an unjust dispossession, Lummis formed the Sequoyah League to provide the two tribes with a new homeland. He attracted to his cause such luminaries as David Starr Jordan of Stanford University, Glacier

National Park advocate and *Forest and Stream* editor George Bird Grinnell, and U.S. Biological Survey head C. Hart Merriam. Muir, too, joined the league, paying membership dues for himself and daughter Helen and lauding Lummis for "the noble work you are doing for our fellow mortals." As a result of his advocacy, Lummis was named to the federal commission that eventually located a reservation for the Warner Ranch tribes in the Pala Valley and acquired it for a little over $46,000 in Interior Department funds.[18]

Lummis's attitude toward Native Americans was paternalistic, for sure; the Sequoyah League's motto was "To Make Better Indians," a phrase dripping noblesse oblige. Still, he respected Indigenous cultures as complete within themselves, and he opposed forced-assimilation strategies like the Carlisle Indian School that stripped Native American children of language, culture, and long hair. Carlisle embodied founder Richard Henry Pratt's strategy to ensure "that all the Indian there is in the race should be dead. Kill the Indian in him, and save the man." Carlisle and boarding schools like it, Lummis argued, severed Indigenous children from their roots and families and prepared them only for life on the lowest rung of the Euro-American world.[19]

When Theodore Roosevelt won the presidential election in 1902, Lummis sent his former Harvard classmate a congratulatory letter holding out hope that, for once, the administration would field a competent Office of Indian Affairs. "I care for Indians not as 'bric-a-brac' but as actual humans," he explained.[20]

Despite his Sequoyah League membership, Lummis's favorable take on the value of Native American ways and on the injustice of pushing tribes off their long-held homelands influenced Muir little. As the connections between the seven tribal nations associated with Yosemite National Park were severed and the people pushed out, Muir failed even to notice their loss. In his view, scenic landscape was all that mattered, and contemplation by spiritually sensitive men of his own background and bent constituted its highest use.[21]

C. Hart Merriam begged to disagree. He, too, was a personal friend and professional acquaintance, yet like his friendship with Lummis, Muir learned little from him about Native Californians. The two knew each other from the Harriman Alaska Expedition, when Merriam, then the chief of the U.S. Biological Survey and a leading field zoologist, tapped Muir as the scientific crew's glaciologist. The following summer, they took a long trip together through Muir's old haunts, crossing back and forth over the spine of the Sierra Nevada four times. Afterward they kept up a correspondence that included Christmas packages of fruit and nuts from Muir's Martinez orchard. Merriam also pitched in to help fight for Hetch Hetchy's preservation.

In 1910 Mary W. Harriman offered to fund Merriam's research, no matter what he pursued, through the Smithsonian's E. H. Harriman Fund, which was something like a contemporary McArthur Genius Grant. Harriman and her philanthropical associates assumed that Merriam would keep working on birds and mammals. What Harriman didn't realize was that since the 1890s Merriam had become more and more interested in investigating the long-overlooked Native Californians. The very same year that Harriman made her offer, Merriam published *The Dawn of the World*, his admiring collection of Miwok mythology. Grasping a rare chance for a midlife career change, Merriam signed on to the financial arrangement that paid more than he was making, resigned from the Biological Survey, and launched in-depth field studies of Native California's peoples, cultures, and languages. The institutional irony was rich: even as Harriman money was paying the bills for Charles Davenport and his white supremacist Eugenics Record Office, it was supporting Merriam's research on, and advocacy for, Native Californians.[22]

Merriam's extensive fieldwork up, down, and across the state led him to realize that Native Californians were far more intelligent and adept than Euro-Americans gave them credit for. Merriam grew to hate the slur "D——" even though federal and state governments still used it officially. He held that tribal nations should be called by the names they gave themselves and not by somebody else's inaccurate and nasty handle. He recognized that "squaw" to a Native woman was as offensive as "skank" or "slut" to a Euro-American. He came to argue, as Kelsey did, that California's tribal nations had been terribly wronged under American conquest and settler colonialism and that they deserved compensation for the land stolen from them. There was no doubt in his mind that "great injustice has been done [to] the Indians of California in that we have confiscated their lands, driven them into remote and inhospitable parts of the State, deprived them of their natural food, imprisoned them for killing deer or taking fish, inoculated them with fatal diseases, and, for a period of at least fifteen years (1849–1864), we hunted and shot them down by hundreds." Further, Euro-Americans could take more than a few lessons from Indigenous peoples: "we have as much to learn from them as they from us, but nevertheless, and entirely apart from their superior knowledge of the food, textile, and medicinal values of animals and plants, they can put us to shame in matters of patience, fairness, honor, and kindness."[23]

Merriam pointed to the reason why Muir looked right past Indigenous peoples: he utterly ignored whole classes of living beings. "While he loved the mountains and everything in them," Merriam wrote in an affectionate memorial to Muir, "his chief interests centered about the dynamic forces that shaped their features and the vegetation that clothed their slopes." This naturalist who worshiped glaciers and trees knew little of the Sierra Nevada's animal life beyond his delight in Douglas squirrels and water ouzels. "For while he liked to see birds and mammals in the wilderness and about his camps, he rarely troubled himself to learn their proper names and relationships," Merriam wrote.[24] Muir simply didn't pay attention to those facets of mountain life that didn't interest him, tribal people included.

Merriam had witnessed Muir's lack of interest on their Sierra trip in the summer of 1900. On the west side of Mono Lake, along a branch of Mill Creek, they came across a Kutzadika'a encampment where two women were preparing mush from acorns they had carried home from a gathering trip on the mountains' western slopes. Fascinated, Merriam filled five pages in his journal with the details of the ornate process of repeated leaching the women used to remove bitter tannins from the nuts and render them edible. He took photographs, too, including one that is the only known image of John Muir with Native people. As for Muir, his journal says not a word about the encounter. To him, unlike Merriam, witnessing the intricacy of the women's work offered nothing notable.[25]

The key to grasping Muir's take on the peoples indigenous to the lands he wanted to preserve as pristine reserves centered on his dismissal of the Kutzadika'as in Bloody Canyon: "somehow they seemed to have no right place in the landscape, and I was glad to see them fading out of sight down the pass." Muir considered the people who had traveled through Bloody Canyon for millennia as distracting interlopers, while he himself, and other Anglo-Saxon adventurers of right mind had every lawful claim to this wild landscape. True wilderness required the absence of a continuing human presence woven into it by the daily business of life. This was a sanctuary to be visited, not lived in, and only by those spiritually adept enough to grasp how close they were coming to the miracle of Creation. The essence of wilderness was not only that it was untamed; it was also that it lay outside human presence and influence. The Indigenous peoples who had once called it home, who hunted its venison and fished its trout, who harvested edible roots and seeds and gathered basketry materials, and who built villages within its forests and meadows seemed to Muir "not a whit more natural in their lives than we civilized whites." If wild country was to be raised up into wilderness worthy of contemplation, its Indigenous people simply did not belong.

This idea didn't start with Muir. Its roots reach deep into the American myth that Native Americans lived off nature's bounty in a pristine country that remained much as the Divine had created it. The legal phrase justifying settler colonialism, *terra nullius,* "no one's land," signified that the landscape Euro-Americans sought to occupy was uninhabited. The continent was theirs for the taking, empty and unpossessed. Wilderness preservation kept it that way, virginal and pristine.

Given the speed and thoroughness with which settlers logged, cleared, dammed, and plowed, Euro-American writers advocating for the ravaged land saw human presence as the original sin against nature. George Perkins Marsh, one of the first American environmental writers, declared in his 1864 book *Man and Nature* that "man everywhere is a disturbing agent. Wherever he plants his foot, the harmonies of nature are turned to discords." Marsh was certain that North America was destined for the same fate as the homelands of its colonial conquerors. "It is certain that a desolation, like that which has overwhelmed many once beautiful and fertile regions of Europe, awaits an important part of the territory of the United States," he wrote, "unless prompt measures are taken to check the action of destructive causes already in operation."[26] Time was running out, and the continent's fate was at stake.

Muir and his preservationist allies were not the only ones to answer Marsh's call to action. Utilitarian foresters like Gifford Pinchot, wildlife preservationists like George Bird Grinnell, and avid hunters like Theodore Roosevelt and Madison Grant devoted serious time and energy to protecting

America's fast-disappearing natural resources through the national forest system, wildlife refuges, and national parks and monuments, particularly in the West. In the middle of the twentieth century, the novelist Wallace Stegner stood atop this legacy to proclaim an even bolder vision for the wildest of the United States' wild lands. "I want to speak for the wilderness idea as something that has helped form our character and that has certainly shaped our history as a people," he wrote. "For an American, insofar as he is new and different at all, is a civilized man who has renewed himself in the wild. The American experience has been the confrontation by old peoples and cultures of a world as new as if it had just risen out of the sea." America should take "pleasure in the fact that such a timeless and uncontrolled part of the earth is still there." Referring to Britain's ambassador to the United States in the early twentieth century, Stegner declared that "if the national park is, as Lord Bryce suggested, the best idea America ever had, wilderness preservation is the highest refinement of that idea."[27]

The concept Stegner articulated—that wilderness is a wild space ever and always outside human influence, resplendent in its pristine, unmanaged, day-of-Creation state—became legally enshrined in the 1964 Wilderness Act. To protect wilderness, the law first had to define what it was. Unlike those regions of the planet dominated by humankind and its many works, wilderness is a place where humans are only visitors, never residents. Essential to wilderness is "its primeval character and influence, without permanent improvements or human habitation."[28] No roads, no dams, no four-wheelers, and, Lord knows since John Muir's time, no people native to what is preserved, no matter how long they have lived in and cared for it.

Yet there is another strategy for effective preservation, one that centers the Indigenous peoples who have long been excluded from lands they once called home. This story reaches across the West to Yosemite, and it begins in Bears Ears.

14

Bettering America's Best Idea

I know who I am. I don't need the federal government to tell me.

—SANDRA CHAPMAN, SOUTHERN SIERRA MIWUK NATION CHAIR, 2022

The year was 2010, and U.S. Sen. Robert Bennett, Republican of Utah, had just launched a planning process for public lands in seven eastern counties of his home state. Seeing an opportunity to have their voices heard on land use for the first time, Utah's Diné (Navajo) leaders drafted a proposal and put it before Bennett. It died, as did Bennett's initiative, when the Tea Party rebellion swamped the senator at the state GOP convention and he lost his seat. Not all the effort was wasted, however.

Utah Diné Bikéyah (UDB), a grassroots nonprofit, arose from this campaign to channel tribal voices on land use. One of UDB's goals became protecting the Bears Ears region—so named for a prominent pair of distinctive red-rock buttes—as a wild and cultural landscape of great spiritual significance. The organization aimed to preserve Bears Ears either as a national conservation area through Congress or as a national monument by presidential action under the Antiquities Act of 1906. UDB members began meeting regularly with the commissioners of San Juan County, where Bears Ears is located, to develop a proposal that would incorporate both tribal and settler interests in preserving the land. Things soon went south. In October 2011, commissioner Phil Lyman told UDB board members coldly that the tribes had "lost the war" back in the day and with it any right to have a say on public-land use.

As hostile as that was, things only got worse. In early 2013 U.S. Rep. Robert Bishop picked up where Bennett left off and again launched a public lands initiative for eastern Utah. At a community meeting organized by Utah members of the House of Representatives, white residents of San Juan County lobbed racial epithets at tribal attendees. The congressional delegation added to the insult by failing to intervene, effectively sanctioning the slurs. The racist writing on the wall told Native Utahans the time had come for a different approach.[1]

In the summer of 2015, Hopis, Dinés, Uintah and Ouray Utes, Ute Mountain Utes, and Zunis—all federally recognized tribal nations that maintain sovereign relations with the federal government—joined forces as the Bears Ears Inter-Tribal Coalition (BEITC). Given the Lyman-animated hostility of San Juan County, the dismissive actions of Representative Bishop and the Utah congressional delegation, and the pending bills in the Utah legislature designating parts of the Bears Ears landscape as oil and gas resources, BEITC aimed to skip over all of them and put a proposal for a national monument on Pres. Barack Obama's desk.[2]

That document, delivered to the White House on October 15, 2015, broke new ground for protecting public lands. "Tribes have never before petitioned for a presidentially declared national monument, much less one of the size and scope we propose here," the proposal made clear right at the top. The 1.9 million acres included in the proposal represented not only little-visited, roadless areas that fit the standard notion of wilderness but also lands shaped and held sacred by the five tribes over millennia. The proposal noted, "The rampant looting and destruction of the villages, structures, rock markings, and gravesites within the Bears Ears landscape saddened and sickened our ancestors, and that sense of loss and outrage continues today." By declaring Bears Ears a national monument, the president "would honor the worldviews of our ancestors, and Tribes today, and their relationships with this landscape."

To deliver on this unique purpose, the "new monument must be managed under a sensible, entirely workable regime of true Federal-Tribal Collaborative Management." Equal power sharing between federal and tribal governments was essential. The proposal argued that "for the Bears Ears National Monument to be all it can be, the Tribes must be full partners with the United States in charting the vision for the monument and implementing that vision." This unique relationship would set the context for "the creation of a world-class institute on systems of land management that accounts for both Western science and Traditional Knowledge."[3]

Fourteen months later, in the closing days of his second term, Obama issued an executive proclamation creating Bears Ears National Monument. "Rising from the center of the southeastern Utah landscape and visible from every direction are twin buttes so distinctive that in each of the native languages of the region their name is the same: Hoon'Naqvut, Shash Ja´a, Kwiyagatu Nukavachi, Ansh An Lashokdiwe, or 'Bears Ears,'" the proclamation opened. This landscape was "profoundly sacred to many Native American tribes, including the Ute Mountain Ute Tribe, Navajo Nation, Ute Indian Tribe of the Uintah Ouray, Hopi Nation, and Zuni Tribe." As the proclamation recited many natural and cultural wonders of Bears Ears, its prose rose into praise songs that John Muir would have admired: "From earth to sky, the region is unsurpassed in wonders. The star-filled nights and natural quiet of the Bears Ears area transport visitors to an earlier eon. Against an absolutely black night sky, our galaxy and others more distant leap into view. As one of the most intact and least-roaded areas in the contiguous United States, Bears Ears has that rare and arresting quality of deafening silence." Still, the president's vision was less ambitious than that of the tribes. The proclamation trimmed Bears Ears to 1.35 million acres, which represented "the smallest area compatible with the proper care and management of the objects to be protected" as the Antiquities Act requires, and it stopped short of management by federal-tribal partnership. Rather, the monument fell under the authority of the Interior and Agriculture secretaries guided by recommendations from the Bears Ears Commission, which would consist of one elected officer from each of the five tribes. Importantly, "the Secretaries shall carefully and fully consider integrating the traditional and historical knowledge and special expertise of the Commission or comparable entity" into the monument's management. Should they refuse the commission's recommendations, the secretaries had to explain their reasoning in writing. The arrangement stopped short of partnership, but it did give the tribes a strong voice in all matters Bears Ears.[4]

Once Donald Trump became president, he couldn't let even so tempered a proclamation stand. For one thing, the new president made a point of undoing his predecessor's work. For another, he was beholden to mining and petroleum interests that had long turned a profit-oriented eye toward Bears Ears. To create an illusion of deliberative policymaking, Trump dispatched Interior Secretary Ryan Zinke to seek stakeholder input on Bears Ears as well as twenty-six other national monuments. Zinke was picky about who he listened to, tilting to fossil fuel executives and county officials of the Lyman persuasion. On Bears Ears, Zinke held zero public meetings and met with BEITC leaders for a mere hour. It was hardly surprising that he recommended massively cropping Bears Ears and cutting it into two much smaller, disconnected units. And to make it appear that he wasn't singling out this good tribal idea for bad treatment, he also proposed lopping neighboring Grand Staircase-Escalante National Monument as well as two other smaller, less-known monuments.[5]

BEITC called out Zinke's recommendation as the insult it was. "For us, Bears Ears is a homeland. It always has been and still is. The radical idea of breaking up Bears Ears National Monument is a slap in the face to the members of our Tribes and an affront to Indian people all across the country," the coalition responded. "The Bears Ears region is not a series of isolated objects, but the object itself, a connected, living landscape, where the place, not a collection of items, must be protected. You cannot reduce the size without harming the whole. Bears Ears is too precious a place, and our cultures and values too dignified and worthy, to backtrack on the promises made in the Presidential Proclamation."[6]

Ignoring BEITC's objections, Trump translated Zinke's recommendation into a December 2017 proclamation that added some 11,200 acres to the monument, then slashed-and-burned Bears Ears from 1.35 million acres to just 201,876, or only fifteen percent of the original. It also broke the national monument into two disconnected units as Zinke wanted and the tribes hated. Trump held that Obama's proclamation violated the Antiquities Act by setting aside far more land than the minimum good management required. Since Obama's Bears Ears boundaries, Trump argued, included sites that are hardly unique—*once you've seen one kiva, you've seen them all, right*—and preserved other features that faced little risk and already enjoyed protection under existing federal law, his proclamation added up to a federal land grab. And the administration complained that Obama had given the tribes too much power on the ground. Trump limited the Bears Ears Commission's scope to the shrunken monument's Shash Jáa unit and required that, besides the tribal officers, it include one commissioner from San Juan County, a nemesis to the five tribes.

Notably, the Trump proclamation lacked the least hint of Obama's praise song; it was all about shrinking both acreage and awe. It turned the living, breathing Bears Ears landscape into a few low-budget museum exhibits and grade-school dioramas. Even that was window dressing for making profit from a tribal homeland. Trump declared that in sixty days more than 1.1 million acres of newly unprotected land would be opened to mining and drilling leases. Energy industry lobbyists had won the day.[7]

Lawsuits challenging Trump's legal authority to dismember Bears Ears and Grand Staircase-Escalante were still making their slow way through the courts even as he lost the 2020 election. Soon after his inauguration, Pres. Joseph R. Biden asked Interior Secretary Deb Haaland (Laguna Pueblo), the first Native American to hold a cabinet-level office, to review the two Utah monuments Trump had shrunk. She recommended that both be restored to their original boundaries, including the 11,200 acres Trump had included in Bears Ears. Biden made her recommendation official policy with two October 2021 presidential proclamations. In the case of Bears Ears, the restoration wasn't just about a landscape "profoundly sacred to sovereign Tribal Nations and indigenous people of the southwest region of the United States," according to the proclamation. It also turned on ensuring tribal "participation in the care and management" of the monument by re-establishing the Bears Ears Commission as all-tribal, without the San Juan County representative Trump had added.[8]

Carleton Bowekaty (Zuni Tribe of the Zuni Indian Reservation), BEITC co-chair, believes restoring the monument is an act of healing. "Today, instead of being removed from a landscape to make way for a public park, we are being invited back to our ancestral homelands to help repair them and plan for their resilient future," he told the House Committee on Natural Resources. "Instead of continuing with a policy to erase our language and way of life, we are being asked to apply our traditional knowledge to the ecological challenges (drought, extinction, erosion, etc.) that are daily becoming more prominent and unavoidable." Bears Ears represents a "brand new arrangement," centered on "a combined land management plan that is based on, and reflects upon, our collective 'Traditional Ecological Knowledge.'"[9]

On June 18, 2022, that new arrangement resulted in the signing of an intergovernmental agreement between the five Bears Ears Commission tribes and the Agriculture and Interior Departments, the U.S. Forest Service, and the Bureau of Land Management to ensure "consistent, effective and collaborative management" of the national monument by "centering Indigenous voices, including increasing the recognition of the value of traditional Indigenous knowledge and empowering Tribal Nations to make decisions for their cultural, natural, and spiritual values." The next month, BEITC unveiled a collaborative land management plan for Bears Ears that gives Indigenous knowledge equal weight with science-based management. The vision BEITC first articulated seven years earlier was coming into being.[10]

That vision is making waves beyond Bears Ears. In March 2023 Pres. Biden set aside more than five hundred thousand acres of sacred and wild lands at the southern tip of Nevada as Avi Kwa Ame National Monument. Called by the Mojave name for Spirit Mountain, the monument's landscape is sacred to ten Yuman-speaking tribes along the Colorado River who make Avi Kwa Ame part of their creation stories, as well as to the Hopis and Chemehuevi Paiutes. Beginning in the 1990s, the tribes built a coalition to advance the national monument proposal, forming alliances with three towns in the area, the Nevada state legislature, recreation and tourism interests, and conservation organizations. When President Biden announced the national monument designation, Fort Mojave Indian Tribal Chair Timothy Williams joined him on the podium, underscoring the reality that Avi Kwa Ame, like Bears Ears, was the tribes' idea.[11]

Then in August 2023 Biden proclaimed yet another tribally inspired national monument. The name Baaj Nwaavjo I'tah Kukveni–Ancestral Footprints Grand Canyon encompasses three languages: Havasupai (baaj nwaavjo, or "where tribal peoples roam"), Hopi (i'tah kukveni, or "the ancestors' footprints"), and English. Covering approximately one million acres in Arizona north and south of Grand Canyon National Park and protecting a major section of the Colorado River watershed from future uranium mining, the coalition that developed the proposal and carried it forward over decades of work included not only the Havasupai Tribe and the Hopi Tribe but also the Hualapai Tribe, Kaibab Paiute Tribe, Las Vegas Band of Paiute Tribe, Moapa Band of Paiutes, Paiute Indian Tribe of Utah, Navajo Nation, San Juan Southern Paiute Tribe, Yavapai-Apache Nation, Pueblo of Zuni, and the Colorado River Indian Tribes. The area is sacred to all twelve tribes and includes more than three thousand known cultural and historical sites.[12]

The world is paying attention to what Bears Ears set in motion. In January 2022 BEITC was named to the first cohort of grantees in a one-million-dollar fund established by the Indigenous Earth Fund to support tribal organizations using traditional wisdom to combat climate change.[13] More and more, the old way is looking like the best way, and the tribes are showing America how to do it.

Unlike Bears Ears, Avi Kwa Ame, and Baaj Nwaavjo I'tah Kukveni, most national parks and monuments are rooted in America's legacy of Indigenous extermination and dispossession. David Treuer (Leech Lake Band of Ojibwe), a respected novelist and nonfiction writer, encapsulates this history in one sentence: "The American West began with war but concluded with parks." The in-between wasn't pretty. "Viewed from the perspective of history," Treuer makes clear, "Yellowstone is a crime scene." He takes a strong stand on the best way to draw restorative justice from this legacy of killing and thievery by titling his essay "Return the National Parks to the Tribes."

Treuer argues that the eighty-five million acres making up the national park system—with a few exceptions, such as the National Mall—should be turned over to a consortium representing all federally acknowledged tribes. The tribal consortium would be responsible for stewarding the parks and managing access and use. But there's more to this proposal than real estate, since "it would restore dignity that was rightfully ours. To be entrusted with the stewardship of America's most precious landscapes would be a deeply meaningful form of restitution. Alongside the feelings of awe that Americans experience while contemplating the god-rock of Yosemite and other places like it, we could take inspiration in having done right by one another," Treuer explains.

Lest preservationists shudder at the thought of Yellowstone and Yosemite being turned into tribal sacrifice zones, Treuer recognizes that "the transfer should be subject to binding covenants guaranteeing a standard of conservation that is at least as stringent as what the park system enforces today, so that the parks' ecological health would be preserved—and improved—long into the future." And this new arrangement would give the American political system a much-needed environmental-justice reboot. "The national parks are the closest thing America has to sacred lands, and like the frontier of old, they can help forge our democracy anew. More than just America's 'best idea,' the parks are the best of America, the jewels of its landscape. It's time they were returned to America's original peoples," he concludes.[14]

Radical as Treuer's idea of turning wild lands over to their former Indigenous owners sounds, it is already working on the flip side of the globe. Australia's Uluru-Kata Tjuta National Park, once known as Ayers Rock, is owned and operated by the Anangu people, the Aboriginals whose homeland encompasses the park. Uluru is managed by a twelve-member commission, with eight of the seats tribal and the remaining four governmental. New Zealand (Aotearoa) melds tribal and government management for the Whanganui River, the country's longest navigable fresh waterway, and for Te Urewara, a park in the North Island's eastern mountains and the homeland of the Tūhoe Maori people.[15]

Australia, New Zealand, and the United States share histories of settler colonialism in which newcomers from Europe took the land from its Indigenous owners. Australia and New Zealand are showing a path forward to recognizing and reconciling this bloody past. Slow to start, the United States is beginning to catch up.

As Secretary of the Interior, Deb Haaland is responsible for both national parks and tribal nations; early in her tenure, she pulled those policy concerns together. Haaland and Agriculture Secretary Thomas J. Vilsack, whose agency oversees the Forest Service, issued the Joint Secretarial Order on Fulfilling the Trust Responsibility to Indian Tribes in the Stewardship of Federal Lands and Waters. Order No. 3403 recognizes that treaties and trusts are inherent to federal lands management, promotes the benefit of "Tribal expertise and Indigenous knowledge," and establishes co-stewardship with tribes as a working model. Haaland also named Charles Sams III (Confederated Tribes of the Umatilla Indian Reservation) to head the National Park Service (NPS), a tribal-citizen first.

In a March 2022 hearing before the House's Natural Resources Committee, Sams outlined where he saw tribes and national parks intersecting in a future that looks more and more like Australia and New Zealand. "As Director of the NPS, I am committed to seeking ways to increase opportunities for co-stewardship with Tribes in the interest of all peoples of the United States and in accordance with the laws and policies governing the NPS," Sams told the committee. "The NPS works cooperatively with Tribes in the stewardship of national parks. This co-stewardship takes many forms, including co-management obligations in law, collaborative and cooperative agreements, and self-governance agreements."

Co-management is already a fact of life at four national park and monument sites. The best known is Arizona's Canyon de Chelly, a national monument that sits on the Navajo Reservation and is owned by the Navajo Nation with the National Park Service overseeing park operations. This arrangement dates to 1931, when Pres. Herbert Hoover, with the consent of the Navajo Nation's tribal council, signed the proclamation to turn the place the Dinés know as Tseyí into a national monument. Diné people continue to live inside the monument's boundaries, raise crops, and graze livestock just as they have done for generations. In 2023 the Park Service, the Navajo Nation, and the Bureau of Indian Affairs began developing a management plan likely to follow the model set by Australia's Uluru-Kata Tjuta National Park.

In Alaska's Glacier Bay National Park, the Park Service and the Hoonah Tlingit Indian Association negotiated a co-management agreement after the passage of a 2014 law allowing traditional and sustainable harvesting of glaucous-winged gull eggs inside the park. The egg harvest not only offers a desirable source of springtime nutrition, but it also reinforces tribal connections to homeland and passes traditional wisdom down from the elders to younger generations.

Situated along the Lake Superior shoreline and cozying up to the U.S.-Canada border, Grand Portage National Monument is co-managed by the Grand Portage Band of Chippewa (Ojibwe) Indians and NPS. That fits since the monument memorializes both the ancient homeland of the Ojibwe peoples and the fur trade that was once an economic engine in North America and employed both tribal people and Europeans. The monument's 713 acres, which sit in the middle of the Grand Portage reservation, were donated by the tribe. Tribal members provide maintenance, interpretation, and resource management on the reservation, in the national monument, and at nearby Isle Royale National Park.

Most of the formal relationships between tribes and the NPS are not co-management arrangements but collaborations and partnerships built upon agreements between tribal and federal governments. Currently, these arrangements total about eighty, with the number expected to grow in the coming years.[16]

In a groundbreaking partnership along Northern California's coast, the Yurok Tribe leads a program with NPS and the U.S. Fish and Wildlife Service to bring California condors back to the skies of the Pacific Northwest. The great birds have been extinct in the region since the 1890s, destroyed by settlers who shot them down or poisoned them with arsenic-and strychnine-laced carcasses intended to kill wolves and bears. It didn't help matters that settlers killed seventy-five percent of the Yurok (Yúruks, Pue-leek-la') people through murder and epidemic and took over their lands. That put an end to the tribe's stewardship practices, like cultural burns to maintain prairies that sustain the large herbivores condors scavenge. To the Yuroks, who are now California's largest federally acknowledged tribe, the condor's loss stands as a spiritual catastrophe. The great bird—*prey-go-neesh* in the Yurok tongue—has been woven into the *Hlkelonah*, the Yuroks' cultural and ecological landscape, since the world began. Condors play important roles in the tribe's creation stories, and songs related to the birds, like their feathers, are important components in Yurok world renewal ceremonies that seek ecological balance.

As with Bears Ears and the five tribes, condor restoration started with the Yuroks. The work began in 2003 with an elders council's vision to bring the sacred birds back and their commitment to do whatever it would take to make the vision real. From that beginning the Yurok Wildlife Department did the hard work of assessing the habitat to be occupied by reintroduced condors and learning the intricacies of caring for birds whose lifestyles are both solitary and communal. Since the condors would range well beyond Yurok country, community meetings were held as far north as Portland, Oregon, and as far south as Sacramento, California. Once attendees were assured that the enormous condors—their nine-foot wingspans make them the largest of all North American land birds—posed no danger to people or their dogs, cats, and backyard chickens, popular response to the idea of bringing back the majestic creatures grew into enthusiasm. Buoyed by public acceptance of the program, the Yurok Tribe concluded a memorandum of understanding with sixteen public and private entities ranging from the NPS and the Bureau of Land Management to Pacific Gas and Electric and the Ventana Wildlife Society. After fourteen years of work, including a five-year National Environmental Protection Act review process that involved the tribe as an equal and sovereign partner with NPS and Fish and Wildlife, the Yuroks received approval to bring back the long-missing birds.

The tribe built a release facility and other infrastructure in a remote location within Redwood National Park, which overlaps with the tribe's ancestral territory. The first bird to arrive was Condor 746, an eight-year-old adult male nicknamed *Paaytoquin* (Come Back) and borrowed from an Idaho breeding program to mentor the younger birds being prepared for release. Their life lessons learned, the first two condors A2 and A3—named *Nes-kwe-chokw'* (He Who Returns) and *Poy'-we-son* (He Who Goes Out Ahead)—were set free on May 3, 2022, to roam, soar, feed, and settle into their new home. On May 25 condor A0 *Ney-gem' 'Ne-chween-kah* (She Who Carries Our Prayers) took to the skies, and on July 14 A1 *Hlow Hoo-let* (At Last We Fly) followed. In October the first four released birds were joined by two more: A4, a confident young male aptly named *Cher-perhl So-nee-ne-pek'* (I Feel Strong), and A5, a milder bird that likes to check things out and goes by *Neee'n* (Watcher) In November, A7 *He-we-che* (I'm Healthy, a name given after minor surgery for a bill infection) and A6, whose cautious personality earned him the name *Me-new-kwek'* (I'm Shy), rounded out the first year's cohort.

Three more condors were set free in November 2023, and the plan is to release four to six birds each year for two decades, tracking and monitoring the slow-growing population along the way. Over time, mature condors will extend their territory, mate, nest, and raise their young, leading to the long, slow return of these magnificent and majestic birds to the skies over northern California, much of Oregon, and northwest Nevada. Across that great reach of their longtime habitat, condors will be extinct no longer.

Risks to the birds remain, in part because of what humans do. The carcasses of two poached elk left in the condors' range in November 2022 contained enough lead fragments from illegal ammunition to kill several birds. Fortunately, the contaminated meat was discovered and removed before the condors found it and dove into a fatal feast.

Then, in early 2023, the virus known as highly pathogenic avian influenza killed twenty-one of the 118 Arizona and Utah condors that soared over the Grand Canyon and Zion National Park. So far, the disease has yet to appear in condors in California or Baja California. Still, when the virus was detected in other bird species in Yurok country, Condor 746 was transferred to the safer locale of the Oakland Zoo to protect his life and genetics for future generations. The Yurok Condor Recovery Program is now taking new precautions to prevent accidental spread of the virus from human handlers and building isolation pens in case any of the birds fall sick. In addition, the program is testing for the virus at the condors' twice-yearly health checks and inoculating them, as well as all new birds to be released in the future, now that the bird flu vaccine has been approved for use in condors.

For Tiana Williams-Claussen, the Harvard-educated director of the Yurok Tribe Wildlife Department who has led the tribe's effort from the beginning, the restoration is both personal and communal. "I have a five-year-old daughter. She is going to grow up with condors in her sky for her entire life," Williams-Claussen said. "She is not going to know what it is to miss condors. She will always live in relationship with condors, which is really what this project is all about—bringing condor home, back into our communities, back into our conversations, back into our households, and into the minds and hearts of our children on behalf of the hearts of our elders."

Importantly, the condor restoration effort has legs beyond Yurok country. "We're creating a template for how other parks and tribes can work together," Williams-Claussen continued. "They can look at what we've done and the success we're having and build their own programs on this foundation."[17]

Things have changed and are changing from Muir's time to our own. Still, getting all the way to equality and justice is a slog, and America's public lands remain a place of struggle for tribal survival. Just ask the Timibisha (Tümpisa) Shoshones.

The Timibishas positively hate the name Death Valley. For one thing, Death Valley is a settler name imposed on what they know and revere as

Tupippüh, or homeland. For another, it's simply not done. The Timbishas refrain from speaking about the dead, preferring to describe the departed as "the one it has happened to." And the name Death Valley, according to Timbisha elder Pauline Esteves, amounted to unwarranted denigration. The valley isn't about those it has happened to. Rather, she wrote, "this is a place about life. It is a powerful and spiritual valley that has healing powers, and the spirituality of the valley is passed on to our people."

Esteves was a child when her home village at Furnace Creek was absorbed into Death Valley National Monument in 1933. Her tribal legacy reached back much further than her own personal story. "Our people, the Timbisha, have always lived here. The Creator, Appü, placed us here at the beginning of time," she made clear.

When Pres. Herbert Hoover signed the proclamation that established Death Valley, neither he nor anyone else in the federal government gave a thought to the Timbishas' title to Tupippüh. Like many California tribes, the Timbishas lacked a reservation and had no legal status with the federal government. They, along with the other Western Shoshone tribes, signed an 1863 peace treaty with the United States in Ruby Valley, Nevada, but that agreement gave them no land. Even though Hoover's proclamation made the Timbisha homeland part of the national monument, NPS felt it owed these reservation-free, tribal people nothing. If anything, the Timbishas posed a problem. NPS saw them as a threat to the scarce water supplies needed for a growing stream of tourists, and the poverty the tribe lived in at Furnace Creek, right next door to the monument's Furnace Creek headquarters and the upscale Furnace Creek Inn, amounted to an unwelcome eyesore. To lessen the effect of subsistence activities on the purportedly pristine environment of the park, NPS banned hunting and gathering by the Timbishas. And the people dubbed an "eyesore" were moved to forty acres outside the tourist viewshed, where NPS settled them in eleven adobe houses. The accommodations were primitive: no electricity, indoor plumbing, or heating and cooling. The only water came from a single, communal tap.

When American policy in the 1950s set out to terminate reservations, Death Valley Superintendent Fred W. Binnewies launched an under-the-table policy to force the Timbishas out of Furnace Creek one adobe at a time. NPS began collecting rents and forbidding the Timbishas from making repairs or improvements without permission, and it required them to apply for permits to occupy their homes. NPS even turned firehoses on adobes whose residents had made the usual summer migration to the cooler, higher-elevation Wildrose Canyon, thus washing the unoccupied residences away.

Meanwhile, NPS had rid Yosemite of the Yosemites and Grand Canyon of the Havasupais. Bucking the trend, Esteves and the elders organized Furnace Creek's residents to protest their shabby treatment, lobbied for their cause outside the national monument, and won the support of the Inter-tribal Council of California, California Indian Legal Services, and the Native American Rights Fund. When the Bureau of Indian Affairs launched its new federal acknowledgment process in 1978, the Timbisha legal team filed a petition. In 1983 the Timbisha Shoshone Tribe became the one and only California tribe ever to win acknowledgment.

Recognition delivered no reservation, however. The first step toward that goal came with the California Desert Protection Act of 1994 that elevated Death Valley from monument to park, expanded it into the largest park outside Alaska, protected 1.2 million acres from further development, and— owing to the Timbishas' savvy lobbying of Hawaii Senator Daniel Inouye to insert an amendment they wanted—instructed the Interior secretary to find the tribe a reservation. It came to be in 2000 with the Timbisha Homeland Act, which set aside five land parcels in California and Nevada totaling 7,754 acres, including 314 at Furnace Creek. The law also recognized Timbisha subsistence activities within the park as a tribal right that contributes to improved land stewardship.

Today the Death Valley website, run by the same NPS that once worked to expel the Timbishas by fire-hosing their adobes, declares them "active partners with Death Valley National Park in preserving the land they have always called their homeland." Things have changed.[18]

They've changed, too, in Yosemite, the park synonymous with John Muir and one set aside in the era when pristine meant Indigenous-free. As required by administrative law since the early 1980s, Yosemite officials consult every year with a consortium of seven tribes traditionally associated with its lands and waters. That's not ownership, nor co-management. It is nothing more than consultation—a word of ambiguous meaning at best. To their credit, Yosemite's NPS leaders and personnel have been listening more and more to the tribes and recognizing their role not only in the park's past but also in its present. Still, the people who were the Ahwahneechees, became the Yosemites, and now call themselves the Southern Sierra Miwuks remain federally unacknowledged. Not that they haven't tried to fix that.[19]

The bind the Southern Sierra Miwuks find themselves in plagues many California tribes. When the U.S. Senate refused in July 1852 to ratify the eighteen treaties signed by at least 119 tribal signatories, then locked the repudiated agreements in a secret archive, the treaty relationship that commonly underpinned tribal acknowledgment evaporated. The Southern Sierra Miwuks' ancestors signed three of the treaties, but they, like the other tribes who signed on, learned what had happened in the Senate only much later. Nor did they know that under the 1851 California Land Claims Act they had only two years to advocate for aboriginal title to their lands before it went legally extinct. Even though neither federal nor state government made the least effort to inform the tribes of the legal requirement, popular opinion held that the tribes' failure to present their case moved every acre they occupied into the public domain. Legally, Native Californians became landless. Later, a few reservations were established, mostly in Southern California, and funds were allocated to buy small rancherias for some, but by no means all, landless Northern California tribes.[20]

The Yosemites had neither reservation nor rancheria, but since many were living and working in Yosemite Valley, they did have a de facto land base. That came to a flaming end in 1969 when NPS burned down the last of the cabins in Wahhoga. This was the era of termination, when the federal government was shutting down reservations and rancherias and, in an unnamed bureaucrat's words, "getting out of the Indian business." The NPS was going with the anti-tribal flow.

A few years after Wahhoga's fiery demise, the former tribal residents of Yosemite Valley established the nonprofit American Indian Council of Mariposa County. The council helped fund an effort to win federal acknowledgment under the tribal name of the Southern Sierra Miwuk Nation (SSMN). SSMN filed a letter of intent to petition for federal acknowledgment in 1982 and delivered the application itself two years later.[21]

Now the Southern Sierra Miwuks had to wait. And wait they did, producing documents and other evidence to support the petition all the while and at their own considerable expense. Not until November 2010 did the Bureau of Indian Affairs' Office of Federal Acknowledgement (OFA) place the petition under active consideration. Regulations require that acknowledgment be decided within eighteen months. Instead, OFA suspended consideration six times just because it could, then dragged the process out further with seventeen unexplained extensions. The SSMN's lawyers—led by Stephen Quesenberry, who also worked on the successful acknowledgment effort for Death Valley's Timbisha Shoshones—complained in a September 2017 letter to OFA about the irregular procedures and the improperly extended process. Fourteen months later, OFA responded with its proposed finding. Eight years of bureaucratic process had produced a proposed finding of a mere twenty-seven pages plus bibliography, a whimper of a response at best. Worse, the finding recommended against acknowledgment.

OFA did so on grounds as narrow and bizarre as they were brief. The law requires that the application of a tribe seeking acknowledgment be evaluated according to seven criteria that range from demonstrating descent from a distinct tribe or tribes to producing a tribal government document. OFA seized upon the single criterion requiring the applicant to comprise a distinct community continuously since 1900. The proposed finding declared that the Southern Sierra Miwuks failed to demonstrate their existence between 1982 and 2011, a span OFA chose to define as "at present." Obviously, OFA was failing to consider SSMN's existence as evidenced by its long-term and ongoing relationship with NPS during those very years. And, although the law requires the application to be evaluated according to all seven criteria, OFA failed to look at the remaining six, claiming, wrongly, that its guidance documents allowed it to do so.[22]

Oddly, despite all the unexplained delays, the SSMN application had previously looked to be faring well, according to insiders. Aldo E. Salerno, a former OFA historian who peer-reviewed the tribe's case, said that the office drafted a proposed finding that ran two hundred pages and affirmed acknowledgment on all seven criteria. Mark A. Nicholas, also a former OFA historian who worked on the SSMN petition, agreed with Salerno that the evidence was all there and it qualified the tribe for acknowledgment. The approval draft went for legal review, then came back cut to only twenty-seven pages denying acknowledgment. Gordon M. Schoepfle, who had served on the three-member evaluation team in his days an an OFA cultural anthropologist, decried the proposed finding's selective documentation. He wrote that it was no longer in "my best interests to be associated with the evaluation processes suggested by this sort of OFA-originated document." Further, he said, this in no way typified the OFA he had worked for. Nicholas declared the review process broken and asserted that OFA's attorneys had improperly interfered with the fact-finding process. Salerno went public online and decried the proposed finding as a sham.[23]

In his letter of protest, SSMN attorney Stephen Quesenberry demonstrated that OFA had broken its own rules by failing to evaluate the application on all seven criteria and focusing instead on only one requirement. Then he excoriated OFA for failing, as required, to supply SSMN with the documents on which it based the finding. Instead, Quesenberry had to file a Freedom of Information Act (FOIA) request to get what the law requires. Then there was the matter of "unambiguous previous federal acknowledgement," or UPFA in the arcana of Indian law. Regulations require OFA to determine whether the applicant produced adequate evidence that the federal government has dealt with the tribe in a way demonstrating its UPFA status. Signing a treaty with the tribe is one way to demonstrate UPFA; that happened with the Southern Sierra Miwuks three times in the 1850s. Although a 2016 letter from OFA stated that the tribe had been acknowledged unambiguously as of 1857, the proposed finding walked back that determination and said that the tribe still had to produce evidence for UPFA. As for the disputed years of 1982–2011, SSMN had, at OFA's request, provided hundreds of documents to support its existence as a community. OFA never even acknowledged receiving the evidence.

To correct this injustice, Quesenberry argued, the proposed finding should be withdrawn, all FOIA documents provided to SSMN promptly, additional evidence of UPFA and present community reviewed, and a new and updated proposed finding consistent with regulations and principles issued.[24] In short, *get your act together, cut the crap, and let's see the Southern Sierra Miwuk Nation acknowledged as the tribe it is.*

"It's almost as if the acknowledgement process is designed to stop the tribes," Quesenberry said. "With all the legal and scholarly support it takes to file an acknowledgement application, the process becomes at least a $1 million proposition. For Indigenous peoples who lack financial resources and a land base, who are struggling just to maintain their culture and their existence, that's absurd."[25]

And the stakes are major. Acknowledgment would deliver major benefits to SSMN, including protection under the Indian Child Welfare Act, annual income of $1.1 million from the Indian Gaming Revenue Sharing Trust Fund to support non-casino tribal government services, access to the Indian Health Service, and participation in any number of BIA programs. And acknowledgment would fundamentally change the connection between SSMN and Yosemite National Park by formalizing a sovereign government-to-government relationship. At the moment, SSMN is working on restoring the historic village of Wahhoga, including constructing a ceremonial round-house with traditional methods and materials. Acknowledgment would place SSMN on an equal footing with NPS on the Wahhoga restoration and on all matters coming before Yosemite's tribal consortium.[26]

When the proposed finding denying acknowledgment to SSMN became public, a wide array of groups and individuals expressed both support of the tribe and dismay at OFA's position. Mariposa County's Board of Supervisors protested to OFA that the county had worked with SSMN for decades and that the proposed finding was ludicrous in light of that history. Other county groups, including Yosemite Gateway Partners, foster care advocacy nonprofit CASA, the Spiritual Assembly of the Bahá'ís of Mariposa County, the county's Office of Sheriff-Coroner Public Administrator, and the Sierra Foothill Conservancy weighed in on behalf of SSMN. So did fellow members of Yosemite's tribal consortium: the neighboring Jackson Rancheria Band of Miwuk Indians and the Mono Lake Kootzaduka'a Tribe. Plant scientist M. Kat Anderson of the University of California, Davis, said that *Tending the Wild*, her groundbreaking book on the myriad environmental benefits of Indigenous land stewardship, was rooted in the years she spent absorbing the long-held ecological wisdom of SSMN elders. Park Superintendent Michael Reynolds let OFA know that Yosemite had been consulting with SSMN for over forty years on the general management plan and other significant environmental matters, and the park had signed a thirty-year agreement with SSMN in 2018 to restore and maintain Wahhoga. And five members of the

House Committee on Natural Resources informed the Interior Department that they were keeping a concerned congressional eye on the SSMN process and recommending an extended public comment period in response to the denial—basically saying, *give these folks a fair shake already.*[27]

The rising pressure has nudged the federal needle at least a little. In early May 2022, R. Lee Fleming, OFA's director, let SSMN know that the deadline for resubmitting the acknowledgment application had been extended from mid-May to November 2022. Then, as the November deadline approached, Fleming granted the tribe's requests for two more deadline extensions. Although OFA had agreed to produce all the documents covered by the FOIA request, it was slow to deliver them. One tranche contained almost six thousand images that required weeks of work to analyze. The latest batch, turned over in May 2023, was heavily redacted, but it did contain a treasure trove of more than a hundred public-comment letters supporting SSMN acknowledgment based on personal histories from local families and knowledge of the tribe's connection to Yosemite from authors, federal agency professionals, and state and local officials.[28]

With only minutes to spare, the legal team pulled the materials together to file an updated petition on the December 6, 2023, deadline. How long it will take OFA to respond is anyone's guess. SSMN's four-decade effort to receive federal acknowledgment continues to drag on, and one wonders why something so obvious and so lawful has taken so absurdly—and so unjustly—long.

Even without federal acknowledgment, the tribe has been working for decades to support community members with programs including health care services, language and cultural preservation, and food distribution. In addition, SSMN is building a campaign that will help tourists realize that Yosemite's full history begins well before John Muir.

Barely had the embers from the Wahhoga fire cooled when three tribal elders—Jay Johnson, Les James, and Bill Tucker—set to lobbying NPS to include a restoration of the village, complete with ceremonial roundhouse, in what over time became the Yosemite National Park General Management Plan of 1980. "The park didn't see that coming," Sandra Chapman, the tribal chair, made clear. "But that was the elders' vision, and that's what we've been doing. We persevere, we keep on going."

In 2009 ground was broken to build the roundhouse with traditional methods and materials to ensure its spiritual and cultural integrity. Two years later, then-Park Superintendent Don Neubacher shut the project down by claiming that the roundhouse ran afoul of national building codes. And so the partially built structure sat, open to the elements, for five years. That's when Mike Reynolds, who had grown up in the park with the SSMN elders and supported the Wahhoga restoration, replaced Neubacher. That same year the Wenaha Group, a Native American-owned construction management and consulting firm based in the Seattle area, certified the roundhouse's structural soundness. Construction resumed with an all-Native crew volunteered by the Jackson Rancheria Band of Miwuk Indians. In 2018 Superintendent Reynolds signed the Thirty-Year General Agreement for Wahhoga with SSMN, and as of this writing construction of the roundhouse continues.

In May 2023 SSMN and the park returned the Wilson Cabin, the only one of the original structures to escape the 1969 fire because it had been moved out of the village, back to its original location and dedicated it to the twenty-nine SSMN military veterans who once lived in the village. In addition, the new Wahhoga Indian Cultural Center will be connected to Yosemite Valley's utilities to accommodate visitors, with a goal completion date of 2026. The center will host traditional ceremonies for tribal members in the roundhouse, and non-tribal tourists will, with the help of tribal guides and docents, learn that SSMN remains a vital part of today's Yosemite. "People coming here will slow down and have a chance to experience the peace and calm that is Wahhoga. It's what we call healing," Chapman said.

"It really bothers me when people think Yosemite began with John Muir," she continued. "Our ancestors were here long, long before he ever heard of this sacred place. Tourists who come to Wahhoga will see we're still here."[29]

When OFA's proposed finding against SSMN acknowledgment went public, one of the groups joining the outcry against it was the executive committee of the Sierra Club's Tehipite Chapter, which is based in Mariposa County. Authorized by the national Sierra Club to speak on its behalf, the Tehipite leaders voted to support federal acknowledgment for the tribe as an action "consistent with the Sierra Club's recognition of the importance of environmental justice as a concern for the Club and our members."[30]

In taking that stand, the Sierra Club was reversing the legacy of its own creation. Founder John Muir had endorsed the Mariposa Battalion's violence against the Yosemites, ancestors of the Southern Sierra Miwuks, as both self-defense against rustling and murder and as a step toward transforming the valley into a pristine, ahistorical temple of nature. That was then. Now Muir's Sierra Club is recognizing the injustice done to the Yosemites and joining in the campaign to acknowledge their tribal descendants as the Southern Sierra Miwuk Nation.

John Muir's reaction to this turnabout is unknowable. He may have remained stuck in his view of the tribes as having "no right place in the landscape" and disapproved of the Sierra Club's support of SSMN. Then again, knowing now what he did not know then, such as the genocidal injustice done to the tribes and the benefits Indigenous land stewardship provides to the very landscape he loved, Muir may have applauded the organization he founded and raised his own voice in support of acknowledgment. Only one thing is sure: over the past hundred-plus years the ground beneath Muir's feet, and ours, has shifted mightily.

Epilogue

THE VIEW FROM SHEEPY RIDGE, TWO

This narrative ends where it began, atop the lookout where John Muir beheld the wild sweep of northeastern California in the chilly twilight of early December 1874, and where I, too, have stood. Much has happened here in the nearly 150 years between Muir's visit and my own.

Tule Lake, which Muir beheld as a purple sheet reaching north into Oregon, has shrunk from over one hundred thousand acres to fifteen thousand at best. In bad water years, it dries up completely. Most of the lake was drained over a century ago by the Bureau of Reclamation to turn the exposed lakebed into farm fields, and what remains is a drain for irrigation runoff tainted with agricultural chemicals. Still, the surviving wetlands of the Klamath Basin remain a waypoint and destination for geese and ducks migrating along the Pacific Flyway. Down on the sagebrush flats south of Tule Lake, in the rain and snow shadow of Mount Shasta, wintering mule deer and coyotes range through the season. Wolves from Oregon have roamed over this area and likely will settle in and raise pups here someday soon.

Change has come, too, to the seat of the Modoc War, which lies below the ridge and extends out over the volcanic landscape Muir found downright creepy. Today it forms Lava Beds National Monument. Signage and trails guide visitors to landmarks that include Captain Jack's Stronghold, where the Modocs held out against a vastly larger military for months, and the Canby Cross that venerates the general killed during peace negotiations gone awry. Muir had wanted to set aside the whole sweep of Mount Shasta and the now Indigenous-free volcanic lands to the east as a national park, but his wasn't the vision that prompted the creation of the national monument in 1925. Rather, it focused on Euro-America's commemoration of military victories that killed off Native Americans and removed the survivors from their homelands.

For a time, that settler-colonial strategy held brutal sway. When Muir stood here, the insurgent half of the Modoc nation had been exiled to Oklahoma, where many died from disease and malnutrition worsened by heartbreak. The other half remained on the Klamath Reservation—an area that extended north and east from Oregon's Upper Klamath Lake over 880,000 acres and existed as one of the United States' largest reservations. The Modocs shared that land with the Yahooskin Paiutes (Goyatöka) and the Klamaths (Eukshikni, Auksni). Their reservation, however, no longer exists. Its vast forests of ponderosa pine proved too tempting for the federal government and private timber interests to leave in Indigenous hands when the post-World War II housing boom expanded the lumber market. Against the will of the three tribes, the 1954 Klamath Termination Act ended the reservation in return for a one-time payment to tribal citizens. The law also stripped Klamaths, Modocs, and Yahooskins of their status as federally acknowledged tribes.

After a long legal and bureaucratic effort, the three nations regained federal acknowledgment in 1986. The Klamath Indian Tribe Restoration Act, however, returned none of the taken land. The Klamath Tribes have since established a tribal center in Chiloquin, Oregon, acquired other portions of their former reservation, and built businesses and social services around the KLA-MO-YA Casino. These days, the tribes comprise some five thousand enrolled members and contribute fifty million dollars every year to the local economy.[1] Despite all the violence against them, the Klamath Tribes have done far more than simply survive. They are succeeding on their own terms.

Should you wish to see the landscape where all this has taken place, be sure to climb Sheepy Ridge on a clear evening, just as Muir did. With any luck, you'll get a distant glimpse of the snowy peaks of the South Warner Wilderness to the east. It's the most remote wilderness area in California and one little visited. Decades ago, I retreated into the South Warners, hoping to heal the soul injury left by my closest friend's suicide. Over the course of a week's backpacking, I looped about the wild crest of those mountains, with their deep forests, rugged escarpments, and ice-blue lake. I was as solitary as Muir liked to be, and, like him on an extended saunter, I let the place and its wonders in. I emerged with the re-discovery of the big thing Muir got so right: the awe that wild spaces call up connects us to the cosmos and shines a beacon through the black holes of human existence.

Where Muir went wrong was in assuming that this soulful connection to the wild belonged solely to people who traced their ancestry to northern Europe. He was hardly alone in this belief. Many of his friends and allies supported the spurious faux-scientific racism of the time and even, like Joseph C. LeConte, Henry Fairfield Osborn, and Madison Grant, advanced it. Muir never was the sort to hide behind a KKK hood for a lynching or join a vigilante posse for a dawn murder raid. Such personal hate found no place in him. Still, the effect of his blinkered thinking, writing, and advocacy was to celebrate the removal of Indigenous peoples from their homelands and to preserve these now-"pristine" wildernesses for Euro-Americans. That puts Muir squarely in the main channel of America's tortuous campaign to extend white supremacy to wildlands.

The Sierra Club, founded by Muir himself, is beginning to address this reality in an often-contentious struggle over calling out his racial attitudes and addressing their continuing harm. That fight has cost one executive director his job and for a time divided the organization's board of directors, sometimes nastily. That's the bad news. The good is that Muir, the Sierra Club, and other environmental organizations—all of them former bastions of outdoorsy white supremacy—saved stunning landscapes and ecosystems from for-profit destruction and passed them on to benefit all Americans. At the same time, Indigenous peoples are adding to the wild lands management paradigm the ecological wisdom they draw from millennia of living on this continent. Bears Ears National Monument, the Hoonah Tlingits gull's egg harvest in Glacier Bay, the Yurok Tribe's condor-restoration program, and other tribal efforts are shaping new, planet-saving strategies built on ancient ways.[2]

Perhaps Muir would scoff at these developments, show himself unwilling to admit he got only part of it right, and arch a skeptical eyebrow over letting all the wrong people into the wild. Then again, I like to imagine standing shoulder-to-shoulder with him atop cold, twilit Sheepy Ridge and looking out across the Lava Beds, a landscape he finally finds enthralling.

He would absorb this wild glory, then turn and give me a sly Scottish smile. From the same high perch bridging an eventful century and a half, we may be beginning to understand one another and realize, together, how far we still have to travel.

NOTES

To reduce distraction of note numbers in the text, single source notes cover all text since the preceding note.

PROLOGUE

1. Muir, "Modoc Memories."
2. Muir, "Modoc Memories"; McNally, *Modoc War*, 212–20.
3. Muir, "Modoc Memories"; Muir, My First Summer in the Sierra, 226.
4. Muir, *Steep Trails*, 104.

1. FROM OLD WORLD TO NEW

1. Muir, *Boyhood and Youth*, 53–54.
2. Turner, *Rediscovering America*, 7–12; Worster, *Passion for Nature*, 19–23; Muir, *Boyhood and Youth*, 12.
3. Turner, *Rediscovering America*, 28–29; Jennings, *Origins and Early History*, 54.
4. Worster, *Passion for Nature*, 37–40; Simpson, *Yearning for Land*, 49–51.
5. Devine, *To the Ends of the Earth*, 104, 142.
6. Wolfe, *Settler Colonialism*, 1–2; Wolfe, "Settler Colonialism," 388.
7. Muir, *Boyhood and Youth*, 58–59; U.S. Census Bureau, "Following the Frontier Line."
8. Simpson, *Yearning for Land*, 61, 65–66; Wolfe, *Son of the Wilderness*, 30; Bieder, *Native American Communities*, 135.
9. Bieder, *Native American Communities*, 53–58, 77.
10. Bieder, *Native American Communities*, 145–46; Ostler, *Surviving Genocide*, 297–308.
11. Wyman, *Wisconsin Frontier*, 160–61; Bieder, *Native American Communities*, 132.
12. Bieder, *Native American Communities*, 153–54.

13. Wyman, *Wisconsin Frontier*, 201–7.

14. Campbell, *Popular Lectures*, 24–26, 170, 174–75; Hensley, "Disciples of Christ."

15. Muir, *Boyhood and Youth*, 218–20.

16. Quoted in Wolfe, *Son of the Wilderness*, 28.

17. Muir, *Boyhood and Youth*, 81–82.

18. Muir, *Boyhood and Youth*, 88–89, 103–5, 113–14, 169–70.

19. Muir, *Boyhood and Youth*, 63–64, 71.

20. Muir, *Boyhood and Youth*, 200–203, 76–77.

21. Muir, *Boyhood and Youth*, 226–27, 230, 232–34.

2. A WIDENING WORLD DARKENS

1. Muir, *Boyhood and Youth*, 202.

2. Muir, *Boyhood and Youth*, 247–71; Worster, *Passion for Nature*, 69.

3. Muir, *Boyhood and Youth*, 274.

4. Badè, *Life and Letters*, 1:93–94.

5. Tuck, "Battle Cry of Peace," 20–26; Austin, "Prelude to War"; Jennings, *Origins and Early History*, 321–22.

6. Aaron Hathaway, "Confederate Captives in Madison: Camp Randall's History as Civil War Prisoner-of-War Camp," *Badger Herald*, January 21, 2016, https://badgerherald.com/banter/2016/01/21/confederate-captives-in-madison-camp-randalls-history-as-civil-war-prisoner-of-war-camp/; Turner, *Rediscovering America*, 107.

7. Badè, *Life and Letters*, 1:93.

8. Lee and Ahtone, "Land-Grab Universities"; Wisconsin data from https://www.landgrabu.org/universities/university-of-wisconsin.

9. Muir, *Boyhood and Youth*, 283.

10. Turner, *Rediscovering America*, 104–7.

11. Worster, *Passion for Nature*, 86–91; Muir, *Boyhood and Youth*, 287.

12. Simpson, *Yearning for Land*, 88–90.

13. Muir, *Thousand-Mile Walk*, x.

14. Wood, "Muir a Draft Dodger?"; Stanley, "Muir and Civil War."

15. Muir to David G. Muir, May 7 and August 12, 1866; italics in the originals.

16. Worster, *Passion for Nature*, 107.

17. Badè, *Life and Letters*, 1:154.

18. American Academy of Ophthalmology, "Sympathetic Ophthalmia."

19. Badè, *Life and Letters*, 1:154; Muir, *Letters to a Friend*, 19.

20. Quoted in Williams, "John Muir," 70; Badè, *Life and Letters*, 1:155.

21. Muir, *Letters to a Friend*, 9; Wulf, *Invention of Nature*, 1–9.

22. Muir, *Thousand-Mile Walk*, xv–xvii.

23. Muir, *Thousand-Mile Walk*, xix–xx, 1–2, 17–18; Worster, *Passion for Nature*, 120.

24. Muir, *Thousand-Mile Walk*, 16, 19, 39, 95, 164.

25. Wisconsin Historical Society, "Black History in Wisconsin" and "Population of Wisconsin, 1820–1990."

26. Muir, *Thousand-Mile Walk*, 3–4. In this case and others like it where Muir used offensively racist language, it is elided.

27. Muir, *Thousand-Mile Walk*, 9, 51, 60.

28. Worster, *Passion for Nature*, 103; Muir, *Thousand-Mile Walk*, 52–53.

29. Muir, *Thousand-Mile Walk*, 59.

30. Muir, *Thousand-Mile Walk*, 94, 110.

31. Muir, *Thousand-Mile Walk*, 103–4.

32. Muir, *Thousand-Mile Walk*, 96–99.

33. Muir, *Thousand-Mile Walk*, 95, 109.

34. Muir, *Thousand-Mile Walk*, 105–7, 110.

35. Muir, *Thousand-Mile Walk*, 43.

36. Ostler, *Surviving Genocide*, 267–74; Hicks, *Toward the Setting Sun*, 301–4, 306–14.

37. Garvey, "Mediating Citizenship," 461–69; Muir, *Thousand-Mile Walk*, 42–43; Nobel, "Miseducation of Muir."

38. Muir, *Thousand-Mile Walk*, 73, 80–81.

39. Muir, *Thousand-Mile Walk*, 84.

40. Muir, *Thousand-Mile Walk*, 89.

41. Holmes, *Young John Muir*, 171–73, 261–63; Muir, *Thousand-Mile Walk*, 78.

42. Muir, *Thousand-Mile Walk*, 156, 167–68.

43. Muir, *Thousand-Mile Walk*, 169–70.

44. Muir, *Thousand-Mile Walk*, 187.

45. LeMenager, "Crossing the Panama Isthmus," 7; Bertin, "Abolitions of Slavery."

46. Thomas and Thomas, *Anywhere Wild*, 6.

3. THE UNGODLINESS OF DIRT

1. Muir, *Thousand-Mile Walk*, 15, 42, 161, 189.

2. Owen, "Muir and Edenic Narrative," 26.

3. Merchant, *Reinventing Eden*, 2, 133–37; Thoreau, *Walden*, 195; Owen, "Muir and Edenic Narrative," 33.

4. Muir, *Thousand-Mile Walk*, 190–91.

5. Anderson, *Tending the Wild*, 3.

6. Wolfe, *Son of the Wilderness*, 105.

7. Worster, *Passion for Nature*, 153–55; Muir, *Thousand-Mile Walk*, 194–210.

8. Muir, *Thousand-Mile Walk*, 211–12; Holmes, *Young John Muir*, 178–79; Williams, *God's Wilds*, 85.

9. Muir, *First Summer in the Sierra*, 5–6.

10. Chan, "Contributions of Chinese Immigrants in Yosemite," 301.

11. Lönnberg, "Digger Stereotype"; Heizer, *They Were Only Diggers*, xiv–xv; Muir, *First Summer in the Sierra*, 9–10.

12. Muir, *First Summer in the Sierra*, 16.

13. Muir, *First Summer in the Sierra*, 27–31.

14. "The Act to Prevent the Sale of Fire-arms and Ammunition to Indians" was in effect from 1854 to 1913; see Madley, *American Genocide*, 227.

15. Muir, *First Summer in the Sierra*, 53–55, 58–59.

16. Ewart, "Mono Pass."

17. Muir, *First Summer in the Sierra*, 117–18, 122–23, 156–57.

18. Muir, *First Summer in the Sierra*, 129–30, 205–6.

19. Thoreau, "Walking, and the Wild," 5–6; *Online Etymological Dictionary*, "John Muir and 'Saunter.'"

20. Muir, "By-Ways of Yosemite," 271–72.

21. Muir, *First Summer in the Sierra*, 236, 247, 264.

22. Hughes and Swan, "How Much of Earth Is Sacred Space?" 247–48.

23. Muir, *First Summer in the Sierra*, 196; Solnit, *Savage Dreams*, 246.

24. Muir, *First Summer in the Sierra*, 95.

25. Owen, "Muir and Edenic Narrative," 33; Merchant, *Reinventing Eden*, 152–53; Lundberg, "John Muir and Yosemite's 'Castaway Book,'" 48–49.

4. YOSEMITE'S GENOCIDAL BACKSTORY

1. Bokovoy, *San Diego World Fairs*, 1–54; Madley, *American Genocide*, 36; Castillo, *Cross of Thorns*, 169; Sandos, *Converting California*, 57, 110–27.

2. González, *This Small City*, 28; Madley, *American Genocide*, 39–40; Bancroft, *California*, 91.

3. Kroeber and Heizer, *Almost Ancestors*, 29.

4. Lindsay, *Murder State*, 128–31, 271; Madley, *American Genocide*, 3, 38; Belich, *Replenishing the Earth*, 312–17; Barcott, "The Real Story of the 49ers."

5. Madley, *American Genocide*, 45–48.

6. Madley, *American Genocide*, 115–38; Akins and Bauer, *We Are the Land*, 136–37.

7. Lindsay, *Murder State*, 248–55; Madley, *American Genocide*, 157–63.

8. Lindsay, *Murder State*, 272–77; Madley, *American Genocide*, 12, 163–71; Heizer, "Eighteen Unratified Treaties," 1–5.

9. Nokes, *Troubled Life of Peter Burnett*, 1–6, 65–70, 168–69.

10. Burnett, "State of the State Address."

11. Nokes, *Troubled Life of Peter Burnett*, 165–69.

12. Lemkin, *Axis Rule*, 79.

13. Lemkin, *Axis Rule*, 8; McDonnell and Moses, "Raphael Lemkin"; McNally, "Dark History Hits Home," 79–80.

14. United Nations, "Convention on the Prosecution and Prevention of the Crime of Genocide."

15. Madley, *American Genocide*, 354.

16. Madley, *American Genocide*, 207–8, 354–55, 529–50; McNally, "Bret Harte's Voice for the Wiyots."

17. Lindsay, *Murder State*, 128.

18. Bunnell, *Discovery of the Yosemite*, 17.

19. Bunnell, *Discovery of the Yosemite*, 23–24.

20. Kelly, *Lafayette Bunnell, M.D.*, 180–91; Bunnell, *Discovery of the Yosemite*, 33; Madley, *American Genocide*, 190.

21. Solnit, *Savage Dreams*, 328–48; Shaler, "Mariposa and the Invasion of Yosemite," 126–27; Mitchell, "Maj. James D. Savage and the Tulareños," 324–26.

22. Bunnell, *Discovery of the Yosemite*, 20–21; Shaler, "Mariposa and the Invasion of Ahwahnee," 14, 163–65; Bill Coate, "Murdered Jim Savage Buried Four Times," *Madera Tribune*, December 31, 2017.

23. Bunnell, *Discovery of the Yosemite*, 24.

24. Bunnell, *Discovery of the Yosemite*, 37–40.

25. Bunnell, *Discovery of the Yosemite*, 42.

26. Hull, "Quality of Life," 237–38; Bunnell, *Discovery of the Yosemite*, 49–50; Spence, *Dispossessing the Wilderness*, 103–4; Hull, *Persistence and Pestilence*, 63, 151–53.

27. Bunnell, *Discovery of the Yosemite*, 51–52.

28. Shaler, "Mariposa and the Invasion of Ahwahnee," 224–25; Bates, "Names and Meanings for Yosemite Valley;" Fragnoli, "Naming Yosemite"; "A Bit of Indian History, as told by Della Hern," *Mariposa Gazette & Miner*, August 20, 1987.

29. Bunnell, *Discovery of the Yosemite*, 53, 56–58, 62.

30. Bunnell, *Discovery of the Yosemite*, 92–96.

31. Bunnell, *Discovery of the Yosemite*, 39.

32. Bunnell, *Discovery of the Yosemite*, 115–16, 147.

33. Bunnell, *Discovery of the Yosemite*, 108–16.

34. Bunnell, *Discovery of the Yosemite*, 121–25.

35. Grover, Conway, and Russell, "Early Years in Yosemite," 332–35; Bunnell, *Discovery of the Yosemite*, 141–43; Shaler, "Mariposa and the Invasion of Ahwahnee," 286–89.

36. Bunnell, *Discovery of the Yosemite*, 150–51; Russell, *One Hundred Years in Yosemite*, 46–48; Greene, *Yosemite*, 26; Sanborn, *Yosemite*, 59–60.

37. Gaskell, Brochini, and Johnson, "Five Decades," 12; Gaskell, "Indigenous Peoples and National Parks," 7–10; Merriam, "Indian Villages and Camp Sites," 202–8.

38. Cameron, Kelton, and Swedlund, *Beyond Germs*, 3–4; Jones, "Virgin Soils Revisited," 705; Ostler, "Never Been Just Disease."

39. La Pena, Bates, and Medley, *Legends of the Yosemite Miwok*, viii, 23–25.

40. Pierini, "Hetch Hetchy Project Impact Native Americans?"; Shaler, "Mariposa and the Invasion of Ahwahnee," 32–38.

5. RETURN TO THE GARDEN

1. Merchant, *Reinventing Eden*, 2, 118, 133–36; Outka, *Race and Nature*, 27–30; Muir quoted in Nijhuis, "Don't Cancel John Muir."

2. Yosemite Act of 1864.

3. Farquhar, "Exploration of the Sierra Nevada," 13.

4. King, *Vacation Among the Sierras*, 7–8.

5. Muir to Sarah Muir Galloway, April 5, 1871, in Badè, 1:247–48.

6. Worster, *Passion for Nature*, 167–69.

7. Worster, *Passion for Nature*, 177–79.

8. Muir, *Our National Parks*, 144–50.

9. Muir's annotated copy available at the Beinecke Rare Book and Manuscript Library at Yale University.

10. Painter, "Ralph Waldo Emerson's Saxons," 77–85.

11. Emerson, *English Traits*, 49–59; quoted in Painter, *History of White People*, 139–40; quoted in Nicoloff, *Emerson on Race and History*, 187–88.

12. Emerson, *Prose Works*, 1:28, 41, 509, 517, 518.

13. Branch, "'Angel Guiding Gently,'" 133.

14. Muir, "Reminiscences of Joseph LeConte," 210–11; LeConte, *Journal of Ramblings*, 73–74.

15. Carozzi, "Agassiz's Amazing Geological Speculation."

16. Muir, "Yosemite Glaciers"; Worster, *A Passion for Nature*, 194.

17. Carr to Muir, July 10, 1870, italics in the original; LeConte, *Journal of Ramblings*, 59; Muir, "Reminiscences of Joseph LeConte," 210.

18. Armes, *Autobiography of Joseph LeConte*, 12–13.

19. Armes, *Autobiography of Joseph LeConte*, 104, 130, 143.

20. Armes, *Autobiography of Joseph LeConte*, 144–53, italics in the original.

21. Quoted in Wallis, "Black Bodies, White Sciences," 104.

22. Quoted in Lurie, "Louis Agassiz and the Races of Man," 239.

23. Morton, *Crania Americana*, 6, 81–82.

24. Nott and Gliddon, *Types of Mankind*, 283, 79, italics in the original.

25. Lurie, "Louis Agassiz and the Races of Man," 227–42.

26. Armes, *Autobiography of Joseph LeConte*, 181, 221.

27. Armes, *Autobiography of Joseph LeConte*, 230–31, 234, 239.

28. Lee and Ahtone, "Land-Grab Universities"; Royster, "This Land Is Their Land."

29. Muir, "Reminiscences of Joseph LeConte," 212–13.

30. Lopez, *Horizon*, 259–60; LeConte, *Evolution*, 301; LeConte, "Effect of Mixture of Races," 85–86, italics in the original.

31. LeConte, "Effect of Mixture of Races," 100.

32. LeConte, *Evolution*, 86, italics in the original.

33. LeConte, *Race Problem in the South*, 360–61.

34. Gretchen Kell, "UC Berkeley's LeConte and Barrows Halls Lose Their Names" *Berkeley News*, November 18, 2020, https://news.berkeley.edu/2020/11/18/uc-berkeleys-leconte-and-barrows-halls-lose-their-names/; Hilgard, "Biographical Memoir of Joseph LeConte," 211.

35. Muir, "Reminiscences of Joseph LeConte," 211–12.

36. Douglass, *Claims of the Negro*, 15. In *Stamped from the Beginning*, Kendi writes of this statement, "Douglass, amazingly, summed up the history of racist ideas in a single sentence," 199.

37. Greene, *Yosemite*, 1:26–27; Spence, "Dispossessing the Wilderness," 27–39; Merriam, "Indian Villages and Campsites," 202.

38. Muir, *Yosemite*, 226–35.

39. Hassrick, "Art, Agency, and Conservation," 8.

40. Palmquist, "California Indian in Three-Dimensional Photography," 101–3.

41. Gordon-Cumming, *Granite Crags*, 133, 143, 151; a black-and-white version of *Indian Camp* appears on 132.

42. Castillo, "Petition to Congress," 273–77.

43. Clark, *Indians of the Yosemite Valley*, 63.

44. Muir, "Yosemite Valley," 58–59.

45. Badè, *Life and Letters*, 1:259–60.

46. Muir, Journal 5, August–October 1872, 47; Badè, *Life and Letters*, 2:29; Worster, *Passion for Nature*, 222–23; McNally, "John Muir in Klamath Country," 107–8.

6. WELL DONE FOR WILDNESS!

1. Muir, "Shasta in Winter."
2. Muir, "Wild Sheep of California," 358.
3. Muir, "Shasta Game."
4. Cohen, *Pathless Way*, 173–76; Muir, "Wild Wool," 361–65, italics in the original.
5. Cohen, *The Pathless Way*, 28–29, 131–32, 140–42.
6. Williams, *God's Wilds*, 34.
7. Muir, *Steep Trails*, 41, 43.
8. Bernbaum, *Sacred Mountains*, 148–50; Houck, "Salmon Repatriation," 23.
9. Muir, "Mt. Shasta," 174.
10. Muir, *Steep Trails*, 300–305, 321–23, 312, 273–74, 250.
11. Jacoby, *Crimes Against Nature*, 81–82; Kerns, *Texas Jack*, 236–40; Nabokov and Loendorf, *American Indians and Yellowstone*, 188.
12. Louisiana Strentzel to Muir, June 18, 1878; Muir to Strentzels, July 11, 1878.
13. Muir, *Our National Parks*, 210.
14. Catlin, *North American Indians*, 1:289–90, 292–95, italics in the original. See also Nash, "American Invention of National Parks," 728–30.
15. Thoreau, *Maine Woods*, 160. See also Nash, "American Invention of National Parks," 732–33.
16. U.S. Congress, "An Act to Set Apart a Certain Tract of Land."
17. Nabokov and Loendorf, *Restoring a Presence*, 29–30, 53; Nabokov and Loendorf, *American Indians and Yellowstone*, 35–236.
18. Nabokov and Loendorf, *Restoring a Presence*, xiii–xiv, 34–38.
19. Burnham, *Indian Country, God's Country*, 20–21; Muir, *Our National Parks*, 44.
20. Anderson, *Tending the Wild*, 1, 108; Stewart, *Forgotten Fires*, 37–42.
21. Muir, "The Yosemite Valley," 49; Muir, *Yosemite*, 8, 148, 87–90.
22. Olmsted, *Yosemite and the Mariposa Grove*, 15–20.
23. Taylor, "Return of the Last Survivor."
24. Quoted in Anderson, *Tending the Wild*, 157–58.
25. McCarthy, "Managing Oaks and the Acorn Crop," 220–24; Anderson, *Tending the Wild*, 169, 179–85; Lewis, "Patterns of Indian Burning," 75, 105–11.
26. Kroeber and Heizer, *Almost Ancestors*, 24.
27. Muir, *Letters to a Friend*, 73, 148.

7. MISSIONARY TO THE TLINGITS

1. Henry, *Across the Shaman's River*, 122–23, 131–32; Hinckley, "Presbyterian Leadership in Pioneer Alaska," 745, n. 11.
2. Muir, *Travels in Alaska*, 13.

3. Muir, *Travels in Alaska*, 19–27, italics in the original.

4. Muir, *Travels in Alaska*, 20–21.

5. Hinckley, "Early Alaskan Ministry of S. Hall Young," 175–79; Young, *Alaska Days with John Muir*, 11; Young, *Hall Young of Alaska*, 52, 259; Henry, *Across the Shaman's River*, 82–88.

6. Young, *Alaska Days with John Muir*, 12–13.

7. History Channel, "This Day in History"; Henry, *Across the Shaman's River*, 91–92.

8. Grinëv, *Tlingit Indians in Russian America*, 15–28, 64, 100, 116–23.

9. Henry, *Across the Shaman's River*, 46–48.

10. Grinëv, *Tlingit Indians in Russian America*, 193.

11. Hinckley, *Canoe Rocks*, 67, 100–102, 111–13; Jones, "Bombardment of Kaachx an.áak'w."

12. Muir, Journal 29, July 14, 1879, 20–21.

13. Muir, *Letters from Alaska*, 22, 25–26.

14. Muir, *Travels in Alaska*, 70–75; Engberg and Merrell, *John Muir*, 38–40.

15. Muir, *Travels in Alaska*, 46–55; Young, *Alaska Days with John Muir*, 37–51.

16. Muir, *Travels in Alaska*, 33–36; Mike Dunham, "How John Muir Became an Indian Chief—or Not," *Anchorage Daily News*, December 8, 2016, https://www.adn.com/alaska-life/2016/12/08/how-john-muir-became-an-indian-chief-or-not/#.

17. Muir, *Travels in Alaska*, 114–16; Young, *Alaska Days with John Muir*, 68–70; Genealogy Trails, "Welcome to Wrangell Borough, Alaska."

18. Muir, *Travels in Alaska*, 124–26, 131, 138, 198.

19. Muir, *Travels in Alaska*, 134–36; Muir, Journal 31, October 23, 1879, 14–15.

20. Muir, *Travels in Alaska*, 161–63.

21. Muir, Journal 31, November 3, 1879, 31–33; Muir, *Travels in Alaska*, 171, 173; Henry, *Across the Shaman's River*, 170–82.

22. Young, *Hall Young of Alaska*, 211–12.

23. Muir, Journal 31, November 3, 1879, 32–34.

24. Young, *Alaska Days with John Muir*, 120–21.

25. Young, *Hall Young of Alaska*, 216–18; Muir records the perilous passage, but not To'watte's scolding, in Journal 31, November 19, 1879, 47–49.

26. Worster, *A Passion for Nature*, 254–56.

27. Muir, *Stickeen*, 4; Young, *Alaska Days with John Muir*, 133–34, 136.

28. Young, *Alaska Days with John Muir*, 170–71.

29. Muir, *Travels in Alaska*, 234; Henry, *Across the Shaman's River*, 8; Dunham, "How John Muir Became an Ice Chief—or Not."

30. Muir, *Stickeen*, 17–74.

31. Muir, *Travels in Alaska*, 195.

32. Muir, *Travels in Alaska*, 197.

33. Petroff, *Report*, 40, 33.

34. Ross, *Pioneering Conservation in Alaska*, 176–78; Hinckley, "The Inside Passage," 68–70.

35. Muir, "Alaska Gold Fields"; Henry, *Across the Shaman's River*, 191–92.

8. ONE SAVAGE LIVING ON ANOTHER

1. Badè, *Life and Letters of John Muir*, 2:161–62.

2. Muir to Louie, May 16, 1881, in Badè, *Life and Letters of John Muir*, 2:165.

3. Tammiksaar, Sukhova, and Stone, "Hypothesis Versus Fact," 237–43; Sachs, "Humboldt Current," 495–500; Newcomb, *Our Lost Explorers*, 17–19.

4. Worster, *Passion for Nature*, 263.

5. Muir, *Cruise of the Corwin*, 8–16.

6. Muir, *Cruise of the* Corwin, 19–20.

7. Muir, *Cruise of the* Corwin, 26–29, 32.

8. Muir, *Cruise of the* Corwin, 32–33.

9. Muir, *Cruise of the* Corwin, 36.

10. Muir, *Cruise of the* Corwin, 37–38, 45.

11. Muir, *Cruise of the* Corwin, 45; Morgan, "'Some Could Suckle over Their Shoulder,'" 167–92.

12. Muir, *Cruise of the* Corwin, 76–77, 80–81.

13. Muir, *Cruise of the* Corwin, 89–91.

14. Muir, *Cruise of the* Corwin, 102–6.

15. Smithsonian Institution Archives, "Edward William Nelson."

16. Muir, *Cruise of the* Corwin, 117, 119–20; Nelson, *Eskimo About Bering Strait*, 270.

17. Muir, *Cruise of the* Corwin, 121.

18. Juzda, "Skulls, Science, and the Spoils of War," 156–67; McNally, *The Modoc War*, 242–43.

19. Muir, *Cruise of the* Corwin, 121; Crimmel, "No Place," 172–74, 177–78.

20. Nelson, *Eskimo About Bering Strait*, 269.

21. Hooper, *Report of the Cruise*, 11–12.

22. Crowell and Oozevaseuk, "St. Lawrence Famine and Epidemic," 1–19.

23. Rosse, *First Landing*, 177, 187, 202–11.

24. Muir, *Cruise of the* Corwin, 142–43, 152, 156, 176–77.

25. Muir, *Cruise of the* Corwin, 184, facing 195.

26. Muir, *Cruise of the* Corwin, 206.

27. Znamenski, "'Vague Sense of Belonging,'" 21–26; Muir, *Cruise of the* Corwin, 225–31.

28. Muir, *Cruise of the* Corwin, 237–39.

29. Newcomb, *Our Lost Explorers,* 111–25; Sachs, "Humboldt Current," 499–500.

30. Muir, *Cruise of the* Corwin, facing 190.

31. Ross, *Pioneering Conservation in Alaska,* 91.

9. THE GRAPES OF WEALTH

1. Foley, "Paradise in the Alhambra Valley," 14–18; *History of Contra Costa County,* 506–7.

2. *History of Contra Costa County,* 508; Foley, "Paradise in Alhambra Valley," 31; Milliken, Shoup, and Ortiz, "Ohlone/Costanoan Indians," 5, 20, 107–10, 115.

3. Foley, "Paradise in the Alhambra Valley," 19–25; *History of Contra Costa County,* 508.

4. Quoted in Hickman, "John Muir's Orchard Home," 340–42.

5. Foley, "Paradise in the Alhambra Valley," 28.

6. Sandos, *Converting California,* 1–3, 8; Stoll, *Fruits of Natural Advantage,* 56; Olmstead and Rhode, "A History of California Agriculture," 1.

7. Martinez Historical Museum, *Martinez,* 26; Wickson, *California Fruits,* 79–80.

8. Chan, *This Bittersweet Soil,* 325–27.

9. Hickman, "John Muir's Orchard," 342.

10. "The Storm—the Trains—the River" and "The Great Flood!," *Marysville Daily Appeal,* January 22, 1875; Muir, "Flood-Storm in the Sierra," 494–95. When Muir republished this essay in *Mountains of California* as Chapter 11, "The River Floods," he deleted this section.

11. Stoll, *Fruits of Natural Advantage,* 94; Young, *Alaska Days with John Muir,* 207.

12. Young, *Alaska Days with John Muir,* 204.

13. Dosch, "The Mystery of John Muir's Money," 61–64.

14. Sandos, *Converting California,* xiv–xv, 13; Street, *Beasts of the Field,* 54–55.

15. Street, *Beasts of the Field,* 101–5.

16. Madley, *American Genocide,* 157–63.

17. Street, *Beasts of the Field,* 119; Bell, *Reminiscences of a Ranger,* 34–36; Frances Dinkelspiel, "Op-Ed: Los Angeles Owes Native Americans an Apology," *Los Angeles Times,* June 21, 2019, https://www.latimes.com/opinion/op-ed/la-oe-dinkelspiel-newsom-apology-native-americans-los-angeles-20190621-story.html.

18. Madley, *American Genocide,* 332–33; Lindsay, *Murder State,* 128.

19. Chan, *This Bittersweet Soil,* 16–20, 25–26; Chan, "Chinese Livelihood in Rural California," 57.

20. Takaki, *Iron Cages*, 216–17.

21. Chan, "Chinese Livelihood in Rural California," 57; Waite, "Forgotten History of the Western Klan."

22. Chan, "Chinese Livelihood in Rural California," 69; Barry, *Documentary History*, 4–5; Stoll, *Fruits of Natural Advantage*, 124–26; Street, *Beasts of the Field*, 258–89, 353–54.

23. Chan, "Chinese Livelihood in Rural California," 62; Chan, *This Bittersweet Soil*, 129, 327–28; Barry, *Documentary History*, 10–14.

24. *Contra Costa Gazette*, April 29 and May 3, 1882, reprinted at http://frederickbee.com/martinezriotccg.html; Sides, *Backcountry Ghosts*, 148; Takaki, *Iron Cages*, 230–31; Chan *This Bittersweet Soil*, 332–33; Street, *Beasts of the Field*, 341–42.

25. Sarah Muir Galloway to Muir, November 20, 1885; Killion and Davidson, *Cultural Landscape Report*, 1:73, 77, 121; Muir to Louie Muir, July 9, 1887.

26. Street, *Beasts of the Field*, 311; Daniels, *Asian America*, 48–54.

27. John Muir Papers MS 48, box 15: Published & Precursor Works; Unpublished Works; Miscellaneous Notes, 1903–ca. 1910, 3.15.45.10931: [World Trip: The Chinese], 1904.

28. Dosch, "Mystery of John Muir's Money," 62; Hickman, "John Muir's Orchard Home," 352.

29. Dosch, "Mystery of John Muir's Money," 20–21.

30. Muir to Millicent Shinn, April 18, 1883; Young, *Alaska Days with John Muir*, 204.

31. Badè, *Life and Letters of John Muir*, 1:217; Baker, "John Muir," 377.

32. Martinez Historical Museum, *Martinez*, 35.

10. WILDERNESS INFLUENCER

1. Rossetti Archive, "Century Illustrated Monthly Magazine."

2. Johnson, *Remembered Yesterdays*, 280–89.

3. Muir, "Treasures of the Yosemite" and "Features of the Proposed Yosemite National Park."

4. Johnson, *Remembered Yesterdays*, 288–89; Worster, *Passion for Nature*, 219–22; Allegheny Forest Alliance, "Forest Reserve Act of 1891."

5. Collins, "Native Americans in the Census"; Turner, *Significance of the Frontier*, 227.

6. Taylor, *Rise of Conservation*, 34–35.

7. Walker, "Restriction of Immigration."

8. Roosevelt, *Winning of the West*, 1:100, 105; Bederman, *Manliness & Civilization*, 44, 181–82.

9. Dunlap, "Sport Hunting and Conservation," 51–52, 54.

10. Punke, *Last Stand*, 3, 109–10, 165–66; Taliaferro, *Grinnell*, 96–98, 103–4, 116, 118–19, 167–69.

11. Merchant, "Grinnell's Audubon Society," 10–18; Taliaferro, *Grinnell*, 149–55.

12. Jones, *John Muir and the Sierra Club*, 3–5, 306–7.

13. LeConte, "Sierra Club," 135–39; Jones, *John Muir and the Sierra Club*, 5–10, 170; Cohen, *History of the Sierra Club*, 8–9.

14. Jones, *John Muir and the Sierra Club*, 10–11; Taylor, *Rise of the American Conservation Movement*, 306–7.

15. Worster, *Passion for Nature*, 329–30; Powell, "From Barbarism to Civilization," 109, 123, italics in the original; Haller, *Outcasts from Evolution*, 100–101, 107–8; Pico, "The Darker Side of John Wesley Powell"; Jacobson, *Barbarian Virtues*, 140, 146–47.

16. Sierra Club, "Sierra Club Award Winners," 32–33.

17. Runte, *Yosemite*, 57–61; Hampton, *U.S. Cavalry Saved National Parks*, 146–52.

18. Muir, "National Parks and Forest Reservations," 3–5.

19. Spence, "Dispossessing the Wilderness," 45; Muir, *Our National Parks*, 210–11.

20. Muir, *Our National Parks*, 45.

21. Muir, *Letters to a Friend*, 80–81, italics in the original.

22. Muir, *Our National Parks*, 15; Cohen, "John Muir's Public Voice," 179–80.

23. Muir, *Our National Parks*, 32, 58; Muir, *Yosemite*, 226–35.

24. Deluca and Demo, "Imagining Nature," 553–54; Merchant, "Shades of Darkness," 380–83.

25. Muir, *Mountains of California*, 79, 90–93, 148, 198–99, 220–22.

26. Muir to Louie Muir, June 12, 1893; Johnson, *Remembered Yesterdays*, 314.

11. ON TOP OF THE WORLD

1. Merriam, "To the Memory of John Muir," 147; Muir to Clinton L. Merriam, August 20, 1871.

2. Klein, *Life & Legend of E. H. Harriman*, 214–15; Taliaferro, *Grinnell*, 269–70.

3. Gannett, "Harriman Expedition," 344–45; Lindsey, "Harriman Expedition of 1899," 383–86; Hinckley, "Inside Passage," 70–71.

4. Young, *Hall Young of Alaska*, 243–44.

5. Usher, "William Duncan," abstract.

6. Burroughs, "Narrative of the Expedition," 24–26.

7. Grinnell, "Natives," 152–56.

8. Quoted in Taliaferro, *Grinnell*, 267–68.

9. Muir, Journal 58, June 2, 1899, 4.

10. Muir, Journal 58, June 12, 1899, 16–18.

11. Muir, Journal 58, June 14, 1899, 19.

12. Goetzmann and Sloan, *Looking Far North*, 97–98.

13. Muir, Journal 58, June 24 and 25, 1899, 33–35.

14. Goetzmann and Sloan, *Looking Far North*, 113–14.

15. Goetzmann and Sloan, *Looking Far North*, 120–22.

16. Muir, Journal 59, July 4 and 19, 1899, 14. 39.

17. Goetzmann and Sloan, *Looking Far North*, 4, 135–37; Muir, Journal 59, July 11, 1899, 29.

18. Muir, Journal 59, July 12, 1899, 30–32; Goetzmann and Sloan, *Looking Far North*, 141–44.

19. Muir, Journal 59, July 23, 1899, 43.

20. Adams, *Tip of the Iceberg*, 277; Goetzmann and Sloan, *Looking Far North*, 161–70.

21. Gleach, "From Cape Fox, Alaska"; Cape Fox Corporation, "Our Past"; Worl, "Standing with Spirits," 31–39; Gmelch, *Tlingit Encounter*, 40–44.

22. Muir, Journal 60, July 26, 1899, 4; Goetzmann and Sloan, *Looking Far North*, 38.

23. Muir, Journal 60, July 27, 1899, 4; Keenan, "Yellowstone Kelly," 15–27.

24. Muir, "Notes on Pacific Glaciers"; Merriam, "To the Memory of John Muir," 147; Barrus, "With John o' the Birds."

25. Ostler and Jacoby, "After 1776," 9; Gilio-Whitaker, *As Long as Grass Grows*, 57–59; Thornton, "Native American Demographic and Tribal Survival," 23–24.

26. Orsi, "'Wilderness Saint' and 'Robber Baron,'" 143; Muir, *Edward Henry Harriman*, 3, 33, 39.

27. Eckenrode and Edmunds, *E. H. Harriman*, 80, 181; Olin, *California's Prodigal Sons*, 191, n. 7; Mowry, *California Progressives*, 10–18.

28. Muir to E. H. Harriman, January 5, 1905.

29. Muir to R. U. Johnson, February 24, 1905.

30. Orsi, "'Wilderness Saint' and 'Robber Baron,'" 149–52; Roosevelt, *Winning of the West*, 4:53.

31. Muir, *Edward Henry Harriman*, 21–27.

32. Sides, *Backcountry Ghosts*, 111. Kennan, *Salton Sea*, tells the saga of Harriman against the Colorado.

33. Quoted in Adams, *Tip of the Iceberg*, 293.

12. RIVER OUT OF EDEN

1. Muir, "Hetch Hetchy Valley," "Features of the Proposed Yosemite National Park," 664, and "Tuolumne Yosemite," 486; Davis-King, "Grass Called Hetch Hetchy"; Davis-King and Snyder, "Silver Thread," vii, 82–84, 37–41, 156–57; Pierini, "Hetch Hetchy Project Impact Native Americans?"; Medeiros, "Hetch Hetchy"; Hofmann, "Notes on Hetch Hetchy Valley"; National Park Service, *Voices of the People*, 175–76.

2. Clements, "Politics and the Park," 186–87.

3. Simpson, *Dam!*, 112–14.

4. Worster, *Passion for Nature*, 418–19, 422; Duncan and Burns, *National Parks*, 122.

5. Worster, *Passion for Nature*, 422–23.

6. Simpson, *Dam!*, 137, 141; Clements, "Politics and the Park," 190–91.

7. Smith, "Value of a Tree," 759–68; Muir, "Tuolumne Yosemite," 488; Muir, "Hetch Hetchy Valley," 220.

8. Quoted in Simpson, *Dam!*, 150–51; Phelan, "Hetch-Hetchy," 283–84.

9. "Harriman, Builder of Railroad Empire," *New York Times*, September 10, 1909; Campbell, *Mary Williamson Harriman*, 1–4, 13, 17–18.

10. Campbell, *Mary Williamson Harriman*, 21–25, 42–45; Spiro, *Defending the Master Race*, 126–27; Kevles, *In the Name of Eugenics*, 45, 54–55; Okrent, *The Guarded Gate*, 118–26; Allen, "Eugenics Record Office," 235.

11. Jacobson, *Barbarian Virtues*, 154–63. Source includes Davenport quotations from *Heredity in Relation to Eugenics*.

12. Stocking, *Race, Culture, and Evolution*, 180–81, 250–51; Bokovoy, *San Diego World's Fairs*, 87–88.

13. Jordan to Muir, December 9, 1909; Johnson, *Dark, Gray City*, 90–93, 152–53; Powell, *Vanishing America*, 82–84.

14. Strange Science, "Henry Fairfield Osborn"; Milligan, "Henry Fairfield Osborn," 5–6.

15. Osborn, *Impressions of Great Naturalists*, 197; Osborn quoted in Milligan, "Henry Fairfield Osborn," 19.

16. Osborn, *Impressions of Great Naturalists*, 199–200, 183.

17. Osborn, *Man Rises to Parnassus*, 169, 171–72, italics in the original; Osborn, *Impressions of Great Naturalists*, xvi–xvii, 197, 204.

18. Osborn, *Man Rises to Parnassus*, 185–86.

19. Spiro, *Defending the Master Race*, xii, 5, 7–19; Allen, "'Culling the Herd,'" 39–45; Okrent, *Guarded Gate*, 204–10.

20. Regal, "Madison Grant," 317–26; Spiro, *Defending the Master Race*, 157–61; Okrent, *Guarded Gate*, 210–18.

21. Spiro, *Defending the Master Race*, 145–57; Grant, *Passing of the Great Race*, xxi, 263.

22. Osborn, *Man Rises to Parnassus*, fig. 50 facing 109; Grant, *Passing of the Great Race*, 17–18.

23. Hitler quoted in Spiro, *Defending the Master Race*, 357; Offit, "Loathsome American Book."

24. Gessner, *Leave It as It Is*, 82–83; Simpson, *Dam!*, 155–56; Clayton, *Natural Rivals*, 150–55; Spence, "Crown of the Continent"; Taliaferro, *Grinnell*, 223–26; West, "Starvation Winter of the Blackfeet," 2.

25. Quoted in Branch, *John Muir's Last Journey*, 15–16; Worster, *Passion for Nature*, 441; Muir, *Yosemite*, 255; Muir to Helen Muir Funk, June 28, 1911.

26. Branch, *John Muir's Last Journey*, 34, 128.

27. Branch, *John Muir's Last Journey*, 114 footnote, 147; Muir, Journal 77, November 20, 1911, and January 20, 1912.

28. Branch, *John Muir's Last Journey*, 37–38, 49, 52–53.

29. Whitaker, "Report on the Prevention and Punishment of Genocide," 9; Norimitsu Onishi and Melissa Eddy, "A Forgotten Genocide: What Germany Did in Namibia, and What It's Saying Now," *New York Times*, May 29, 2021; Brown, "Natives Have Provided . . . ," *San Jose Daily Mercury News*, June 16, 1904; "African Savages Defeated," *Los Angeles Herald*, August 4, 1904; "Hereros Meet with Defeat," *San Francisco Call*, August 17, 1904; "Africans Fight Stubbornly," *Press Democrat*, January 8, 1905; Muir, Journal 77, January 10–11, 1912; Worster, *Passion for Nature*, 446.

30. Muir, Journal 77, January 24 January 29, 36–37; February 7, 42; February 13, 1912, 48.

31. Clements, "Politics and the Park," 203–12; Simpson, *Dam!*, 162; Muir to Harriman, June 21, 1913; Harriman to Muir, August 7, 1913; Muir to Kelloggs, September 15, 1913.

32. Muir to Kelloggs, December 27, 1913; Muir to Osborn, January 4, 1914.

13. LEAVE FOOTPRINTS, TAKE PICTURES

1. National Park Service Organic Act of 1916, section 1.

2. Simpson, *Dam!*, 318; Righter, *Battle over Hetch Hetchy*, 152.

3. National Park Service, *Voices of the People*, 31–32; Cothran, "Working the Indian Field Days," 209–10.

4. Cothran, "Working the Indian Field Days"; Spence, *Dispossessing the Wilderness*, 116–23; Merriam, "Indian Village and Camp Sites," 205–6; Gaskell, Brochini, and Johnson, "Five Decades," 8–9; Lasky, "Sierra Club Supports Federal Recognition," 1.

5. Spence, *Dispossessing the Wilderness*, 120–30, italics in the original; Pavlik, "In Harmony with the Landscape," 189–91; Margolin, *Deep Hanging Out*, 205; Gaskell, Brochini, and Johnson, "Five Decades," 14–16.

6. Fleck, *Henry Thoreau and John Muir*, 28–70; Fleck, "John Muir's Evolving Attitudes."

7. Muir, "By-Ways of Yosemite," 272.

8. Muir, "Passes of the Sierra," 649–52.

9. Muir, "Passes of the High Sierra," 24–33.

10. Muir, *Mountains of California*, 90–93.

11. Holmes, *Young John Muir*, 253–59; Holmes, "Rethinking Muir's First Summer," 153–64; Muir, *My First Summer*, 218–20, 225–28.

12. Trafzer, "John Muir's Missed Opportunity," 14–15; Burns, "Address to a Haggis."

13. National Parks Service, *Voices of the People*, 128–29.

14. Kelsey, "Rights and Wrongs of California Indians," 419; Madley, *American Genocide*, 165; Heizer, "Eighteen Unratified Treaties," 1–2; Advisory Council on California Indian Policy, "Historical Overview," 11.

15. Kelsey, "Rights and Wrongs of California Indians," 424.

16. Kelsey, "Census of Non-reservation California Indians," i–iii; Miller, "Primary Sources on C. E. Kelsey"; Miller, "Native American Land Ownership," 4–8; Sackman, *Wild Men*, 84–85.

17. Lummis, *Tramp Across the Continent*, 142.

18. Muir to Lummis, April 8, 1905.

19. Pratt, "Advantages of Mingling Indians with Whites," 46.

20. Lummis quoted in Pierce, *Making the White Man's West*, 101.

21. Padget, "Travel, Exoticism, and the Writing of Region"; Karr, "Warner Ranch's Indian Removal," 24–32; Pierce, *Making the White Man's West*, 95–117.

22. Merriam, *Dawn of the World*, 1–16; Camp, "C. Hart Merriam"; Davis-King, "Perspectives on Native American Historical Information," 30–31; Davis-King, "Native American Ethnographic Research," 24; Osgood, "Biographical Memoir of Clinton Hart Merriam," 19–23; Palmer, "In Memoriam: Clinton Hart Merriam."

23. Merriam, "Ethnographic Notes," 39–40, 41, 64–66.

24. Merriam, "To the Memory of John Muir," 146–47.
25. Davis-King, email to the author, July 11, 2022; Mike Wurtz, University of the Pacific Libraries, Special Collections, email to the author, June 24, 2022; Merriam, journal, summer 1900, August 31, 65–70; Muir, Journal 50, August 31, 1900.
26. Quoted in Stegner, *Where the Bluebird Sings*, 123.
27. Stegner, "Wilderness Letter"; Stegner, *Where the Bluebird Sings*, 128; MacEachern, "Who Had 'America's Best Idea'?"
28. U.S. Congress, "The Wilderness Act," Section 2c.

14. BETTERING AMERICA'S BEST IDEA

1. Thompson, "A Reluctant Rebellion."
2. Bears Ears Inter-Tribal Coalition, "Threats"; Hoffmann, "Fracking the Sacred," 341.
3. Bears Ears Inter-Tribal Coalition, "Proposal to President Barack Obama," 1–4.
4. U.S. President, Proclamation, "Establishment of the Bears Ears National Monument, Proclamation 9558."
5. Turrentine, "Zinke's Western 'Listening' Tour"; U.S. Department of the Interior, "Secretary Zinke Submits 45-Day Interim Report"; Zinke, "Final Report," 10–11, 13–14.
6. Bears Ears Inter-Tribal Coalition, "Bears Ears Inter-Tribal Coalition Condemns Zinke Recommendation."
7. U.S. President, Proclamation, "Modifying the Bears Ears Monument, Proclamation 9681"; Juliet Eilperin, "Uranium Firm Urged Trump Officials to Shrink Bears Ears National Monument," *Washington Post*, December 8, 2017, https://www.washingtonpost.com/national/health-science/uranium -firm-urged-trump-officials-to-shrink-bears-ears-national-monument/2017 /12/08/2eea39b6-dc31-11e7-b1a8-62589434a581_story.html?utm_term= .ff0dad6cd902.
8. Rikert, "President Biden Takes Sec. Haaland's Recommendation"; U.S. President, Proclamation, "Bears Ears National Monument, Proclamation 10285."
9. Bowekaty, "The Testimony of the Zuni Tribe," 2–4.
10. Bureau of Land Management, "Intergovernmental Cooperative Agreement," 2, 6; Bears Ears Inter-Tribal Coalition, "Collaborative Land Management Plan," i–ii.
11. Benallie, "Biden Declares Avi Kwa Ame"; Conservation Lands Foundation, "Avi Kwa Ame"; Avi Kwa Ame Coalition, "Celebrate Avi Kwa Ame"; Botts, "Biden Designates Two National Monuments."

12. U.S. President, Proclamation, "A Proclamation on Establishment of the Baaj Nwaavjo I'tah Kukveni–Ancestral Footprints of the Grand Canyon National Monument, Proclamation 1606"; Grand Canyon Coalition, "Tribes Propose New Baaj Nwaavjo I'tah Kukveni Grand Canyon National Monument."

13. Bears Ears Inter-Tribal Coalition, Newsletter, Spring 2022, membership update; Indigenous Earth Fund, "First Cohort."

14. Treuer, "Return the National Parks to the Tribes."

15. Andersson, Cothran, and Kekki, "Traditional Indigenous Knowledge," 2–3; Coombes, "Personifying Indigenous Rights in Nature?" 29–31.

16. Haaland and Vilsack, "Order 3403"; Sams, "Statement Before House Committee"; National Park Service, "Canyon de Chelly"; Brugge and Wilson, *Administrative History of Canyon de Chelly*, appendices 6 and 7; "NAU Team Facilitates Joint Agreement."

17. Yurok Tribe, "Yurok Condor Restoration Program"; Fritts, "Thanks to the Yurok Tribe"; U.S. Fish and Wildlife, "For the First Time in a Century"; U.S. Fish and Wildlife Service, "Endangered and Threatened Plants and Wildlife"; Steve Kirkland, U.S. Fish and Wildlife Service, email to the author, February 10, 2022; Tiana Williams-Claussen, interviews with the author, March 1, 2022, and August 2, 2023, and emails with the author, March 15 and March 23, 2022, and August 22, 2023; "Condors Soar Again over Northern California"; Levy, "How the Yurok Tribe Is Bringing Back"; Kimberly Wear, "Condor A6 Joins Growing North Coast Flock in the Wild," *North Coast Journal*, November 17, 2022, https://www.northcoastjournal .com/NewsBlog/archives/2022/11/17/condor-a6-joins-growing-north -coast-flock-in-the-wild; "Mentor Condor 746 Being Moved due to Bird Flu Concerns." *North Coast Journal*, December 13, 2022, https://www. northcoastjournal.com/NewsBlog/archives/2022/12/13/mentor-condor- 746-being-moved-due-to-bird-flu-concerns, "Local Condor Tests Include Exams for Deadly Avian Flu," North Coast Journal, May 17, 2023, https:// www.northcoastjournal.com/NewsBlog/archives/2023/05/17/condor -exams-underway-include-tests-for-deadly-avian-flu; and "Caring for the Condors," *North Coast Journal*, May 23, 2023, https://www.northcoastjournal .com/humboldt/caring-for-the-condors/Content?oid=26776152; Battaglia, "String of Poached Elk"; Grable, "Newest Flock."

18. Esteves, "Preface to the Draft"; Death Valley National Park, "Timbisha"; Miller, "The Timbisha Shoshone"; Miller, *Forgotten Tribes*, 123–55; Stringfellow, "How the Timbisha Shoshone Got Their Land Back"; Clarke, "When Green Groups Fought Native Rights."

19. National Archives, "Native American Relationships Policy"; Scott Gediman, Yosemite National Park Public Affairs Office, interview with the author, March 14, 2022.

20. Gaskell, "Real-Time Mapping"; Advisory Council on California Indian Policy, "ACCIP Historical Overview Report," 5–15.

21. Southern Sierra Miwuk Nation, "Federal Recognition."

22. Bureau of Indian Affairs, "Proposed Finding Against Acknowledgement," 1–2.

23. Salerno to Haaland, April 29, 2021; Nicholas to Assistant Secretary of Indian Affairs, April 12, 2019; Schoepfle to Assistant Secretary of Indian Affairs, March 21, 2019; Salerno, "A 'Sham.'"

24. Quesenberry to Newland, June 25, 2021, and September 29, 2021.

25. Stephen Quesenberry, interview with the author, February 17, 2022.

26. Southern Sierra Miwuk Nation, "Federal Recognition," and "Wahhoga."

27. Comments and letters linked on Southern Sierra Miwuk Nation, "Federal Recognition."

28. Stephen Quesenberry, emails to author, May 8 and August 21, 2023.

29. Sandra Chapman, Southern Sierra Miwuk Nation, interview with the author, May 24, 2022; Southern Sierra Miwuk Nation, "Wahhoga"; Wahhoga Committee, "Long Live Wahhoga"; Jeannie Tyrrell, "Coming Home: Wahhoga Historic Wilson Cabin Returns After a Long, Painful Wait," *Mariposa Gazette*, May 18, 2023, https://www.mariposagazette.com/articles/coming-home-2/.

30. Lasky, "Sierra Club Supports Federal Recognition," 1.

EPILOGUE

1. Bojorcas, Counter, and DeGross, "Oregon Termination"; KLA-MO-YA Casino, "Tribal History."

2. Brune, "Pulling Down Our Monuments"; Solnit, "Muir in Native America"; Brown, "Sierra Club Executive Director Resigns"; Mair, Hanson, and Nelson, "Who Was John Muir, Really?"; Colman, "'It's Just Wrong'"; Tobias, "At the Sierra Club, a Fierce Dispute"; NoiseCat, "Environmental Movement Needs to Reckon."

BIBLIOGRAPHY

UNPUBLISHED SOURCES

Bureau of Indian Affairs. "Proposed Finding Against Acknowledgement of the Southern Sierra Miwuk Nation a.k.a. American Indian Council of Mariposa County (Petitioner #82)." November 16, 2018.

Davis-King, Shelly. "The Grass Called Hetch Hetchy." Draft manuscript, January 2021.

———. "Native American Ethnographic Research for Stages 1 and 2 of the East Sonora Bypass." Standard CA: Davis-King Associates, June 2003.

———. "Perspectives on Native American Historic Information from Independence to Haiwee Reservoir in Owens Valley." Standard CA: Davis-King Associates, August 2003.

Davis-King, Shelly, and James B. Snyder. "The Silver Thread—Upper Tuolumne River American Indian Land Use in Yosemite National Park." Standard CA: Davis-King Associates, February 2010.

Frederick Bee History Project. http://frederickbee.com/index.html.

Gaskell, Sandra. "Indigenous Peoples and National Parks: Yosemite Southern Sierra Miwuk Nation of the 7 Affiliated Tribes of Yosemite." Roundtable presented at Annual Meeting of the Organization of American Historians, Sacramento CA, April 2018. https://www.academia.edu/38184337 /Indigenous_in_the_nps_Yosemite_4_14_2018_pdf.

———. "Real-Time Mapping the Boundaries of the California Treaties of 1851, Treaty M, Treaty N, & Treaty E." Society of California Archaeology. https://www .academia.edu/4215114/esri_uc_2009_and_Society_of_California_Archaeology _2009_Real_Time_Mapping_of_California_Treaties_M_N_and_E_the_paper.

Gaskell, Sandra, Anthony C. Brochini, and Danette Johnson. "Five Decades of Historic, Archaeological, Cultural, Material, and Sacred Sites of Wah-ho-ga Village [CA-Mrp-305], Yosemite, California, U.S." Presented to the Society

for California Archaeology, 2009. https://www.academia.edu/1852204/Five
_Decades_in_Wahoga_Village_Yosemite.

Heizer, Robert F. "The Eighteen Unratified Treaties of 1851—1852, Between the
California Indians and the United States Government." University of California, Archaeological Research Facility, 1972.

Kelsey, C. E. "Census of Non-Reservation California Indians, 1905–1906." Berkeley, CA: Archaeological Research Facility, 1971.

Muir, John. Journals, notebooks, writings, correspondence, drawings, etc. University of the Pacific Library's Holt-Atherton Special Collections and Archives. ©
1984 Muir-Hanna Trust. https://scholarlycommons.pacific.edu/muir/.

Nicholas, Mark A., to Assistant Secretary, Indian Affairs. Department of the Interior, April 12, 2019. https://www.southernsierramiwuknation.org/_files/ugd
/060079_cc572e4153a04ed6bbd251628ee37fdb.pdf.

Owen, Russell. "John Muir and the Edenic Narrative: Towards an Understanding
of Class and Racial Bias in the Writing of a Preeminent Environmentalist."
Master's thesis, University of Montana, 1998. https://scholarworks.umt.edu
/etd/6625/?utm_source=scholarworks.umt.edu/etd/6625&utm_medium=
pdf&utm_campaign=pdfcoverPages.

Quesenberry, Stephen, to Bryan Newland, Assistant Secretary of Indian Affairs,
Department of the Interior, June 25 and September 29, 2021.

Sachs, Aaron Jacob. "The Humboldt Current: Avant-Garde Exploration and
Environmental Thought in 19th-Century America." PHD diss., Yale University, 2004.

Salerno, Aldo D., to Interior Secretary Deb Haaland, April 29, 2021.
https://www.southernsierramiwuknation.org/_files/ugd/060079
_3ee14c25466b4310b11e6c19251a4ad9.pdf.

Schoepfle, Gordon M., to Assistant Secretary of Indian Affairs Tara Sweeney,
March 21, 2017. https://www.southernsierramiwuknation.org/_files/ugd
/060079_8394b966129d49b893a2a262960fd0d2.pdf.

Shaler, Andrew. "Mariposa and the Invasion of Ahwahnee: Indigenous Histories
of Resistance, Resilience, and Migration in Gold Rush California." PhD diss.,
University of California, Riverside, 2019.

Southern Sierra Miwuk Nation. "Federal Recognition." https://www
.southernsierramiwuknation.org/federal-recognition.

———. "Wahhoga." https://www.southernsierramiwuknation.org/wahhoga.

Trafzer, Clifford. "John Muir's Missed Opportunity: Ignoring Native American
Cultural and Environmental Knowledge." Unpublished paper, 2022.

Tuck, Darin A. "The Battle Cry of Peace: The Leadership of the Disciples of Christ Movement During the American Civil War, 1861–1865." Master's thesis, Kansas State University, 2007. https://core.ac.uk/download/pdf/5168103.pdf.

Usher, Jean. "William Duncan of Metlakatla: A Victorian Missionary in British Columbia." PhD diss., University of British Columbia, 1969.

Published Sources

Adams, Mark. *Tip of the Iceberg: My 3,000-Mile Journey Around Wild Alaska, the Last Great American Frontier.* New York: Dutton, 2018.

Advisory Council on California Indian Policy. "The ACCIP Historical Overview Report: The Special Circumstances of California Indians." September 1997. https://cthcupdates.files.wordpress.com/2021/05/accip-historical-overview -report-1.pdf.

Akins, Damon B., and William J. Bauer, Jr. *We Are the Land: A History of Native California.* Oakland: University of California Press, 2021.

Allen, Garland E. "'Culling the Herd': Eugenics and the Conservation Movement in the United States, 1900–1940." *Journal of the History of Biology* 46, no. 1 (Spring 2013): 31–72.

———. "The Eugenics Record Office at Cold Spring Harbor, 1910–1940: An Essay in Institutional History." *Osiris* 2 (1986): 225–64.

American Academy of Ophthalmology. "Sympathetic Ophthalmia." EyeWiki, June 17, 2023. https://eyewiki.aao.org/Sympathetic_Ophthalmia.

Anderson, M. Kat. *Tending the Wild: Native American Knowledge and the Management of California's Natural Resources.* Berkeley: University of California Press, 2005.

Andersson, Rani-Henrik, Boyd Cothran, and Saara Kekki. "Traditional Indigenous Knowledge and Nature Protection." In *Bridging Cultural Concepts of Nature: Indigenous People and Protected Spaces of Nature,* edited by Rani-Henrik Andersson, Boyd Cothran, and Saara Kekki, 1–25. Helsinki: Helsinki University Press, 2021. https://doi.org/10.33134/ahead-1-1.

Allegheny Forest Alliance. "Forest Reserve Act of 1891." https://alleghenyforestalliance .org/wp-content/uploads/2019/07/Forest-Reserve-Act-of-1891.pdf.

Armes, William Dallam, ed. *The Autobiography of Joseph Le Conte.* New York: D. Appleton and Company, 1903.

Bertin, Yvan. "Abolitions of Slavery." Atlas Caribbean. http://atlas-caraibe.certic .unicaen.fr/en/page-117.html.

Austin, Thad S. "A Prelude to War: The Religious Nonprofit Sector as a Civil Means of Debate over Slavery, Christian Higher Education, and Religious

Philanthropy in the Stone-Campbell Movement." *Religions* 9, no. 8 (2018). https://www.mdpi.com/2077-1444/9/8/235.

Avi Kwa Ame National Monument Coalition. "Celebrate Ave Kwa Ame." https://honorspiritmountain.org/.

Badè, William Frederic. *The Life and Letters of John Muir.* 2 vols. Boston: Houghton Mifflin, 1924.

Baker, Ray. "John Muir." *The Outlook* 74, no. 6 (June 6, 1903): 365–77.

Bancroft, Hubert Hugh. *California.* Vol. 2, *1801–1824.* San Francisco: A. L. Bancroft 1885.

Barcott, Bruce. "The Real Story of the 49ers." *The Atlantic* (February 2, 2020). https://www.theatlantic.com/ideas/archive/2020/02/real-story-49ers/605911/.

Barrus, Clara. "With John o' the Birds and John o' the Mountains." *The Century Magazine* 80, no. 4 (August 1910). https://vault.sierraclub.org/john_muir_exhibit/life/john_o_mountains_clara_barrus/.

Barry, Raymond P., ed. *A Documentary History of Migratory Farm Labor in California.* Oakland CA: Federal Writers Project, 1938. http://content.cdlib.org/view?docId=hb88700929;naan=13030&doc.view=frames&chunk.id=div00020&toc.depth=1&toc.id=&brand=calisphere.

Bates, Craig. "Names and Meanings for Yosemite Valley." *Yosemite Nature Notes* 47, no. 3 (1978). http://www.yosemite.ca.us/library/yosemite_nature_notes/47/3/names_and_meanings_for_yosemite_valley.html.

Battaglia, Roman. "String of Poached Elk Threaten Recovering California Condor Population." Jefferson Public Radio, November 24, 2022. https://www.ijpr.org/environment-energy-and-transportation/2022-11-24/string-of-poached-elk-threaten-recovering-california-condor-population.

Bears Ears Inter-Tribal Coalition. "Bears Ears Inter-Tribal Coalition Condemns Zinke Recommendation to Eviscerate Bears Ears National Monument." June 12, 2017. https://www.bearsearscoalition.org/bears-ears-inter-tribal-coalition-condemns-zinke-recommendation-to-eviscerate-bears-ears-national-monument/.

———. "A Collaborative Land Management Plan for the Bears Ears National Monument." July 5, 2022. https://www.bearsearscoalition.org/beitc-land-management-plan/.

———. Newsletter, Spring 2022. https://www.bearsearscoalition.org/wp-content/uploads/2022/03/Spring-Newsletter-2022.pdf.

———. "Proposal to President Barack Obama for the Creation of Bears Ears National Monument." October 15, 2015. https://bearsearscoalition.org/wp-content/uploads/2015/10/Bears-Ears-Inter-Tribal-Coalition-Proposal-10-15-15.pdf.

———. "Threats." https://www.bearsearscoalition.org/threats/.

Bederman, Gail. *Manliness & Civilization: A Cultural History of Gender and Race in the United States, 1880–1917.* Chicago: University of Chicago Press, 1995.

Belich, James. *Replenishing the Earth: The Settler Revolution and the Rise of the Anglo-World, 1783–1939.* Oxford: Oxford University Press, 2009.

Bell, Major Horace. *Reminiscences of a Ranger: Or Early Times in Southern California.* Santa Barbara: Wallace Hebberd, 1927.

Benallie, Kalle. "Joe Biden Designates Avi Kwa Ame National Monument." *Indian Country Today*, March 21, 2023. https://ictnews.org/news/biden-designates-avi-kwa-ame-a-national-monument.

Bernbaum, Edwin. *Sacred Mountains of the World.* Berkeley: University of California Press, 1997.

Bieder, Robert E. *Native American Communities in Wisconsin, 1600–1960: A Study of Tradition and Change.* Madison: University of Wisconsin Press, 1995.

Bojorcas, Robert, Robert Counter, and Dennis DeGross. "Oregon Termination: Study of the Process and Effects of the Federal Government's Policy of Termination on the Lives of Oregon Indians." In *Report on Terminated and Nonfederally Recognized Indians*, edited by Jo Jo Hunt et al., 17–70. Washington DC: Government Printing Office, 1976.

Bokovoy, Matthew F. *The San Diego World Fairs and Southwestern Memory, 1880–1940.* Albuquerque: University of New Mexico Press, 2005.

Botts, Lindsey. "President Biden Designates Two National Monuments in Nevada and Texas." *Sierra*, March 21, 2023. https://www.sierraclub.org/sierra/president-biden-designates-two-national-monument-nevada-and-texas-avi-kwa-ami-castner-range.

Bowekaty, Carlton R. "Testimony of the Zuni Tribe Before the U. S. House of Representatives Committee on Natural Resources Legislative Hearing on Examining the History of Federal Lands and the Development of Tribal Co-Management." March 8, 2022. https://democrats-naturalresources.house.gov/imo/media/doc/Bowekaty,%20Carleton%20-%20Testimony%20-%20FC%20Ovr%20Hrg%203.08.22.pdf.

Branch, Michael P. "'Angel Guiding Gently': The Yosemite Meeting of Ralph Waldo Emerson and John Muir, 1871." *Western American Literature* 32, no. 2 (Summer 1997): 126–49.

———. *John Muir's Last Journey: South to the Amazon and East to Africa.* Covelo CA: Island Press/Shearwater Books, 2001.

Brown, Allen. "Sierra Club Executive Director Resigns amid Upheaval Around Race, Gender, and Abuses." *The Intercept*, August 19, 2021. https://theintercept.com/2021/08/19/sierra-club-resignation-internal-report/.

Brugge, David M., and Raymond Wilson. *Administrative History: Canyon de Chelly National Monument, Arizona.* Washington DC: National Park Service, 1976.

Brune, Michael. "Pulling Down Our Monuments." Sierra Club, July 22, 2020. https://www.sierraclub.org/michael-brune/2020/07/john-muir-early-history-sierra-club.

Bunnell, Lafayette H. *Discovery of the Yosemite and the Indian War of 1851.* 3rd ed. New York: Fleming H. Revell Company, 1892.

Bureau of Land Management. "Intergovernmental Cooperative Agreement Between the Tribal Nations Whose Representatives Comprise the Bears Ears Commission, the Hopi Tribe, Navajo Nation, Ute Mountain Ute Tribe, Ute Indian Tribe of the Uintah and Ouray Reservation, and the Pueblo of Zuni and the United States Department of the Interior, Bureau of Land Management, and the United States Department of Agriculture, Forest Service, for the Cooperative Management of the Federal Lands and Resources of the Bears Ears National Monument." June 18, 2022. https://www.blm.gov/sites/blm.gov/files/docs/2022-06/BearsEarsNationalMonumentInter-GovernmentalAgreement2022.pdf.

Burnett, Peter. "State of the State Address." January 1851. https://governors.library.ca.gov/addresses/s_01-Burnett2.html.

Burnham, Philip. *Indian Country, God's Country: Native Americans and the National Parks.* Covelo CA: Island, 2000.

Burns, Robert. "Address to a Haggis." https://www.scottishpoetrylibrary.org.uk/poem/address-haggis/.

——. "For a' That and a' That." Poetry Foundation. https://www.poetryfoundation.org/poems/43805/for-a-that-and-a-that.

Burroughs, John. "Narrative of the Expedition." In *Alaska: Narrative, Glaciers, Natives,* edited by C. Hart Merriam, 1:1–118. New York: Doubleday, 1901.

Cameron, Catherine M., Paul Kelton, and Alan C. Swedlund. *Beyond Germs: Native Depopulation in North America.* Tucson: University of Arizona Press, 2015.

Camp, Charles L. "C. Hart Merriam, 1855–1942." *California Historical Society Quarterly* 21, no. 3 (September 1942): 284–86.

Campbell, A., Rev. *Popular Lectures and Addresses.* Philadelphia: James Challen & Son, 1863.

Campbell, Persia. *Mary Williamson Harriman.* New York: Columbia University Press, 1960.

Cape Fox Corporation. "Our Past." https://www.capefoxcorp.com/about-us/.

Carozzi, Albert V. "Agassiz's Amazing Geological Speculation: The Ice-Age." *Studies in Romanticism* 5, no. 2 (Winter 1966): 57–83.

Castillo, Ed. "Petition to Congress on Behalf of the Yosemite Indians." *Journal of California Anthropology* 5, no. 2 (Winter 1978): 271–77.

Castillo, Elias. *A Cross of Thorns: The Enslavement of California's Indians by the Spanish Missions.* Fresno CA: Craven Street, 2015.

Catlin, George. *North American Indians: Being Letters and Notes on Their Manners, Customs, and Conditions Written During Eight Years' Travel Amongst the Wildest Tribes of Indians in North America, 1832–1839.* 2 vols. Philadelphia: Leary, Stuart, 1913.

Chan, Sucheng. *This Bittersweet Soil: The Chinese in California Agriculture, 1860–1913.* Berkeley: University of California Press, 1986.

———. "Chinese Livelihood in Rural California: The Impact of Economic Change, 1860–1880." In *Working People of California*, edited by Danial Conford, 57–83. Berkeley: University of California Press, 1995. https://publishing.cdlib.org/ucpressebooks/view?docId=ft9x0nb6fg&chunk.id=d0e1777&toc.id=d0e1777&brand=ucpress.

Chan, Yenyen F. "Interpreting the Contributions of Chinese Immigrants in Yosemite National Park's History." *George Wright Forum* 34, no. 3 (2017): 299–307.

Clark, Galen. *Indians of the Yosemite Valley and Vicinity: Their History, Customs and Traditions.* 4th ed. Yosemite Valley: Galen Clark, 1910.

Clarke, Chris. "When Green Groups Fought Native Rights: The Timbisha Shoshone in Death Valley." KCET, January 2, 2017. https://www.kcet.org/shows/tending-the-wild/when-green-groups-fought-native-rights-the-timbisha-shoshone-in-death-valley.

Clayton, John. *Natural Rivals: John Muir, Gifford Pinchot, and the Creation of America's Public Lands.* New York: Pegasus, 2019.

Clements, Kendrick A. "Politics and the Park: San Francisco's Fight for Hetch Hetchy, 1908–1913." *Pacific Historical Review* 48, no. 2 (May 1978): 185–215.

Cohen, Michael P. *The History of the Sierra Club, 1892–1970.* San Francisco: Sierra Club Books, 1988.

———. "John Muir's Public Voice." *Western American Literature* 10, no. 3 (Fall 1975): 177–87.

———. *The Pathless Way: John Muir and American Wilderness.* Madison: University of Wisconsin Press, 1984.

Collins, James P. "Native Americans in the Census, 1860–1890." *Genealogy Notes* 38, no. 2 (Summer 2006). https://www.archives.gov/publications/prologue/2006/summer/indian-census.html.

Colman, Zack. "'It's Just Wrong': Internal Fight over Sierra Club Founder's Racial Legacy Roils Organization." *Politico*, August 16, 2021. https://www.politico.com/news/2021/08/16/sierra-club-racist-internal-fight-505407.

"Condors Soar Again over Northern California Coastal Redwoods." Associated Press, May 3, 2022. https://apnews.com/article/travel-california-wildlife-parks-national-fefbd6b9ed15698c0b6507fa6f60317d.

Conservation Lands Foundation. "Avi Kwa Ame." https://www.avikwaame.com/.

Coombes, Brad. "Personifying Indigenous Rights in Nature?" In *Bridging Cultural Concepts of Nature: Indigenous People and Protected Spaces of Nature*, edited by Rani-Henrik Andersson, Boyd Cothran, and Saara Kekki, 29–60. Helsinki: Helsinki University Press, 2021. https://doi.org/10.33134/ahead-1-1.

Cothran, Boyd. "Working the Indian Field Days: The Economy of Authenticity and the Question of Agency in Yosemite Valley." *American Indian Quarterly* 34, no. 2 (Spring 2010): 194–223.

Crimmel, Hal. "No Place for 'Little Children and Tender, Pulpy People': John Muir in Alaska." *Pacific Northwest Quarterly* 92, no 4 (Fall 2001): 171–80.

Crowell, Aron L., and Estelle Oozevaseuk. "The St. Lawrence Island Famine and Epidemic, 1878–80: A Yupik Narrative in Cultural and Historical Context." *Arctic Anthropology* 43, no. 1 (2006): 1–19.

Daniels, Roger. *Asian America: Chinese and Japanese in the United States Since 1850*. Seattle: University of Washington Press, 1988.

Death Valley National Park. "Timbisha." https://www.nps.gov/museum/exhibits/death_valley/Timbisha.html.

Deluca, Kevin, and Anne Demo. "Imagining Nature and Erasing Class and Race: Carleton Watkins, John Muir, and the Construction of Nature." *Environmental History* 6, no. 4 (October 2001): 541–60.

Devine, T. M. *To the Ends of the Earth: Scotland's Global Diaspora, 1750–2010*. Washington DC: Smithsonian, 2011.

Dippie, Brian W. *The Vanishing American: White Attitudes and U. S. Indian Policy*. Lawrence: University Press of Kansas, 1982.

Dosch, Arno. "The Mystery of John Muir's Money." *Sunset* 36 (February 1916): 20–22, 61–64.

Douglass, Frederick. *The Claims of the Negro, Ethnologically Considered*. Rochester NY: Lee, Mann, Daily American Office, 1854.

Duncan, Dayton, and Ken Burns. *The National Parks, America's Best Idea: An Illustrated History*. New York: Alfred A. Knopf, 2009.

Dunlap, Thomas R. "Sport Hunting and Conservation." *Environmental Review* 12, no. 1 (Spring 1988): 51–60.

Eckenrode, H. J., and Pocahontas Wright Edmunds. *E. H. Harriman: The Little Giant of Wall Street*. New York: Greenberg, 1933.

Emerson, Ralph Waldo. *English Traits.* New and revised edition. Boston: Houghton, Mifflin, 1886.

———. *The Prose Works of Ralph Waldo Emerson.* New and rev. ed. 2 vols. Boston: Fields, Osgood, 1870.

Esteves, Pauline. "Preface to the Draft Secretarial Report to Congress," February 28, 2015. https://www.nps.gov/deva/learn/management/esteves_preface.htm.

Ewart, Dick. "Mono Pass and Bloody Canyon." *Yosemite Nature Notes* 47, no. 3 (1978). https://www.yosemite.ca.us/library/yosemite_nature_notes/47/3 /mono_pass_bloody_canyon.html.

Farquhar, Francis P. "Exploration of the Sierra Nevada." *California Historical Quarterly* 4, no. 1 (March 1925): 3–58.

Fleck, Richard F. *Henry Thoreau and John Muir Among the Indians.* Hamden CT: Archon, 1985.

———. "John Muir's Evolving Attitudes Toward Native American Cultures." *American Indian Quarterly* 4, no. 1 (February 1986): 19–31.

Foley, Mark A. "A Paradise in the Alhambra Valley." In *John Muir in Historical Perspective,* edited by Sally M. Miller, 13–34. New York: Peter Lang, 1984.

Fox, Stephen. *John Muir and His Legacy: The American Conservation Movement.* Boston: Little, Brown, 1981.

Fritts, Rachel. "Thanks to the Yurok Tribe, Condors Will Return to the Pacific Northwest." *Mongabay,* September 21, 2021. https://news.mongabay.com/2021 /09/thanks-to-the-yurok-tribe-condors-will-return-to-the-pacific-northwest/.

Fragnoli, Delfine P. "Naming Yosemite." *ATQ* 18, no. 4 (December 2004): 263–75.

Gannett, Henry. "The Harriman Alaska Expedition." *Journal of the American Geographical Society of New York* 31, no. 4 (1899): 344–55.

Garvey, T. Gregory. "Mediating Citizenship: Emerson, the Cherokee Removals, and the Rhetoric of Nationalism." *Centennial Review* 41, no. 3 (Fall 1997): 461–69.

Genealogy Trails. "Welcome to Wrangell Borough, Alaska." http:// genealogytrails.com/alaska/wrangell/borough_history.htm.

Gessner, David. *Leave It As It Is: A Journey Through Theodore Roosevelt's American Wilderness.* New York: Simon & Schuster, 2020.

Gilio-Whitaker, Dina. *As Long as Grass Grows: The Indigenous Fight for Environmental Justice, from Colonization to Standing Rock.* Boston: Beacon, 2019.

Gleach, Frederick W. "From Cape Fox, Alaska, to Cornell University: The Changing Meaning of a Totem Pole," 1995. http://www.gleach.com/totem.html.

Gmelch, Sharon Bohn. *The Tlingit Encounter with Photography.* Philadelphia: University of Pennsylvania Museum of Archaeology and Anthropology, 2008.

Goetzmann, William H., and Kay Sloan. *Looking Far North: The Harriman Expedition to Alaska, 1899.* New York: Viking, 1982.

González, Michael. *This Small City Will Be a Mexican Paradise: Exploring the Origins of Mexican Culture in Los Angeles, 1821–1846.* Albuquerque: University of New Mexico Press, 2005.

Gordon-Cumming, C. F. *Granite Crags of California.* New ed. Edinburgh: William Blackwood and Sons, 1886.

Grable, Juliet. "Newest Flock of California Condors Faces an Old Threat: Lead Poisoning." *Revelator,* February 6, 2023. https://therevelator.org/newest -california-condors-lead/.

Grand Canyon Trust. "Tribes Propose New Baaj Nwaavjo I'tah Kukveni National Monument." https://www.grandcanyontrust.org/blog/tribes-propose-baaj -nwaavjo-itah-kukveni-grand-canyon-national-monument.

Grant, Madison. *The Passing of the Great Race: or, The Racial Basis of European History.* 4th Rev. ed. New York: Charles Scribner's Sons, 1916, 1918, 1921.

Greene, Linda Wedel. *Yosemite: The Park and Its Resources.* 3 vols. Denver: National Park Service, 1987. https://catalog.hathitrust.org/Record/007417184.

Grinnell, George Bird. "The Natives of the Alaska Coast Region." In *Alaska: Narrative, Glaciers, Natives,* edited by C. Hart Merriam, 1:137–83. New York: Doubleday, Page, 1902.

Grinëv, Andrei Val'terovich. *The Tlingit Indians in Russian America 1741–1867.* Translated by Richard L. Bland and Katerina G. Solovjova. Lincoln: University of Nebraska Press, 2005.

Grover, Stephen F., John Conway, and Carl P. Russell. "Early Years in Yosemite." *California Historical Society Quarterly* 5, no. 4 (December 1926): 328–41.

Haaland, Deb, and Thomas J. Vilsack. "Order 3403 of November 15, 2021, Joint Secretarial Order on Fulfilling the Trust Responsibility to Indian Tribes in the Stewardship of Federal Lands and Waters." https://www.usda.gov/sites /default/files/documents/joint-so-3403-stewardship-tribal-nations.pdf.

Haller, John S., Jr. *Outcasts from Evolution: Scientific Attitudes of Racial Inferiority, 1859–1900.* Urbana: University of Illinois Press, 1971.

Hampton, H. Duane. *How the U.S. Cavalry Saved Our National Parks.* Bloomington: Indiana University Press, 1971.

Hassrick, Peter H. "Art, Agency, and Conservation: A Fresh Look at Albert Bierstadt's Vision of the West." *Montana: The Magazine of Western History* 68, no. 1 (Spring 2018): 3–26, 90–91.

Heizer, Robert F., ed. *They Were Only Diggers: A Collection of Articles from California Newspapers, 1851–1866, on Indian and White Relations.* Ramona CA: Ballena, 1974.

Henry, Daniel Lee. *Across the Shaman's River: John Muir, the Tlingit Stronghold, and the Opening of the North.* Fairbanks: University of Alaska Press, 2017.

Hensley, Carl Wayne. "Disciples of Christ." *Quarterly Journal of Speech* 61 (October 1975): 250–64.

Hickman, David. "John Muir's Orchard Home." *Pacific Historical Review* 82, no. 3 (August 2013): 335–61.

Hicks, Brian. *Toward the Setting Sun: John Ross, the Cherokees, and the Trail of Tears.* New York: Atlantic Monthly, 2011.

Hilgard, Eugene. "Biographical Memoir of Joseph LeConte, 1823–1901." Read before the National Academy of Sciences, April 18, 1907. http://www.nasonline .org/publications/biographical-memoirs/memoir-pdfs/le-conte-joseph.pdf.

Hinckley, Ted. C. *The Canoe Rocks: Alaska's Tlingit and the Euramerican Frontier, 1800–1912.* Lanham MD: University Press of America, 1996.

———. "The Early Alaskan Ministry of S. Hall Young." *Journal of Presbyterian History (1962–1985)* 46, no. 3 (September 1968): 175–96.

———. "The Inside Passage: A Popular Gilded Age Tour." *Pacific Northwest Quarterly* 56, no. 2 (April 1965): 67–74.

———. "The Presbyterian Leadership in Pioneer Alaska." *Journal of American History* 52, no. 4 (March 1966): 742–756.

History Channel. "This Day in History, August 14, 1784: Russians Settle Alaska." https://www.history.com/this-day-in-history/russians-settle-alaska.

History of Contra Costa County. Los Angeles: Historic Record Company, 1926.

Hofmann, C. F. "Notes on Hetch Hetchy Valley," 1868. https://www.yosemite.ca .us/library/notes_on_hetch-hetchy_valley.html.

Hoffmann, Hillary M. "Fracking the Sacred: Resolving the Tension Between Unconventional Oil and Gas Development and Tribal Culture." *Denver Law Review* 94, no. 2 (April 2017): 319–62.

Holmes, Steven J. "Rethinking Muir's First Summer in Yosemite." In *John Muir in Historical Perspective,* edited by Sally M. Miller, 153–64. New York: Peter Lang, 1984.

———. *The Young John Muir: An Environmental Biography.* Madison: University of Wisconsin Press, 1999.

Hooper, C. L. *Report of the Cruise of the U. S. Revenue-Steamer* Corwin *in the Arctic Ocean.* Washington DC: Government Printing Office, 1881.

Horsman, Reginald. *Race and Manifest Destiny: The Origins of American Racial Anglo-Saxonism.* Cambridge: Harvard University Press, 1981.

Houck, Darcie. "Salmon Repatriation: One Tribe's Battle to Maintain Its Culture and Spiritual Connection to Place." *Natural Resources & Environment* 34, no. 1 (Summer 2019): 23–28.

Hughes, J. Donald, and Jim Swan. "How Much of Earth Is Sacred Space?" *Environmental Review* 10, no. 4 (Winter 1986): 247–59.

Hull, Kathleen L. *Pestilence and Persistence: Yosemite Indian Demography and Culture in Colonial California.* Berkeley: University of California Press, 2009.

———. "Quality of Life." In *Beyond Germs: Native Depopulation in North America,* edited by Catherine M. Cameron, Paul Kelton, and Alan C. Swedlund, 222–48. Tucson: University of Arizona Press, 2015.

Indigenous Earth Fund. "First Cohort of Grantee Partners." https://decolonizingwealth.com/liberated-capital/ief/.

Jacobson, Matthew Frye. *Barbarian Virtues: The United States Encounters Foreign Peoples at Home and Abroad, 1876–1917.* New York: Hill and Wang, 2000.

Jacoby, Karl. *Crimes Against Nature: Squatters, Poachers, Thieves, and the Hidden History of American Conservation.* Berkeley: University of California Press, 2001, 2014.

Jennings, Walter Wilson. *Origin and Early History of the Disciples of Christ.* Cincinnati: Standard, 1919.

Johnson, Benjamin Heber. *Escaping the Dark, Gray City: Fear and Hope in Progressive-Era Conservation.* New Haven: Yale University Press, 2017.

Johnson, Robert Underwood. *Remembered Yesterdays.* Boston: Little, Brown, 1923.

Jones, David S. "Virgin Soils Revisited." *William and Mary Quarterly* 60, no. 4 (October 2003): 703–42.

Jones, Holway R. *John Muir and the Sierra Club: The Battle for Yosemite.* San Francisco: Sierra Club, 1965.

Jones, Zachary R. "The 1869 Bombardment of Kaachx an.áak'w from Fort Wrangell: The U.S. Army Response to Tlingit Law, Wrangell, Alaska." Sealaska Heritage Institute and National Park Service American Battlefield Protection Program, in collaboration with Wrangell Cooperative Association, City and Borough of Wrangell, 2015.

Juzda, Elise. "Skulls, Science, and the Spoils of War: Craniological Studies at the United States Army Medical Museum, 1868–1900." *Studies in History and Philosophy of Biological and Biomedical Sciences* 40 (2009): 156–67.

Karr, Steven M. "The Warner Ranch's Indian Removal: Cultural Adaptation, Accommodation, and Continuity." *California History* 86, no. 4 (2009): 24–43, 82–84.

Keenan, Jerry. "Yellowstone Kelly: From New York to Paradise." *Montana: The Magazine of Western History* (Summer 1990): 15–27.

Kelly, Howard A. *Lafayette Bunnell, M.D., Discoverer of the Yosemite.* New York: Paul B. Hoeber, 1921.

Kelsey, C. E. "The Rights and Wrongs of California Indians." *Transactions of the Commonwealth Club of California* 4, no. 7 (December 1909): 417–29.

Kendi, Ibram X. *Stamped from the Beginning: The Definitive History of Racist Ideas in America.* New York: Bold Type, 2016.

Kennan, George. *The Salton Sea: An Account of Harriman's Fight with the Colorado River.* New York: Macmillan, 1917.

Kerns, Matthew. *Texas Jack: America's First Cowboy Star.* Lanham MD: Two Dot, 2021.

Kevles, Daniel J. *In the Name of Eugenics: Genetics and the Uses of Human Heredity.* Cambridge: Harvard University Press, 1985, 1995.

Killion, Jeffrey, with Mark Davidson. *Cultural Landscape Report for John Muir National Historic Site.* 2 vols. Boston: National Park Service, 2005.

King, Thomas Starr. *A Vacation Among the Sierras: Yosemite in 1860.* http://www.yosemite.ca.us/library/vacation_among_the_sierras/vacation_among_the_sierras.pdf.

KLA-MO-YA Casino. "Tribal History." https://klamoyacasino.com/.

Klein, Maury. *The Life & Legend of E. H. Harriman.* Chapel Hill: University of North Carolina Press, 2000.

Kroeber, Theodora, and Robert Heizer. *Almost Ancestors: The First Californians.* San Francisco: Sierra Club, 1968.

La Pena, Frank, Craig D. Bates, and Steven P. Medley. *Legends of the Yosemite Miwok.* 3rd rev. ed. Yosemite and Berkeley: Yosemite Association and Heyday, 1981, 1993, 2007.

Lasky, Greg. "Sierra Club Supports Federal Recognition of Southern Sierra Miwuk Nation." *Tehipite Topics* 65, no. 1 (December 2019): 1, 6. www.sierraclub.org/tehipite.

LeConte, Joseph C. "The Effect of Mixture of Races on Human Progress." *Berkeley Quarterly* 1 (1880): 81–104.

———. *Evolution: Its Nature, Its Evidences, and Its Relation to Religious Thought.* New York: D. Appleton, 1888, 1891.

———. *A Journal of Ramblings Through the High Sierra of California with the University Excursion Party.* San Francisco: Sierra Club, 1930 [1875].

———. *The Race Problem in the South.* Evolution Series, No. 29. New York: D. Appleton, 1892.

LeConte, Joseph N. "The Sierra Club." *Sierra Club Bulletin* 10, no. 2 (January 1917): 136–43.

Lee, Robert, and Tristan Ahtone. "Land-Grab Universities: Expropriated Indigenous Land Is the Foundation of the Land-Grant University System." *High Country News* 52, no. 4 (April 2020): 33–46. https://www.hcn.org/issues/52.4/indigenous-affairs-education-land-grab-universities.

LeMenager, Stephanie. "Crossing the Panama Isthmus, March 1868." *John Muir Newsletter,* Spring-Summer 2001,1, 4–7.

Lemkin, Raphaël. *Axis Rule in Occupied Europe: Laws of Occupation, Analysis of Government, Proposals for Redress.* Washington: Carnegie Endowment for International Peace, Division of International Law, 1944.

Levy, Sharon. "How the Yurok Tribe Is Bringing Back the California Condor." *Undark*, June 22, 2022. https://undark.org/2022/06/22/how-the-yurok-tribe-is-bringing-back-the-california-condor/.

Lewis, Henry T. "Patterns of Indian Burning in California: Ecology and Ethnohistory." In *Before the Wilderness: Environmental Management by Native Californians*, edited by Thomas C. Blackburn and Kat Anderson, 55–116. Menlo Park CA: Ballena, 1993.

Lindsay, Brendan C. *Murder State: California's Native American Genocide, 1846–1873.* Lincoln: University of Nebraska Press, 2012.

Lindsey, Alton A. "The Harriman Alaska Expedition of 1899, Including the Identities of Those in the Staff Picture." *BioScience* 28, no. 6 (June 1978): 383–86.

Lönnberg, Allen. "The Digger Stereotype in California." *Journal of California and Great Basin Anthropology* 3, no. 2 (1981): 215–23.

Lopez, Barry. *Horizon.* New York: Alfred A. Knopf, 2019.

Lummis, Charles F. *A Tramp Across the Continent.* New York: Charles Scribner's Sons, 1892.

Lundberg, Ann. "John Muir and Yosemite's 'Castaway Book': The Troubling Geology of Native America." *Western American Literature* 36, no. 1 (Spring 2001): 25–55.

Lurie, Edward. "Louis Agassiz and the Races of Man." *Isis* 45, no. 3 (September 1954): 227–42.

MacEachern, Alan. "Who Had 'America's Best Idea'?" https://niche-canada.org/2011/10/23/who-had-americas-best-idea/.

Madley, Benjamin. *An American Genocide: The United States and the California Indian Catastrophe, 1846–1873.* New Haven: Yale University Press, 2016.

Mair, Aaron, Chad Hanson, and Mary Ann Nelson. "Who Was John Muir, Really?" *Earth Island Journal*, August 11, 2021. https://www.earthisland.org/journal/index.php/articles/entry/who-was-john-muir-really/.

Margolin, Malcolm. *Deep Hanging Out: Wanderings and Wonderment in Native California.* Berkeley CA: Heyday, 2021.

Martinez Historical Museum. *Martinez.* Charleston: Arcadia, 2004.

McCarthy, Helen T. "Managing Oaks and the Acorn Crop." In *Before the Wilderness: Environmental Management by Native Californians*, edited by Thomas C. Blackburn and Kat Anderson, 213–28. Menlo Park CA: Ballena, 1993.

McDonnell, Michael A., and A. Dirk Moses. "Raphael Lemkin as Historian of Genocide in the Americas." *Journal of Genocide Research* 7 no. 4 (2007): 501–29.

McNally, Robert Aquinas. "Bret Harte's Voice for the Wiyots." *Wild West* 32, no. 4 (April 2019): 70–75. https://www.historynet.com/bret-hartes-voice-for-the-wiyots.htm.

———. "A Dark History Hits Home." *California History* 96, no. 4 (Winter 2019): 78–87.

———. "John Muir in Klamath Country." *Journal of the Shaw Historical Library* 27 (2014): 106–13.

———. *The Modoc War: A Story of Genocide at the Dawn of America's Gilded Age.* Lincoln: Bison Books, 2017.

Medeiros, Joe. "Hetch Hetchy—Natural History Before the Dam." *Snow Range Reflections* 6, no. 1 (2015). https://ejournals.sierracollege.edu/jsnhb/v6n1/medeiros.html.

Merchant, Carolyn. "George Bird Grinnell's Audubon Society: Bridging the Gender Divide in Conservation." *Environmental History* 15, no. 1 (January 2010): 3–30.

———. *Reinventing Eden: The Fate of Nature in Western Culture.* New York: Routledge, 2003.

———. "Shades of Darkness: Race and Environmental History." *Environmental History* 8, no. 3 (July 2003): 380–94.

Merriam, C. Hart. *The Dawn of the World: Myths and Tales of the Miwok Indians of California.* Cleveland: Arthur H. Clark, 1910; reprt. with an introduction by Lowell J. Bean. Lincoln: Bison Books, 1993.

———. "Ethnographic Notes on California Indian Tribes." Compiled and edited by Robert F. Heizer. Reports of the University of California Archaeological Survey, No. 68, part 1, October 1966.

———. "Indian Village and Camp Sites in Yosemite Valley." *Sierra Club Bulletin* 10, no. 2 (January 1917): 202–9.

———. "To the Memory of John Muir." *Sierra Club Bulletin* 10, no. 2 (January 1917): 146–51.

Miller, Larisa K. "Native American Land Ownership in California's National Forests." *Forest History Today* (Fall 2017): 3–13.

———. "Primary Sources on C. E. Kelsey and the Northern California Indian Association." *Journal of Western Archives* 4, no. 1 (2013): 1–20.

Miller, Mark Edwin. *Forgotten Tribes: Unrecognized Indians and the Federal Acknowledgment Process.* Lincoln: University of Nebraska Press, 2004.

———. "The Timbisha Shoshone and the National Park Idea: Building Toward Accommodation and Acknowledgement in Death Valley National Park, 1933–2000." *Journal of the Southwest* 50, no. 4 (Winter 2008): 415–45.

Milligan, Florence. "Henry Fairfield Osborn, Man of Parnassus." *Bios* 7, no. 1 (March 1936): 4–24.

Milliken, Randall, Laurence H. Shoup, and Beverly R. Ortiz. "Ohlone/ Costanoan Indians of the San Francisco Peninsula and Their Neighbors, Yesterday and Today." Prepared by Archaeological and Historical Consultants, Oakland, California, for National Park Service, Golden Gate National Recreation Area, San Francisco, 2009. https://digitalcommons.csumb.edu /hornbeck_ind_1/6/?utm_source=digitalcommons.csumb.edu%2fhornbeck _ind_1%2f6&utm_medium=pdf&utm_campaign=pdfcoverPages.

Mitchell, Annie R. "Major James D. Savage and the Tulareños." *California Historical Society Quarterly* 28, no. 4 (December 1949): 323–41.

Morgan, Jennifer L. "'Some Could Suckle over Their Shoulder': Male Travelers, Female Bodies, and the Gendering of Racial Ideology." *William and Mary Quarterly* 54, no. 1 (January 1997): 167–92.

Morton, Samuel George. *Crania Americana*. Philadelphia: J. Dobson, 1839.

Mowry, George E. *The California Progressives*. Berkeley: University of California Press, 1951.

Muir, John. "Alaska Gold Fields." *San Francisco Daily Evening Bulletin*, December 23, 1879. https://scholarlycommons.pacific.edu/jmb/144/.

———. "By-Ways of Yosemite Travel: Bloody Cañon." *Overland Monthly* 13, no. 3 (September 1874): 267–73.

———. *The Cruise of the Corwin: Journal of the Arctic Expedition of 1881 in Search of De Long and the* Jeannette. Edited by William Frederick Badè. Boston: Houghton Mifflin, 1918.

———. *Edward Henry Harriman*. Garden City NY: Doubleday, Page, 1912.

———. "Features of the Proposed Yosemite National Park." *The Century Magazine* 40, no. 55 (September 1890): 656–67. https://vault.sierraclub.org/john_muir _exhibit/writings/features_of_the_proposed_yosemite_national_park/.

———. "Flood-Storm in the Sierra." *Overland Monthly* 14, no. 6 (June 1875): 489–96.

———. "The Hetch Hetchy Valley." Boston *Weekly Transcript* (March 25, 1873). https://vault.sierraclub.org/john_muir_exhibit/writings/muir_hh_boston _25mar1873.asp.

———. *Letters from Alaska (A North Coast Book)*. Edited by Robert Engberg and Bruce Merrell. Madison: University of Wisconsin Press, 1993.

———. *Letters to a Friend: Written to Mrs. Ezra S. Carr 1866–1879*. Boston: Houghton Mifflin, 1915.

———. "Modoc Memories." *San Francisco Daily Evening Call*, December 28, 1874. https://scholarlycommons.pacific.edu/jmb/25.

———. *The Mountains of California.* New and enlarged ed. New York: Century, 1894, 1911.

———. "Mt. Shasta." In *Picturesque California: The Rocky Mountains and the Pacific Slope*, edited by John Muir, 3:145–74. New York: J. Dewing, 1888. https://vault.sierraclub.org/john_muir_exhibit/writings/picturesque_california/.

———. *My First Summer in the Sierra.* Boston: Houghton Mifflin, 1911, 1916.

———. "The National Parks and Forest Reservations." Proceedings of the Meeting of the Sierra Club, November 23, 1895. https://vault.sierraclub.org/john_muir_exhibit/writings/nat_parks_forests_1896.aspx.

———. "Notes on Pacific Glaciers." In *Alaska: Narrative, Glaciers, Natives*, edited by C. Hart Merriam, 1:119–25. New York: Doubleday, Page, 1902.

———. *Our National Parks.* Boston: Houghton Mifflin, 1901, 1917.

———. "The Passes of the Sierra." *Scribner's Monthly* 17, no. 5 (March 1879): 644–52.

———. "The Passes of the High Sierra." In *Picturesque California: The Rocky Mountains and the Pacific Slope*, edited by John Muir, 1:19–34, New York: J. Dewing Pulishing, 1888. https://vault.sierraclub.org/john_muir_exhibit/writings/picturesque_california/chapter_2.aspx.

———. "Reminiscences of Joseph LeConte." *University of California Magazine* 7, no. 5 (1901): 209–13.

———. "Shasta Game." *San Francisco Daily Evening Bulletin*, November 29, 1874.

———. "Shasta in Winter." *San Francisco Daily Evening Bulletin*, December 21, 1874.

———. *Steep Trails. Edited by* William Frederick Badè. Boston: Houghton Mifflin, 1918.

———. *Stickeen.* Boston: Houghton Mifflin, 1909.

———. *The Story of My Boyhood and Youth.* Boston: Houghton Mifflin, 1913.

———. *A Thousand-Mile Walk to the Gulf.* Boston: Houghton Mifflin, 1916.

———. "The Treasures of the Yosemite." *The Century Magazine* 40, no. 4 (August 1890): 483–500.

———. "The Tuolomne Yosemite in Danger." *Outlook* (November 7, 1907): 486–89.

———. "The Wild Sheep of California." *Overland Monthly* 12 (April 1874): 358–63.

———. *Travels in Alaska.* Edited by William Frederick Badè. Boston: Houghton Mifflin, 1915.

———. "Wild Wool." *Overland Monthly* 14 (April 1875): 361–65.

———. *The Yosemite.* New York: Century, 1912.

———. "Yosemite Glaciers." *New York Tribune*, December 5, 1871. https://vault.sierraclub.org/john_muir_exhibit/writings/yosemite_glaciers.aspx.

———. "The Yosemite Valley." In *Picturesque California: The Rocky Mountains and the Pacific Slope.* Edited by John Muir, 2:49–88. New York: J. Dewing, 1888.

Nabokov, Peter, and Lawrence Loendorf. *American Indians and Yellowstone National Park: A Documentary Overview.* Yellowstone National Park: National Park Service, Yellowstone Center for Resources, 2002.

———. *Restoring a Presence: American Indians and Yellowstone National Park.* Norman: University of Oklahoma Press, 2004.

Nash, Roderick. "The American Invention of National Parks." *American Quarterly* 22, no. 3 (Autumn 1970): 726–35.

National Archives and Records Administration. "Native American Relationships Policy." *Federal Register* 52 Fed. Reg. 2389. Thursday, 1987, 2452–58. https://www.loc.gov/item/fr052014/.

National Park Service. "Canyon de Chelly: History & Culture." https://www.nps.gov/cach/learn/historyculture/index.htm.

———. National Park Service Organic Act of 1916 (16 USC 1–4). https://www.nps.gov/grba/learn/management/organic-act-of-1916.htm.

———. *Voices of the People: The Traditionally Associated Tribes of Yosemite National Park.* National Park Service: Yosemite National Park, 2019.

"NAU Team Facilitates Joint Agreement for Cooperative Stewardship of Canyon de Chelly." *NAU Review,* July 31, 2018. https://news.nau.edu/joint-agreement -canyon-de-chelly/.

Nelson, Edward William. *The Eskimo About Bering Strait.* Washington DC: Government Printing Office, 1900.

Newcomb, Raymond Lee. *Our Lost Explorers: The Narrative of the Jeannette Arctic Expedition.* Hartford CT: American, 1884.

Nicoloff, Philip L. *Emerson on Race and History: An Examination of English Traits.* New York: Columbia University Press, 1961.

Nijhuis, Michelle. "Don't Cancel John Muir: But Don't Excuse Him Either." *The Atlantic,* April 12, 2021. https://www.theatlantic.com/ideas/archive/2021/04 /conservation-movements-complicated-history/618556/.

Nobel, Justin. "The Miseducation of John Muir." *Atlas Obscura,* July 26, 2016. https://www.atlasobscura.com/articles/the-miseducation-of-john-muir?utm _source=Atlas+Obscura+Daily+Newsletter&utm_campaign=1cac85f705-email _campaign_2020_07_24&utm_medium=email&utm_term=0_f36db9c480 -1cac85f705-66106445&mc_cid=1cac85f705&mc_eid=99a49692b9.

NoiseCat, Julian Brave. "The Environmental Movement Needs to Reckon with Its Racist History." *Vice,* September 13, 2019. https://www.vice.com/en/article /bjwvn8/the-environmental-movement-needs-to-reckon-with-its-racist-history.

Nokes, R. Gregory. *The Troubled Life of Peter Burnett: Oregon Governor and First Governor of California.* Corvallis: Oregon State University Press, 2018.

Nott, J. C., and Geo. R. Gliddon. *Types of Mankind.* 6th ed. Philadelphia: Lippin-cott, Grambo, 1854.

Offit, Paul A. "The Loathsome American Book That Inspired Hitler." *Daily Beast,* August 26, 2017. https://www.thedailybeast.com/the-loathsome-american -book-that-inspired-hitler.

Okrent, Daniel. *The Guarded Gate: Bigotry, Eugenics, and the Law That Kept Two Generations of Jews, Italians, and Other European Immigrants Out of America.* New York: Scribner, 2019.

Olin, Spencer C., Jr. *California's Prodigal Sons: Hiram Johnson and the Progressives, 1911–1917.* Berkeley: University of California Press, 1968.

Olmstead, Alan L., and Rhode, Paul W. "A History of California Agriculture." University of California Agriculture and Natural Resources, December 2017. https://s.giannini.ucop.edu/uploads/giannini_public/19/41/194166a6-cfde -4013-ae55-3e8df86d44d0/a_history_of_california_agriculture.pdf.

Olmsted, Frederick Law. *Yosemite and the Mariposa Grove: A Preliminary Report, 1865.* Introduced by Victoria Post Ranney. Yosemite National Park: Yosemite Association, 1993.

Online Etymological Dictionary. "John Muir and 'Saunter.'" https://www .etymonline.com/columns/post/john-muir-and-'saunter'.

Orsi, Richard J. "'Wilderness Saint' and 'Robber Baron': The Anomalous Partnership of John Muir and the Southern Pacific Company for Preservation of Yosemite National Park." *Pacific Historian* 29, nos. 2–3 (Summer–Fall 1985): 136–56.

Osborn, Henry Fairfield. *Impressions of Great Naturalists: Reminiscences of Darwin, Huxley, Balfour, Cope and Others.* New York: Charles Scribner's Sons, 1924.

———. *Man Rises to Parnassus: Critical Epochs in the Prehistory of Man.* Princeton NJ: Princeton University Press, 1927.

Osgood, Wilfred H. "Biographical Memoir of Clinton Hart Merriam, 1855–1942." *National Academy of Sciences Biographical Memoirs* 24 (Fall 1944).

Ostler, Jeffrey. "Disease Has Never Been Just Disease for Native Americans." *The Atlantic,* April 2020. https://www.theatlantic.com/ideas/archive/2020/04 /disease-has-never-been-just-disease-native-americans/610852/.

———. *Surviving Genocide: Native Nations and the United States from the American Revolution to Bleeding Kansas.* New Haven CT: Yale University Press, 2019.

Ostler, Jeffrey, and Karl Jacoby. "After 1776: Native Nations, Settler Colonialism, and the Meaning of America." *Journal of Genocide Research* (September 2021). https://doi.org/10.1080/14623528.2021.1968143.

Outka, Paul. *Race and Nature from Transcendentalism to the Harlem Renaissance.* New York: Palgrave Macmillan, 2008.

Padget, Martin. "Travel, Exoticism, and the Writing of Region: Charles Fletcher Lummis and the 'Creation' of the Southwest." *Journal of the Southwest* 37, no. 3 (Autumn 1995): 421–49.

Painter, Nell Irvin. *The History of White People.* New York: W. W. Norton, 2010.

———. "Ralph Waldo Emerson's Saxons." *Journal of American History* 95, no. 4 (March 2009): 977–85.

Palmer, T. S. "In Memoriam: Clinton Hart Merriam." *Auk* 71, no. 2 (April 1954): 130–36.

Palmquist, Peter E. "The California Indian in Three-Dimensional Photography." *Journal of California and Great Basin Anthropology* 1, no. 1 (Summer 1979): 89–116.

Pavlik, Robert C. "In Harmony with the Landscape: Yosemite's Built Environment, 1913–1940." *California History* 69, no. 2 (Summer 1990): 182–95.

Petroff, Ivan. *Report on the Population, Industries, and Resources of Alaska.* Vol. 8 of Tenth United States Census. Washington DC: Government Printing Office, 1884.

Phelan, James D. "Hetch-Hetchy for the Wealth-Producer." *California Weekly,* March 26, 1909, 283–84.

Pico, Tamara. "The Darker Side of John Wesley Powell." *Scientific American Blogs,* September 9, 2019. https://blogs.scientificamerican.com/voices/the-darker -side-of-john-wesley-powell/#.

Pierce, Jason E. *Making the White Man's West: Whiteness and the Creation of the American West.* Boulder: University Press of Colorado, 2016.

Pierini, Bruce. "How Did the Hetch Hetchy Project Impact Native Americans?" *Snow Range Reflections: Journal of Sierra Nevada History & Biography* 6, no. 1 (2015). https://ejournals.sierracollege.edu/jsnhb/v6n1/pierini.html.

Powell, J. W. "From Barbarism to Civilization." *American Anthropologist* 1, no. 2 (April 1888): 97–123.

Powell, Miles A. *Vanishing America: Species Extinction, Racial Peril, and the Origins of Conservation.* Cambridge: Harvard University Press, 2016.

Pratt, R. H., Capt. "The Advantages of Mingling Indians with Whites." *Proceedings of the National Conference on Charities and Corrections* 19 (June 1892): 45–59.

Punke, Michael. *Last Stand: George Bird Grinnell, the Battle to Save the Buffalo, and the Birth of the New West.* New York: HarperCollins, 2007.

Regal, Brian. "Madison Grant, Maxwell Perkins, and Eugenics Publishing at Scribner's." *Princeton University Library Chronicle* 65, no. 2 (Winter 2004): 317–42.

Righter, Robert W. *The Battle over Hetch Hetchy: America's Most Controversial Dam and the Birth of Modern Environmentalism.* Oxford: Oxford University Press, 2005.

Rikert, Levi. "President Biden Takes Sec. Haaland's Recommendation." *Native News Online,* October 7, 2021. https://nativenewsonline.net

/currents/president-biden-takes-sec-haaland-s-recommendation-will-sign -proclamation-restoring-bears-ears-and-other-monuments-on-friday.

Roosevelt, Theodore. *The Winning of the West: An Account of the Exploration and Settlement of Our Country from the Alleghenies to the Pacific.* 4 vols. Philadelphia: Gebbie, 1903.

Ross, Ken. *Pioneering Conservation in Alaska.* Louisville: University Press of Colorado, 2006.

Rosse, Irving C. *The First Landing on Wrangel Island; with Some Remarks on the Northern Inhabitants.* New York?: s.n., 1883.

Rossetti Archive. "The Century Illustrated Monthly Magazine." http://www .rossettiarchive.org/docs/ap2.c4.raw.html.

Royster, Hayden. "This Land Is Their Land." *California,* June 8, 2022. https://alumni .berkeley.edu/california-magazine/2022-summer/this-land-is-their-land/.

Runte, Alfred. *Yosemite: The Embattled Wilderness.* Lincoln: University of Nebraska Press, 1990.

Russell, Carl Parcher. *One Hundred Years in Yosemite: The Story of a Great Park and Its Friends.* Yosemite National Park: Yosemite Natural History Association, 1957.

Sackman, Douglas Cazaux. *Wild Men: Ishi and Kroeber in the Wilderness of Modern America.* Oxford: Oxford University Press, 2010.

Salerno, Aldo D. "A 'Sham': Southern Sierra Miwuk Nation Being Denied Federal Recognition." Indianz.com, September 9, 2019. https://www.indianz .com/News/2019/09/09/a-sham-southern-sierra-miwuk-nation-bein.asp.

Sams, Charles F., III. "Statement of Charles F. Sams III, Director, National Park Service, U.S. Department of the Interior, Before the House Committee on Natural Resources, Regarding Tribal Co-management of Federal Lands." March 8, 2022. https://www.doi.gov/ocl/tribal-co-management-federal-lands.

Sanborn, Margaret. *Yosemite: Its Discovery, Its Wonders, and Its People.* New York: Random House, 1981.

Sandos, James A. *Converting California: Indians and Franciscans in the Missions.* New Haven CT: Yale University Press, 2004.

Sides, Josh. *Backcountry Ghosts: California Homesteaders and the Making of a Dubious Dream.* Lincoln: University of Nebraska Press, 2021.

Sierra Club. "Sierra Club Award Winners." https://www.sierraclub.org/sites /www.sierraclub.org/files/Award-winners-by-award-2017.pdf.

Simpson, John Warfield. *Dam!: Water, Power, Politics, and Preservation in Hetch Hetchy and Yosemite National Park.* New York: Pantheon, 2005.

———. *Yearning for the Land: A Search for Homeland in Scotland and America.* New York: Vintage, 2002.

Smith, Michael B. "The Value of a Tree: Public Debates of John Muir and Gifford Pinchot." *Historian* 60, no. 4 (Summer 1998): 757–78.

Smithsonian Institution Archives. "Nelson, Edward William, 1855–1934." https://siarchives.si.edu/collections/auth_per_fbr_eacp192.

Solnit, Rebecca. "John Muir in Native America." *Sierra*, March 2, 2021. https://www.sierraclub.org/sierra/2021-2-march-april/feature/john-muir-native-america.

———. *Savage Dreams: A Journey into the Hidden Wars of the American West.* 20th anniversary ed., with a new preface. Berkeley: University of California Press, 1994, 2014.

Spence, Mark David. "Crown of the Continent, Backbone of the World: The American Wilderness Ideal and Blackfeet Exclusion from Glacier National Park." *Environmental History* 1, no. 3 (July 1996): 29–49.

———. *Dispossessing the Wilderness: Indian Removal and the Making of National Parks.* Oxford: Oxford University Press, 1999.

———. "Dispossessing the Wilderness: Yosemite Indians and the National Park Ideal." *Pacific Historical Review* 65, no. 1 (February 1996): 27–59.

Spiro, Jonathan Peter. *Defending the Master Race: Conservation, Eugenics, and the Legacy of Madison Grant.* Burlington: University of Vermont Press/University Press of New England, 2009.

Stanley, Millie. "John Muir and the Civil War." *John Muir Newsletter* 12, no. 4 (Fall 2002): 1, 5–6. https://vault.sierraclub.org/john_muir_exhibit/john_muir_newsletter/stanley_john_muir_and_the_civil_war.aspx.

Stewart, Omer C. *Forgotten Fires: Native Americans and the Transient Wilderness.* Edited and introduced by Henry T. Lewis and M. Kat Anderson. Norman: University of Oklahoma Press, 2002.

Stegner, Wallace. *Where the Bluebird Sings to the Lemonade Springs: Living and Writing in the West.* New York: Random House: 1992.

———. "Wilderness Letter." https://web.stanford.edu/~cbross/Ecospeak/wildernessletter.html.

Stocking, George W., Jr. *Race, Culture, and Evolution: Essays in the History of Anthropology.* With a new preface. Chicago: University of Chicago Press, 1982.

Stoll, Steven. *The Fruits of Natural Advantage: Making the Industrial Countryside in California.* Berkeley: University of California Press, 1998. https://publishing-cdlib-org.libproxy.berkeley.edu/ucpressebooks/view?docId=ft809nb55n&brand=ucpress.

Street, Richard Steven. *Beasts of the Field: A Narrative History of California Farmworkers, 1769–1913.* Stanford CA: Stanford University Press, 2004.

Stringfellow, Kim. "How the Timbisha Shoshones Got Their Land Back." The Mojave Project, July 2016. https://mojaveproject.org/dispatches-item/how -the-timbisha-got-their-land-back/.

Takaki, Ronald T. *Iron Cages: Race and Culture in Nineteenth-Century America.* New York: Alfred A. Knopf, 1979.

Taliaferro, John. *Grinnell: America's Environmental Pioneer and His Restless Drive to Save the West.* New York: Liveright, 2019.

Tammiksaar, E., N. G. Sukhova, and I. R. Stone. "Hypothesis Versus Fact: August Petermann and Polar Research." *Arctic* 52, no. 3 (September 1999): 237–43.

Taylor, Dorceta. *The Rise of the American Conservation Movement: Power, Privilege, and Environmental Protection.* Durham NC: Duke University Press, 2016.

Taylor, H. J. "Return of the Last Survivor." *University of California Chronicle* 33, no. 1 (January 1931). http://www.yosemite.ca.us/library/the_last_survivor/.

Thomas, Peter, and Donna Thomas. *Anywhere That Is Wild: John Muir's First Walk to Yosemite.* Yosemite National Park: Yosemite Conservancy, 2018.

Thompson, Jonathan. "A Reluctant Rebellion in the Utah Desert." *High Country News,* May 13, 2014. https://www.hcn.org/articles/is-san-juan-countys-phil -lyman-the-new-calvin-black.

Thoreau, Henry David. *The Maine Woods.* 6th ed. Boston: James R. Osgood, 1877.

———. *Walden.* Boston: James R. Osgood, 1878.

———. "Walking, and the Wild." In *In Praise of Walking,* 5–44. London: Arthur C. Fifield, 1905.

Thornton, Russell. "Native American Demographic and Tribal Survival into the Twenty-First Century." *American Studies* 46, nos. 3–4 (Fall–Winter 2005): 23–38.

Tobias, Jimmy. "At the Sierra Club, a Fierce Dispute over Founder's Legacy Continues." *Yahoo! News,* November 18, 2021. https://news.yahoo.com/sierra -club-fierce-dispute-over-104504276.html.

Treuer, David. "Return the National Parks to the Tribes." *The Atlantic* 327, no. 4 (May 2021): 30–45. https://www.theatlantic.com/magazine/archive/2021 /05/return-the-national-parks-to-the-tribes/618395/.

Turner, Frederick. *Rediscovering America: John Muir in His Time and Ours.* New York: Viking, 1985.

Turner, Frederick Jackson. *The Significance of the Frontier in American History.* Annual Report of the American Historical Association for the Year 1893. Washington DC: Government Printing Office, 1894.

Turrentine, Jeff. "Zinke's Western 'Listening Tour' Light on the Listening, Heavy on the Fossil Fuels." Natural Resources Defense Council, May 19, 2017. https://www .nrdc.org/onearth/zinkes-western-listening-tour-light-listening-heavy-fossil-fuels.

United Nations. "Convention on the Prosecution and Prevention of the Crime of Genocide." United Nations Resolution 260 (III) of December 9, 1948. http://www.un-documents.net/a3r260.htm.

U.S. Census Bureau. "Following the Frontier Line." https://www.census.gov /dataviz/visualizations/001/.

U.S. Congress. "An Act to Set Apart a Certain Tract of Land near the Head-waters of the Yellowstone River As a Public Park." March 1, 1872, 42nd Congress, 2nd session, 32–33.

———. "The Wilderness Act." Public Law 88–577 (16 U.S.C. 1131–1136). 88th Congress, Second Session, September 3 1964 (as amended).

———. "Yosemite Act of 1864." S. 203, 38th Congress, Session 1 (June 30, 1864).

U.S. Department of the Interior. "Secretary Zinke Submits 45-Day Interim Report on Bears Ears National Monument and Extends Public Comment Period." Press release, June 12, 2017. https://www.bia.gov/sites/default/files /dup/assets/public/pdf/idc2-064984.pdf.

U.S. Fish and Wildlife Service. "Endangered and Threatened Wildlife and Plants." Code of Federal Regulations, Title 50, ch. 1, sub. B, part 17. https:// www.ecfr.gov/current/title-50/chapter-I/subchapter-B/part-17.

U.S. Fish and Wildlife Service. "For the First Time in a Century, California Condors Will Take Flight in the Pacific Northwest." Press release, March 23, 2021. https://www.fws.gov/press-release/2021-03/first-time-century -california-condors-will-take-flight-pacific-northwest-0.

U.S. President. Proclamation, "Bears Ears National Monument, Proclamation 10285 of October 8, 2021." *Federal Register* 86, no. 197 (October 8, 2021): 57321–34.

———. Proclamation, "Establishment of the Baaj Nwaavjo I'tah Kukveni–Ancestral Footprints of the Grand Canyon, Proclamation 10606 of August 8, 2023." *Federal Register*, August 15, 2023. https://www.federalregister.gov /documents/2023/08/15/2023-17628/establishment-of-the-baaj-nwaavjo -itah-kukveni-ancestral-footprints-of-the-grand-canyon-national.

———. Proclamation, "Establishment of the Bears Ears National Monument Proclamation 9558 of December 28, 2016." *Federal Register* 82, no. 3 (January 5, 2017): 1139–47.

———. Proclamation, "Modifying the Bears Ears National Monument, Procla-mation 9681 of December 4, 2017." *Federal Register* 82, no. 235 (December 8, 2017): 58081–86.

Wahhoga Committee of the American Indian Council of Mariposa County/ Southern Sierra Miwuk Nation. "Long Live Wahogga." *News from Native California* 35, no. 3 (Spring 2022): 32–35.

Waite, Kevin. "The Forgotten History of the Western Klan." *The Atlantic*, April 6, 2021. https://www.theatlantic.com/ideas/archive/2021/04/california-klans -anti-asian-crusade/618513/.

Walker, Francis A. "Restriction of Immigration." *The Atlantic* (June 1896). https://www.theatlantic.com/magazine/archive/1896/06/restriction-of -immigration/306011/.

Wallis, Brian. "Black Bodies, White Science: The Slave Daguerreotypes of Louis Agassiz." *Journal of Blacks in Higher Education* (Summer 1996): 102–6.

West, Helen B. "Starvation Winter of the Blackfeet." *Montana: The Magazine of Western History* 9, no. 1 (Winter 1959): 2–19.

Wickson, Edward J. *The California Fruits and How to Grow Them.* San Francisco: Dewey, 1889.

Whitaker, Ben. "Revised and Updated Report on the Question of the Prevention and Punishment of the Crime of Genocide." United Nations Economic and Social Council, July 2, 1985.

Williams, Dennis C. *God's Wilds: John Muir's Vision of Nature.* College Station: Texas A&M University Press, 2002.

———. "John Muir, Christian Mysticism, and the Spiritual Value of Nature." In *John Muir: Life and Work,* edited by Sally M. Miller, 81–101. Albuquerque: University of New Mexico Press, 1993.

Wisconsin Historical Society. "Black History in Wisconsin." https:// wisconsinhistory.org/Records/Article/CS502.

———. "Population of Wisconsin, 1820–1990." https://www.wisconsinhistory.org /Records/Article/CS1816.

Wolfe, Linnie Marsh, ed. *John of the Mountains: The Unpublished Journals of John Muir.* Boston: Houghton Mifflin, 1938.

———. *Son of the Wilderness: The Life of John Muir.* Madison: University of Wisconsin Press, 1945.

Wolfe, Patrick. "Settler Colonialism and the Elimination of the Native." *Journal of Genocide Research* 8, no. 4 (December 2006): 387–409.

———. *Settler Colonialism and the Transformation of Anthropology: The Politics and Poetics of an Ethnographic Event.* London: Cassell, 1999.

Wood, Harold. "Was John Muir a Draft Dodger?" Sierra Club, John Muir Exhibit, January 2019. https://vault.sierraclub.org/john_muir_exhibit/life/was _john_muir_a_draft_dodger.aspx.

Worl, Rosita. "Standing with Spirits, Waiting." In *The Harriman Alaska Expedition Retraced: A Century of Change, 1899–2001*, edited by Thomas S. Litwin, 31–39. New Brunswick NJ: Rutgers University Press, 2005.

Worster, Donald. *A Passion for Nature: The Life of John Muir.* Oxford: Oxford University Press, 2008.

Wulf, Andrea. *The Invention of Nature: Alexander von Humboldt's New World.* New York: Alfred A. Knopf, 2015.

Wyman, Mark. *The Wisconsin Frontier.* Bloomington: Indiana University Press, 1998.

Young, S. Hall. *Alaska Days with John Muir.* New York: Fleming H. Revell, 1915.

————. *Hall Young of Alaska, "The Mushing Parson": The Autobiography of S. Hall Young.* Introduced by John A. Marquis. New York: Fleming H. Revell, 1927.

Yurok Tribe. "Yurok Condor Restoration Program." https://www.yuroktribe.org /yurok-condor-restoration-program.

Zinke, Ryan F. "Final Report Summarizing Findings of the Review of Designations Under the Antiquities Act." Department of the Interior, n.d. https:// www.doi.gov/sites/doi.gov/files/uploads/revised_final_report.pdf.

Znamenski, Andrei A. "'Vague Sense of Belonging to the Russian Empire': The Reindeer Chukchi's Status in Nineteenth-Century Northeastern Siberia." *Arctic Anthropology* 36, nos.1 & 2 (1999): 19–36.

INDEX